BTS TERTIAIRES
1re ET 2e ANNÉES

NEW ACTIVE BUSINESS TRACKS

CAHIER D'ANGLAIS

Claire **DELAROCQUE**
Marie-Hélène **FOUGERON**

COMMENT ACCÉDER À VOTRE i-MANUEL 2.0 ÉLÈVE

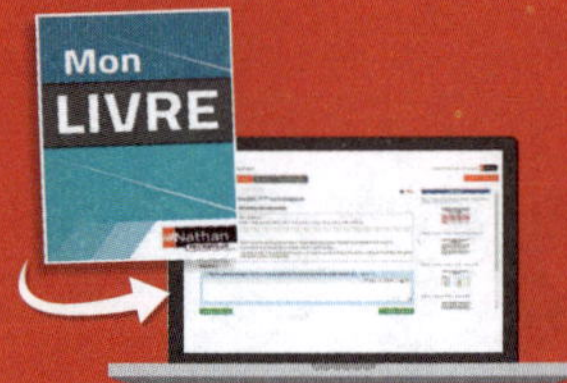

LIVRE + LICENCE NUMÉRIQUE

Votre enseignant souhaite travailler avec le i-Manuel 2.0 ; une fois votre compte créé par votre enseignant, rendez-vous, selon ses indications, sur :

▶ **imanuel.nathan.fr** et connectez-vous à votre espace élève i-Manuel 2.0 avec votre identifiant et votre mot de passe transmis par votre enseignant.

OU

▶ l'ENT ou la plateforme de votre établissement, et accédez directement à votre i-Manuel 2.0.

DÉCOUVREZ LE i-MANUEL 2.0 EN VIDÉO

À NE PAS OUBLIER

Conservez votre identifiant et votre mot de passe pour toutes vos connexions ultérieures

À SAVOIR

Cette licence élève i-Manuel est unique et personnelle. Elle offre un accès pour une période de 12 mois (à compter de la première activation) et ne peut être réutilisée par d'autres élèves les années suivantes. Pour équiper les élèves de nouvelles licences numériques i-Manuel 2.0, connectez-vous sur cns-edu.com.

Pour l'enseignant : rendez-vous sur **www.nathan.fr/i-manuel2** pour contacter votre délégué pédagogique Nathan, disposer de toutes les informations pratiques pour créer vos classes, activer les licences de vos élèves.

Nos équipes de proximité sont également à la disposition des établissements pour les accompagner dans leur projet de digitalisation des parcours de formation.

ISBN : 978-2-09-500084-4

Nathan TECHNIQUE

Avec ce livre, une licence i-MANUEL 2.0

Le i-Manuel 2.0, un outil simple d'utilisation qui reprend l'ensemble des contenus de ce livre sous forme numérique et interactive.

Il permet d'accéder au contenu de ce manuel à tout moment et en tout lieu sur un ordinateur ou une tablette. L'utilisateur peut donc passer du papier au numérique et choisir le support qui lui convient le mieux selon le travail à faire et le lieu où il se trouve.

Une véritable interactivité entre l'enseignant et sa classe

- **Vidéoprojeter** en classe les activités, les documents et les corrections pour animer les cours et travailler collectivement.
- N **Feuilleter le livre papier enrichi et le télécharger** pour un usage sans connexion.
- N Bénéficier d'**une banque de ressources.**
- **Piloter la classe** en assurant le suivi du travail des élèves à distance et en cours (recevoir et envoyer du travail, faire des commentaires, intervenir en temps réel).
- **Intégrer et envoyer à la classe**, à un ou plusieurs élèves, **des documents personnels**.
- **Afficher les corrigés** ou la correction individuelle du travail de l'élève.
- **Imprimer** les documents nécessaires pour mettre les élèves en **situation d'examen**.

Des fonctionnalités innovantes pour favoriser l'intérêt, la motivation et l'implication des élèves

- **Saisir les réponses** en travaillant sur ordinateur ou tablette.
- **Faire les activités et les exercices**, préparer ou réviser le cours **en classe ou à la maison**.
- **Accéder** aux **ressources numériques**, vidéos, fichiers élèves (Word, Excel, GeoGebra...).
- **Sauvegarder** au **format Word** le travail effectué dans un dossier (classeur).
- **Envoyer le travail** au professeur.
- **S'enregistrer** pour les activités orales.
- **S'auto-évaluer**.

Toutes les infos et les tutos sur www.nathan.fr/i-manuel2

Avec ce livre, des ressources numériques en accès direct

Flashez les QR Codes avec votre smartphone ou saisissez les mini-liens associés pour accéder à des vidéos, animations, QCM...

Active Business

Un outil pour l'enseignant et l'étudiant

1 Objectifs BTS

- ✔ Une articulation entre entraînements et évaluations
- ✔ Une préparation efficace à la réussite de l'épreuve d'Anglais dans le cadre du BTS
- ✔ Une pratique de l'Anglais autour des 5 activités langagières
- ✔ Une proposition de gestion de la différenciation
- ✔ Un découpage clair pour une incitation au travail en autonomie
- ✔ La personnalisation d'un sujet blanc spécifique par section de BTS
- ✔ Un cahier sur lequel on écrit, on prend des notes et on conserve une trace de son travail sur deux années.

2 Une unité progressive orientée vers la réussite : Training

Ouverture : entrée dans le thème par une vidéo, un document et des questions. Activités collectives.

Starters : ensemble d'activités faisables en classe, en équipe ou en *pick and choose*, notamment pour prendre en compte la **différenciation** et mettre les étudiants en confiance.

Prep page et text : travail sur les **stratégies de compréhension de l'écrit**. Une grille récurrente représente un cadre rassurant pour les étudiants. Elles les conduit de la lecture à l'analyse d'un texte, au travail sur le lexique et la langue, aux objectifs des examens (résumé, compte rendu, expression orale....)

Audio tracks et Video tracks : entraînement aux **stratégies de compréhension orale**. Décodage phonologique, analyse du document modélisant, mobilisation des savoirs.

Tasks : **activités collaboratives** sur un ensemble d'activités langagières, mise en commun du travail et **prise de parole**.

Background : la **diversité des thèmes** ainsi qu'un **atlas de cartes** permettent de découvrir la richesse du monde anglophone et des enjeux économiques mondiaux.

Powerpoint Presentation et **Role plays** : ciblent les **stratégies d'expression orale** et de réinvestissement des apprentissages des chapitres.

3 Des parcours d'apprentissage riches en documents authentiques : les ressources numériques

55 Audios

27 Videos

Tracks

4 Efficacité pédagogique : un manuel à onglets

TRAINING

Des unités thématiques qui préparent aux 5 activités langagières grâce à des supports choisis (textes, schémas, iconographies, audios, videos) et aux activités qui requièrent les compétences évaluées aux examens (compte rendu, résumé, traduction, exposé, jeu de rôles...).

EXAMS

Un accompagnement méthodologique fort. Les méthodes adaptées aux différentes formes des épreuves de langue, conçues pour être exploitées en classe avec l'appui de l'enseignant puis utilisées par les étudiants en autonomie. Elles proposent la démarche modèle et un réinvestissement.
Une page Mock Test propose, via QR code, un sujet blanc adapté à la section de BTS suivie par l'étudiant.

EXERCISES

10 thèmes de vocabulaire accompagnés d'exercices corrigés
33 thèmes clés de grammaire accompagnés d'exercices corrigés

INTERNSHIP

Préparer sa recherche de stage, son alternance, ou un travail.
Documents modèle puis exercices de réinvestissement (lettre de motivation, cv, demande par mail...)

Contents

TRAINING

3 Companies

4 Work

5 Transports

Contents

EXAMS

EXERCISES

INTERNSHIP

CARTES

CORRIGÉS

Training

Consumers

What are consumers?

Video 01
liennathan.fr/i6b82a

?

1. Find as many words and expressions as you can related to consumers.

2. What definition of the word "consumer" is given in the video?

3. Can a consumer be other than a person?

4. If you buy a product in order to sell it are you a consumer?

5. Tick the right box.
   a. In a consumption society, consumers buy only what they need. ❑
   b. In a consumption society people tend to buy products they don't really need. ❑

Word box

- consumer spending: *les dépenses des consommateurs*
- mid-priced brands: *marques à prix moyens*
- customer's loyalty cards: *cartes de fidélité*

1

TRAINING
EXAMS
EXERCISES
INTERNSHIP

Question

What do you know about Black Friday?

Notes

1 » Starters

Document 1

The Science of Shopping: The Way the Brain Buys

Retailers are making breakthroughs in understanding their customers' minds. Here is what they know about you.

Shoppers already know that everyday items, like milk, are invariably placed towards the back of a store to provide more opportunity to tempt customers. This is why pharmacies are generally at the rear, even in convenience stores. But supermarkets know shoppers know this, so they use other tricks, like placing popular items halfway along a section so that people have to walk all along the aisle looking for them. The idea is to boost "dwell time": the length of time people spend in a store.

■ Adapted from *The Economist*, December, 2008.

1. Identify the document.
2. How do supermarkets appeal to customers? Make a list of the strategies they use.

Document 2

Social media users in the world

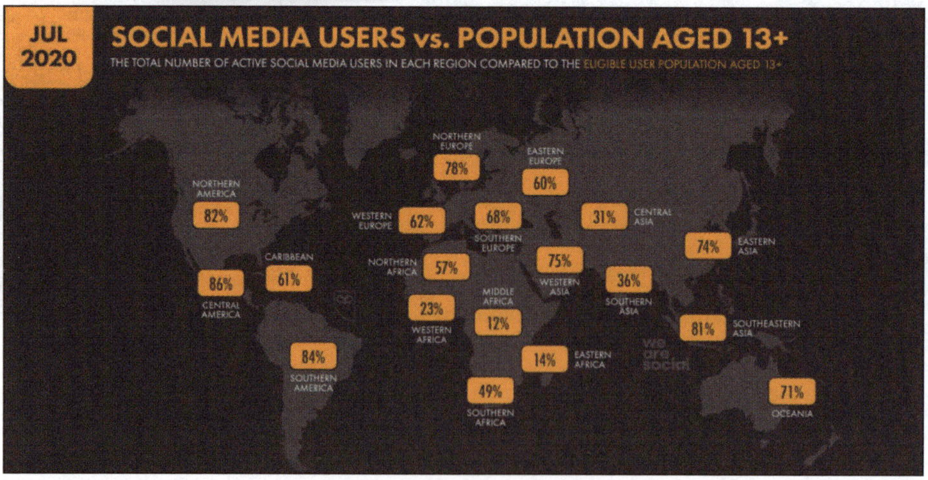

1. What is this graph about?
2. Make a list of the social media you know.
3. What categories of consumers are studied?
4. What countries have the highest percentage of social media users?
5. What countries have the lowest rate of social media users?

Document 3

Consumption Patterns in the EU: a Pie Chart

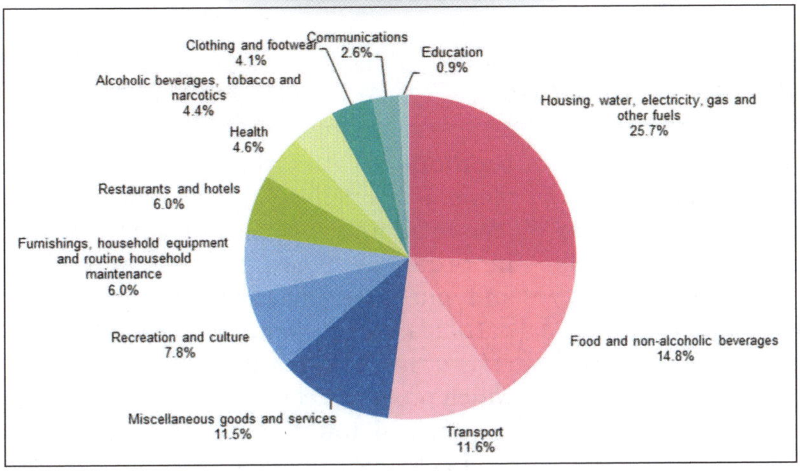

Adapted from ec.europe.eu., 2017.

1. Identify the document.
2. Why is it called a pie chart? What is the equivalent in French?
3. What do Europeans spend more money on?
4. How much in percentage do they spend on clothing?
5. On transport?
6. What percentage of their spending goes to education and health?
7. How can you explain this?

Audio 01
liennathan.fr/62fi2q

Document 4

A Shift in Shopping Habits

1. Identify the document.
2. Explain how the shopping experience has changed.

TRAINING
EXAMS
EXERCISES
INTERNSHIP

1 Prep page

Text

Understanding customers' behaviour

Audio 02
liennathan.fr/h6m95x

In every store, regardless of its layout, there is the traditional main aisle. It is usually located in a way that provides a panoramic sight of the key categories and located in the central area of the store. The main aisle, wide and spacious, improves the experience of the shoppers journey, making sure the search for their favourite products is not only easier but it also allows their shopping cart to move freely throughout the aisle. Therefore, it is imperative to understand the customers behaviour in the main aisle to generate an increase in sales. Understanding the customer behaviour with precision has become a basic need, as a large share of the in-store promotions is located within a few meters in the main aisle. This is possible today thanks to highly sophisticated programs such as Shoppermotion which enables store managers to analyse their customers' behaviour in real time. Consequently, they can improve and optimize their product placement and store layout.

It is highly probable that during the shopper journey, the customers will enter the main aisle directly from the store entrance. Then, having arrived there, they will unconsciously begin to purchase thanks to the in-store marketing promotions attracting their attention. Generally, retailers invest a considerable amount of time designing in-store strategies in order to measure every movement and purchase that happens within this particular zone. Shoppermotion allows to review the customer flow on a daily basis, which provides retailers and manufacturers meaningful information to measure the buying rate of the end caps and evaluate the performance of the promotional campaigns.

It is also true that when people go into most supermarkets, they generally know what they're going to find. In spite of modern shopper tracking technology, items rarely change, and most shoppers have a set shopping list that doesn't change a lot from week to week. But at two of the UK's biggest supermarkets, Tesco and Sainsbury, an entire section of the shop changes completely on a weekly basis. Likewise, both Aldi and Lidl, the biggest German hard discounters, have centre aisles full of miscellaneous products to buy. One week, these aisles could be filled with camping equipment, while the following week it could be paint and rollers.

■ Adapted from *shoppermotion.com*, 2020.

A step-by-step approach

1 Lexical work

a. Find the meaning of the following words in the dictionary.

Layout • aisle • item • purchase • miscellaneous • filled. ....

....

....

b. Find the lexical equivalents in the text:
Allée principale • améliorer • charriot • comportement • ventes • besoin • promotion sur le point de vente • commerçant • investir • taux • tête de gondole.

2 Read the whole text

a. Comment on the title.

b. Who needs to understand customers' behaviour?

3 Check the facts

Tick the right answer.

a. The article is about the strategy used by store managers to understand their customers' behaviour in order to increase their sales. ❑

b. The article is about a new customer surveillance program to prevent shoplifting. ❑

c. The article is about the German hard discounters Aldi and Lidl's strategy. ❑

4 Train for exam

Find the key ideas in each of the three paragraphs.

§1

§2

§3

5 Topic debrief

Use your answers above to write a short account of the article (50 to 100 words).

Language

Futur en *will* → page 184 / Subordonnées relatives → page 200
Auxiliaire modal *can/could* → page 174

Translate into French.

1. Customers **will enter** the main aisle directly from the store entrance.
2. Programs such as Shoppermotion **which** enables store managers to analyse their customers' behaviour.
3. Thanks to in store promotions **attracting** their attention.
4. One week, these aisles **could be filled** with camping equipment, while the following week it **could be paint** and rollers.

TRAINING EXAMS EXERCISES INTERNSHIP

1 Text track

Text

Britons expected to send 235m items of clothing

Audio 03
liennathan.fr/3rw79r

Study finds three-quarters of consumers throw away rather than recycle or donate unwanted garments.

A predicted 235m items of Britons' unwanted clothing are expected to end up in landfill unnecessarily this spring, according to new research. Three-quarters of consumers admit to throw away their unwanted garments, usually because they do not realise that worn-out or dirty clothes can be recycled or accepted by charities.

Consumers are expected to get rid of 680m pieces of clothing as they spring-clean their wardrobes, a survey shows. However, this spring cleaning will be damaging for the environment, with 235m of the garments expected to end up in landfill. Men are more likely to send clothes to landfill, with 82% saying they would throw away items this spring compared with 69% of women.

Over the past 10 years, clothing has been the fastest growing waste category in the UK. In partnership with the charity Oxfam, Sainsbury's is urging consumers to donate unwanted clothes to its collection points alongside the traditional recycling bins in its store car parks. The study also uncovered the reasons people do not donate or recycle clothing, with 49% saying they did not think they could because the clothes were worn out or dirty. A further 16% said they did not have time to visit a charity shop, or could not be bothered to sort items, while 6% did not realise clothing could be recycled.

"If clothes go out with the rubbish, they'll end up in landfill, so we've teamed up with Oxfam to help people become more charitable and environmentally aware this spring," said Paul Crewe, head of sustainability at Sainsbury's. "No matter if they're worn out, we're calling on shoppers to donate their unwanted clothes at recycling points in our stores across the UK."

Marks & Spencer also has a partnership with Oxfam, which began in January 2008. Donors handing old M&S clothing in to Oxfam stores receive a £5 M&S voucher, while its "shwopping" scheme encourages customers to hand over an old or unwanted garment whenever they buy a new one. Figures show that 27m garments have been "shwopped" since 2008.

Adapted from *the Guardian*, 2017.

A step-by-step approach

1 Lexical work

a. Find the lexical equivalents in the text.
Décharge • usé • déchet • partenariat • point de collecte • recycler • trier • donateur.

b. Find synonyms in the text for:
Clothes • waste • throw away.

Notes

c. **Underline the right combination.**
"Shwop" is a combination of the verbs: shop and swap (échanger) • shop and slow (ralentir) • shop and swipe (essuyer).

2 Read the whole text

a. **Comment on the title.**
b. **What do most British people do with their old clothes?**
c. **What could they do instead?**

3 Check the facts

Say if the following statements are true or false.

a. British people have taken the habit of recycling their old clothes. ❑ T ❑ F
b. Women recycle their clothes more than men. ❑ T ❑ F
c. Most people don't recycle because they think it's impossible. ❑ T ❑ F
d. Thrown away clothes damage the environment. ❑ T ❑ F
e. Oxfam is a British supermarket. ❑ T ❑ F
f. Famous supermarket chains are working with charities. ❑ T ❑ F
g. When people recycle their clothes at Oxfam they get a voucher for Marks and Spencer. ❑ T ❑ F

4 Train for the exam

Find the key ideas of each paragraph.

§1 ....
§2 ....
§3 ....
§4 ....
§5 ....

5 Topic debrief

Use the information above to write a 50 to 100 words account of the article.

Notes

Language

Le présent simple → page 190 / La forme passive → page 184
Préfixes et suffixes → page 189 / *Ever* et ses composés → page 182

Translate into French.

a. The study explores the general qualities of the average organic food consumer.
b. Consumers are expected to **get rid** of 680m pieces of clothing.
c. Worn-out or dirty clothes can be recycled or accepted by **charities**.
d. The "shwopping" scheme **encourages** customers to hand over an old or **unwanted** garment **whenever** they buy a new one.

TRAINING EXAMS EXERCISES INTERNSHIP

1 Video track

1 Pronunciation work

Audio 04
liennathan.fr/8mzi64

Listen, repeat the following words and record yourself.
Hierarchy • psychology • behaviour • exemplary • physiological • resources • desire • breathe.

2 Before you start watching the video

a. Think about some basic people's needs and quote them.

....

b. Look at the title and find out more about Maslow.

....

3 Watch the video

Underline the words you hear among the following list:
Theory • hierarchy • stage • behaviour • 1953 • exemplary • physiological needs • motivated • physical needs • safety • reading.

Video

Maslow, the hierarchy of needs

Video 02
liennathan.fr/ed57a2

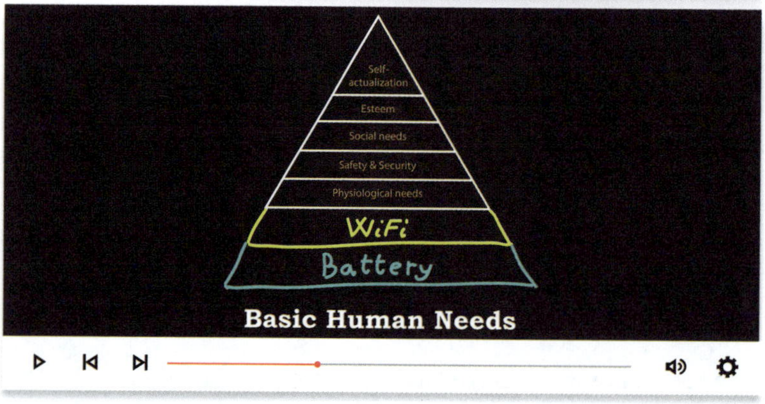

Word box

- breathe: *respirer*
- safety: *sécurité*
- earn money: *gagner de l'argent*
- shelter: *abri*
- seek: *rechercher*
- belong: *appartenir*
- self confidence: *confiance en soi*
- peers: *pairs, semblables*
- brain: *cerveau*
- level: *niveau*
- stand out: *sortir du lot*

4 A step-by-step approach

1. Watch the whole video once

a. Write in French what it is about.

....

2. Watch the video a second time

→ 1'05 – Watch the first part

b. How many stages are there in the Maslow theory?

....

c. What do these stages motivate?

....

d. When did Maslow propose his theory?

....

e. Who inspired him?

....

f. What are the first three stages of Maslow's theory?

....

→ 1'59 – Watch the second part

g. What do people look for in stage 4?

....

h. What do we want to be?

....

i. Does everybody want the same thing? Explain. Quote some of the examples taken.

....

....

j. Under what conditions can we reach stage 5? Describe stage 5.

....

....

→ 1'59 → end – Watch the third part

k. What are the needs which must be fulfilled for a complete life?

....

5 Train for the exam

Oral report: put together all the information you have collected and report to the class.

1 Audio track

1 Pronunciation work

Audio 05
liennathan.fr/4vt97f

Listen to the following words. Then repeat them and record yourself.
Beverages • steadily • highlight • striking • sprouted • exposure • loyalty • affluent • livelihood • sought after.

2 Before listening

a. Look at the visual document and say as much as you can:
– Find out about India's drinking habits. ....
– Find about America's drinking habits. ....

b. Look at the title and rephrase it.

....

3 Listen to the audio

c. Anticipate the topic of the audio.

d. Listen and try to understand the following words:
Beverages • trends • steadily • habit • taste highlight • shift • affluent • hang out • foreign brands • outlets • witnessing • harvested • livelihood • health • herbal teas • household.

e. Write in French what the audio is about.

f. Debrief with the other students and the teacher about their meaning.

Audio

Is India going for coffee and America for tea?

Audio 06
liennathan.fr/k9e88n

A Tea Store in New York

Starbucks in Mumbaï

4 A step-by-step approach

1. Listen to the whole audio once

a. Write in one or two sentences what the interview is about.

....

....

2. Listen to the audio a second time

→ Listen to the first part

b. Collect information about:

– The name of the program. ....

– Who the guests are. ....

– Their role in the interview. ....

– The new habit in India. ....

– The origin of this new habit. ....

– Which age group is concerned. ....

– The brands quoted in the audio. ....

→ Listen to the second part

c. Why is the American guest smiling?

....

d. What is the trend in the USA?

....

e. What are American consumers interested in?

....

f. Why is wellness becoming a powerful market?

....

g. What can be found in many American closets?

....

h. What will be the topic of the next debate?

....

i. Why is it a burning issue?

....

5 Train for the exam

Oral work: speak for at least two minutes about you have just learned.
Put together all the information you have collected.

TRAINING

EXAMS

EXERCISES

INTERNSHIP

1 Tasks

Document 1 Text

Audio 07
liennathan.fr/k9y4h6

One in five UK consumers boycotts brands

LONDON: Every brand knows that establishing trust with their customers is vital, but this point has been reinforced by a new survey that found a fifth (21%) of UK consumers have boycotted a brand following a scandal or negative press. Furthermore, of those who stopped using a brand following adverse headlines, as many as two-thirds (67%) have not returned to it, according to research firm YouGov. The question is what measures can brands take to win consumers back?

According to the findings, one-in-five (26%) consumers went back to the brand they used to trust, but importantly they tended to use it less often, and just 1% used it as much as before.

Tax avoidance and evasion emerged as the main reason for consumers to boycott a brand (48%), but 40% also stopped using a brand if it was perceived to be treating its staff unfairly. Other reasons why respondents said they boycotted a brand included cover ups (40%), workers in the supply chain being treated unfairly (36%), corruption (36%) and faulty products or a product recall (35%).

In terms of winning consumers back, the report found that they have mixed reasons for returning to a boycotted brand. Almost a third (28%) said they returned because the company had changed the practices that started the boycott in the first place, while just under a quarter (24%) said they returned because the brand's product or service had improved.

However, there are also occasions when a brand does not necessarily need to change its practices or alter its approach, the report said, because 29% of former boycotters started to use a brand again because it had become too inconvenient not to.

Adapted from *WARC.com*, April 2017.

Task 1

1. Read the whole text.

2. Underline the sentence corresponding to the document.

a. Consumers can boycott a brand when they think the company is unfair with its workers.

b. Boycotting a brand means to stop buying it because you can't afford it anymore.

c. Boycotting a brand means to buy it online only.

3. Find the key idea(s) in each paragraph.

§1 ....

§2 ....

§3 ....

§4 ....

§5 ....

4. Write an organized account of the article in English (50 to 100 words).

Document 2 Video

Amazon Go opens cashier-free smart grocery store – Dec 2016

Video 03
liennathan.fr/8m6w8g

Word box

to ditch the lines : *se débarrasser de/ sortir des sentiers battus*

Task 2

1. Watch the video.

a. What is new about Amazon?

b. Describe the concept of Amazon Go. What makes it attractive to the consumer?

c. What is the general trend in the grocery retail sector?

d. What products are more likely to be bought in a brick-and-mortar store?

e. What are Amazon's other grocery brands? (2 answers)

f. Name the competitors and number of stores.

2. Organize all the information you have collected and write a report.

Notes

Document 3 Audio

Is the era of big food coming to an end?

Audio 08
liennathan.fr/4e8n2e

Task 3

1. Listen to the whole audio.

a. Anticipate from the title.

b. Focus on the answers to the following questions:

– What type of food are an increasing number of consumers buying and why?

– Give the names of two companies quoted in the interview.

– What are their response to the new consuming trends?

2. Write an organized account in English.

Notes

TRAINING EXAMS EXERCISES INTERNSHIP

1 Background

Who are today's consumers?

An individual who buys products or services for personal use and not for manufacture or resale. A consumer is someone who can make the decision whether or not to purchase an item at the store, either online or offline and someone who can be influenced by marketing and advertisements.

Consumers are now more demanding of products, services and brands than before and are using digital tools to articulate and fulfil their needs.

There are as many consumers as there are people. However, there are trends that must not escape retailers as they enable them to classify consumers and market new product lines.

I How do we consume?

Consuming is about trends, quality, health and taste and **money**. Trends especially in clothing come and go more rapidly. The cosmetic shop, Kiko, has based its business model on the same principle: products go out of trend rapidly at affordable prices. So if price is one criterion, quality is another. The trend for organic, vegan and glutenfree products is moving fast and sometimes generating nutritional debates pointing out excesses of all kinds.

Social networks, especially if you are a millennial or a linkster also known as generation Z, have become the main trend-setters.

II What do we buy?

It depends much on disposable income but it seems that in developed countries more and more is spent on new digital devices and digital-related services. Less is spent on food but quality and variety are more popular than before.

For an increasing number of consumers, buying name-brand items has stopped being a priority when there is an affordable alternative. Some shoppers refuse to pay a "luxury" premium. Others might think it is worth the additional cost as long as the quality is superior.

III Who do consumers buy from?

Consumers are getting more sensitive to the environment, sustainability, animal welfare, and health issues. That is why marketers need to keep a clear focus on the needs and expectations of their customers while following stricter ethical principles. Nevertheless, consumers are a group that's diverse and fragmented, with high expectations and little patience that requires companies to be always on the lookout. To stay competitive you need to be visible, and that's no easy feat. Businesses need to measure sentiment and loyalty of their clients and must come up with **customized** products to meet their audience's needs and interests.

Consumers are being offered a purchasing experience that is facilitated by all sorts of new technological devices increasingly available. Shopping has to be easy, instantaneous and fun.

Conclusion

Consumers are often **unpredictable** but also more and more ethically-oriented. So the retail landscape is difficult to predict in wealthier countries.

"Consumer alert! Consumer alert!
— If it tastes good, spit it out!"

Test

I Say if the following statements are true or false. Write a sentence supporting your answer.

1. The consumer is not necessarily the person who buys the product or service. ❑ T ❑ F

2. There is just one type of consumers. ❑ T ❑ F

3. Consumers are only interested in the price. ❑ T ❑ F

4. Generation Z often decide the trends through social networks. ❑ T ❑ F

5. Retailers must keep up with the new trends if they want to keep their customers. ❑ T ❑ F

6. Kiko is a new clothes brand. ❑ T ❑ F

7. Consumers shopping experience is more and more difficult. ❑ T ❑ F

II Give a detailed answer to each question using the information you learned from the document.

8. What can influence consumers?

9. What are today's consumers more sensitive to?

10. What must brands do to remain competitive?

11. What impact do new technologies have on consumers?

TRAINING

EXAMS

EXERCISES

INTERNSHIP

1 PowerPoint Presentation

Starbucks' SWOT

1. Study Starbucks' SWOT closely.

2. Choose a company in the list below.

TESCO • ALDI • WALMART • OXFAM

a. Prepare a PowerPoint presentation of their SWOT.

b. Present it to the class.

Favourable | Unfavourable

Internal

Strengths

- Provide a gadget brewing range of products
- Very friendly service
- The biggest coffee company in the world
- Strong brand image
- Extensive global supply chain
- Uniqueness of the Starbucks coffee shops comfort and cosiness with free WIFI access
- Innovation: new products on the menu every month

Weaknesses

- Employees are not always told when their shifts are
- Higher price points
- Imitable products
- Too many points of sales leading to market cannibalism

SWOT

External

Opportunities

- Expansion into Indian and Chinese markets
- Use supermarkets as a way of expanding
- Partnerships or alliances or joint-ventures with other firms (ex: Tata Beverage in India)

Threats

- Domestic competition from McDonald's McCafé, Caffe Bene (New York)
- International competition from local start-ups: Mikel Coffee in Greece, Costa Café in London, etc.

Act

Choose one of the following role plays to act in front of the class.

Role play 1

Student A tries to convince his/her/ neighbor to recycle his/her old garments.

Student B does not want to bother and throws them away.

Tips for Student A

You should/ shouldn't; If I were you, I would; I advise you...

Tips for Student B

No time to waste; it is no use; don't believe in recycling...

Role play 2

Student A is trying to convince student B not to spend too much money on shopping for entertainment and clothes.

Student B thinks that spending money on what we like is part of life's pleasures.

Student C's opinion is that today people are tempted to buy things they don't need or can't afford.

Tips: Arguments from the document studied in the chapter can be used.

Role play 3

Student A wants to buy some tea as a gift for an American friend coming to London. He knows that his/her friend is health oriented and also cares about the planet. He/she doesn't know what sort of tea corresponds the best to his / her friend's expectations.

Student B works in a tea shop. He/she needs to understand student A's expectations before giving some advice. Student B knows a lot about the new trends in America and proposes different types of tea each with a specific taste and specific health benefits.

Notes

TRAINING

EXAMS

EXERCISES

INTERNSHIP

Marketing & distribution

The 4 Ps of the marketing mix

Video 04
liennathan.fr/c534qe

1. What are the four Ps of the marketing mix?

2. Is the marketing mix the same for all types of consumers?

Word box

- purchase : *acheter*
- promote : *promouvoir*
- supermarket aisles : *allées de supermarché*
- shelves : *linéaires*
- marketing mix : *plan de marchéage*

2

Tesco in Malaysia

TRAINING EXAMS EXERCISES INTERNSHIP

Questions

1. How can customers purchase/buy products?
2. How do retailers attract customers?
3. Look for information on Tesco.

Notes

2 » Starters

Document 1

Customer loyalty: higher profits and more growth

Loyal, satisfied customers are one of retailers most powerful marketing tools. In the age of e-Commerce and online review websites, positive customer *word-of-mouth is essential to attracting new customers. In fact, 83% of consumers place more trust in personal recommendations than any other form of marketing.

A well-designed and well-executed loyalty programme can help retailers retain existing customers, attract new customers, and generate profits. Nearly 6 in 10 UK adults believe that brands *should* offer loyalty programmes, and almost 60% of internet users cite 'earning rewards' as one of the most valued aspects of the retail shopping experience.

*word of mouth: bouche à oreille

Adapted from the *rocketmarketinggroup.com.*

1. Underline the right answer.
A loyal customer is:

- **a.** Un client fidèle.
- **b.** Un client peu fiable.
- **c.** Un client étourdi.

2. Say if the following statements are true or false. Correct them when they are false.

- **a.** It is very importrant for retailers to establish customer loyalty. ❑ T ❑ F
- **b.** TV advertising is very efficient to attract new customers. ❑ T ❑ F
- **c.** Loyalty programs do not generate profits. ❑ T ❑ F
- **d.** Customers enjoy earning rewards with the loyalty programmes. ❑ T ❑ F

Document 2

Aldi

Audio 09
liennathan.fr/v5xb67

1. Identify the document.

2. How many stores does Aldi plan to open in the US?

3. How would you describe Aldi and what products does it sell?

Document 3
Cooking, Heating, Lighting Fire

"Product diversification, I like that."

1. Identify the document.
2. Who are these sellers?
3. What are the products for sale?
4. What's the difference between the three products?
5. What do the consumers appreciate about them?
6. What does it reveal about some companies' marketing strategies?
7. What does it reveal about consumers' behavior?
8. What does this cartoon make fun of?

Document 4
Brand Marketing

Video 05
liennathan.fr/z99v9t

Word box
- direct selling: *vente directe*
- word-of-mouth: *bouche-à-oreille*

1. Identify the document.
2. Have mothers a lot of free time?
3. How do they get to know new products?
4. Is it an efficient method?

TRAINING
EXAMS
EXERCISES
INTERNSHIP

2 Prep page

Text

Marketing organic food

Audio 10
liennathan.fr/5p2iv3

If consumers are given the choice between buying two different bags of apples, one priced at $5 and one priced at $7, many people would choose the cheaper bag of apples. However, what if the more expensive brand was certified as organic? Would it change some consumers behaviour ?

According to "Who are Organic Food Consumers? A Compilation and Review of Why People Purchase Organic Food," published in *The Journal of Consumer Behavior*, consumers' purchasing decisions are based on subjective experiences and perceptions of organic food. The study explores the general qualities of the average organic food consumer, and the forces and factors that drive consumption of organic food. For regular buyers of organic goods, organic food consumption is a way of life. It represents a range of values and themes they attribute to themselves.

Some of these values include:

- Altruism (Relationships with others)
- Ecology (Harmony with the Universe)
- Universalism (Protection of the welfare of all people/nature)
- Benevolence (Enhancing welfare of loved ones and friends)
- Spirituality (Inner harmony and unity with nature)
- Self Direction (Independent thought and action)

Marketing efforts for organic food usually **focus** on these values, presenting the product as environmentally friendly (Universalism), healthy (Benevolence), and as a means of opposing the system (Independent thought and action).

For example, many organic food companies base their products' images on low environmental impact and local origin. By advertising their food as environmentally safe and local, and presenting the competition as potentially dangerous these organic food producers attract those who identify with environmentalism and alternative lifestyles.

Unfortunately, even if consumers have positive attitudes toward organic goods and wish to purchase them, they might be turned off by the high prices. The study concludes that the best way to increase motivation to purchase goods is to engage in strategic educational marketing campaigns that emphasize the positive attributes of organic goods to the masses.

Adapted from *marketing-schools.org.*

A step-by-step approach

1 Lexical work

Match the words with their French translation.

welfare •	• publicité
average •	• concurrence
advertising •	• moyenne
competition •	• bien-être

2 Read the whole text

a. Comment on the title.

b. What is organic food?

c. Where can you buy it?

d. Is it more or less expensive than industrial food?

3 Check the facts

Underline the right statement.

The main topic of the text is about:

a. The difficulty for organic brands to reach consumers.

b. The increasing number of organic food buyers.

c. The strategy used by organic brands to attract consumers.

4 Train of the exam

Find the key ideas by answering the questions.

§1 Between two similar products at different prices what do most customers choose?

§2 What does organic food represent for most regular buyers?

§3 Quote 3 values associated to organic food.

§4 How do marketers present their organic products?

§5 How do organic food marketers present competition?

§6 What can prevent consumers from buying organic food?

5 Topic debrief

Use your answers above to write a short account of the article (50 to 100 words).

Language

Emploi de *the* → page 172 / Le conditionnel *if* clauses → page 180
Le complément du nom/cas possessif → page 179

Translate into French.

1. **Freedom** is an important value, as well as **altruism** and **animal welfare**.
2. If consumers **had** the choice, they **would choose** cheaper products.
3. Consumers' **purchasing decisions** are difficult to anticipate.

TRAINING
EXAMS
EXERCISES
INTERNSHIP

2 Text track

Text

The rise and fall of the American Mall

Audio 11
liennathan.fr/knp785

America's malls today are empty, ghostly and dead. For decades, the mall was both an economic and social hub. And for many, a way of life. Now, many malls in the United States have either collapsed or are ready to do so. So, how did it happen?

The story of the mall begins in the 1950s, when America was experiencing an unprecedented economic boom. The middle class had more money to spend than ever before, and they were spending it on houses and cars.

Suburban populations rose astronomically, and they needed a place to shop, meet and "hang out". On October 8, 1956, America's first mall, the Southdale Center in Edina, Minnesota, opened its doors. Like no building ever constructed before, the Southdale Center not only had shops, but fountains, art installations, a bird sanctuary, and a sprawling courtyard, all within a single indoor complex.

The mall received mostly enthusiastic reviews, describing it as an attraction like Disneyland, which had just opened a year earlier, in 1955. By 1960, there were 4,500 large shopping complexes in the United States, which means almost three new shopping centers opening every day.

In the 1980s began the mall's golden age. Shopping complexes continued to build at a rate of over 1,000 per year. The American mall would reach its peak in 1992 with its final evolution: the mega-mall.

As the 2000s progressed, consumer habits shifted away from the department store altogether. Macy's, for instance, has been steadily closing stores since 2005, most of them in malls. Department-store-sized vacancies are difficult to refill, and with other, better malls often nearby, there's little that can be done to save a failing mall, which is why hundreds of malls have already been pronounced dead.

The "dead mall" has even become its own aesthetic, capturing the imaginations of several internet photographers and filmmakers. Moreover, in a world of social distancing, even America's most spectacular malls are declining and laying off employees.

Will malls ever recover their status in American culture? Or will we look to new types of third places in our post-pandemic future? Only time will tell, but one thing is certain: there is plenty of space for something new.

Adapted from *the businessinsider.com*, July 2020.

A step-by-step approach

1 Lexical work

a. Find in the lexical equivalents in the text:
Centre commercial • s'effondrer • classe moyenne • habitants des banlieues • trainer • critiques/avis • s'éloigner • grand-magasin • espaces vides • remplir à nouveau • licencier

b. Find the name of the USA's most famous department store in the article.

....

....

....

2 Read the whole text

a. Comment on the title.

....

b. Are malls in the US today as popular as before?

....

3 Check the facts

Say if the following statements are true or false.

a. Malls have never been successful. ❑ T ❑ F

b. Malls became part of the American culture from the 1960s to the end of the 20th century. ❑ T ❑ F

c. Some reviews compared the first mall to Disneyland. ❑ T ❑ F

d. Today consumers' shopping habits have changed. ❑ T ❑ F

e. A lot of malls are closing down but the most spectacular ones are still successful. ❑ T ❑ F

4 Train for the exam

Find the key ideas in each paragraph.

§1 ....

§2 ....

§3 ....

§4 ....

§5 ....

§6 ....

§7 ....

§8 ....

5 Topic debrief

Use the information above to write a 50 to 100 word account of the article.

Notes

Language

Questions ouvertes/fermées → page 201 / *Simple past/past continuous* → page 194

***Present perfect continuous + since/for* → page 192**

Translate into French.

a. How did it happen?

....

b. Suburban populations rose astronomically in the 1950s.

....

c. America was experiencing an unprecedented economic boom.

....

d. Macy's has been closing some of its stores since 2005.

....

TRAINING

EXAMS

EXERCISES

INTERNSHIP

2 Video track

1 Pronunciation work

Audio 12
liennathan.fr/962gga

Listen, repeat the following words and record yourself.
Agriculture • free of genetically-modified organisms • antibiotics • pesticides • healthier • exposure.

2 Before you start watching the video

a. Anticipate on the title of the video.

....

b. Find out more about organic food.

....

3 Watch the video

Underline the words you hear among the following list:
Growth • grocer • labeled • fertilizers • genetically-modified organisms • meat • hormones • antibiotics • outdoors • nutritional benefits • worth • animal feed.

Video

Video 06
liennathan.fr/8h2ff2

Organic food

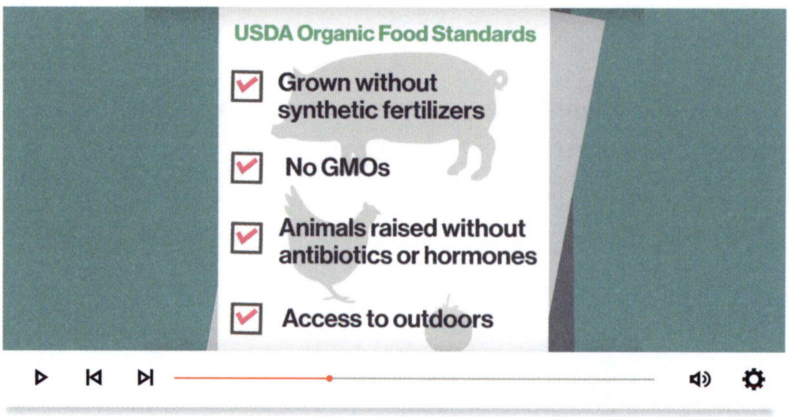

Tips

A definition of the term "organic food"

Organic food is food produced by methods that comply with the standards of organic farming. Organizations regulating organic products may forbid the use of certain pesticides and fertilizers in farming. Special certification is required to market food as organic.

4 A step-by-step approach

1. Watch the whole video once

a. Name the website that posted the video.

....

b. What is required to make a produce organic?

....

c. Why is organic food becoming more popular?

....

2. Watch the video a second time

d. Explain what the big retailers do to increase their sales.

....

e. How much money is spent by the consumer?

....

f. Explain national standards.

....

5 Train for the exam

Write a report or make an oral presentation following the guidelines below.

I. Introduction: What is the topic?
Give the source.

....

....

II. Development

– Organic food is popular: reasons.

....

....

....

– Scientific research questions its healthy impact.

....

....

....

III. Conclusion

....

....

TRAINING
EXAMS
EXERCISES
INTERNSHIP

2 Video track

1 Pronunciation work

Audio 13
liennathan.fr/948pmm

Listen, repeat the following words and record yourself.
Digital • leverage • search engine • focus • content • brand awareness

2 Before you start watching the video

a. **Anticipate on the title of the video.**

....

b. **What do you know about digital marketing?**

....

3 Watch the video

Underline the words you hear among the following list:
Digital • leverage • search engines • channels • device • goals • networks • content • automation • optimization • brand awareness.

Video

What is digital marketing?

Video 07
liennathan.fr/j8g96t

4 A step-by-step approach

1. Watch the whole video once

a. What is the source?

....

b. What is Pete going to explain?

....

2. Watch the video a second time

c. Say if the following statements are true or false. Support your answer with a sentence.

– Digital marketing is intended for people who buy on the net through electronic devices. ❑ T ❑ F

....

– E -mail and social networks are not part of digital marketing. ❑ T ❑ F

....

– SEO means search engine online. ❑ T ❑ F

....

– Marketers should encourage brand awareness. ❑ T ❑ F

....

– There is only one digital channel. ❑ T ❑ F

....

– KPI is an indicator marketers use to measure a company's digital performance. ❑ T ❑ F

....

– Organic traffic measures the number of people who log on a company's website after a Google search. ❑ T ❑ F

....

– Digital marketing is possible only for large companies. ❑ T ❑ F

....

5 Train for the exam

Prepare an oral or a written presentation of the video in English and in French.
Written report: 50/100 words.
Oral report: 1 to 2 minutes.

2 Audio track

1 Pronunciation work

Audio 14
liennathan.fr/95wu6t

Listen to the following words. Then repeat them and record yourself:
Loyalty card • patrons • discount • gathered • worrying • unfortunately • loyal • scheme.

2 Before listening

a. Find out about loyalty cards and give information about your own loyalty cards.

– Do loyalty cards turn the customer into a loyal customer?

....

– Don't loyalty cards compete with each other?

....

– How does a loyalty card make a customer really loyal?

....

3 Listen to the audio

b. Look at the title and say as much as you can.

c. Listen and try to understand the following words:

Junk mail • schemes • cardholders • to be rewarded • bonus points • repeat business • marketing strategies • barcode • keytags • keyrings • application forms • to pay off.

d. Debrief with the other students and the teacher about their meaning.

Audio

Loyalty cards

Audio 15
liennathan.fr/y9bw68

Loyalty cards

Notes

....

4 A step-by-step approach

1. Listen to the whole audio once

a. Write in French what it is about.

2. Listen to the whole audio a second time

→ Listen to the first part

b. Collect information on: place, time, names and figures.

→ Listen to the second part

c. What is the new information we get?

→ Listen to the third part

d. What else do we learn?

5 Train for the exam

Oral work: speak for at least two minutes about you have just leaned.
Put together all the information you have collected.

TRAINING EXAMS EXERCISES INTERNSHIP

2 Tasks

Document 1 Text

Audio 16
liennathan.fr/9y32gt

The boom of e-commerce

Over the last few years, e-commerce has become an indispensable part of the global retail sector. Like many other industries, the retail landscape has undergone an important transformation following the **advent** of the internet, and thanks to the **ongoing** digitalization of modern life, consumers from every country now profit from the **perks** of online transactions. As internet access and adoption are rapidly increasing worldwide, the number of digital buyers keeps climbing every year. In 2020, over two billion people purchased goods or services online, and during the same year, e-retail sales surpassed 4.2 trillion U.S. dollars worldwide.

Internet users can choose from various online platforms to browse, compare, and purchase the items or services they need. Leading the global ranking of online retail websites in terms of traffic is Amazon: The Seattle-based e-commerce giant registered over 5.2 billion visitors in June 2020.

One of the most visible trends in the world of e-commerce is the unprecedented usage of mobile **devices**. In 2021, smartphones accounted for almost 70 percent of all retail website visits worldwide, although desktop and tablet visits generated higher **conversion rates** in 2020. As the adoption of mobile devices is progressing at a rapid pace, mobile integration will continue to shape the shopping experience of the future. **M-commerce** is particularly popular across Asia, with countries like South Korea generating up to 65 percent of their total online transactions via mobile traffic.

Adapted from *statista.com*, October 2021.

Word box

- ongoing: *en cours*
- advent (n): *avènement*
- perk (n): *avantage*
- device(n): *dispositif*

Task 1

1. Read the whole text.

2. Write the equivalent in French for:

– digital (adj): ......

– digitalization (n): ......

3. Find the key idea(s) in each paragraph.

§1 ......

§2 ......

§3 ......

4. Write an organized account of the article in French (50 to 100 words).

Document 2 Audio

Ruby Chocolate is the new black

Audio 17
liennathan.fr/6u4z9k

Word box

- concoction: *préparation/ mélange/concoction*
- shade: *teinte*
- a trade secret: *un secret de fabrication*
- skeptical: *sceptique*

Task 2

1. Listen to the whole audio.

a. Take down notes about what you believe is important.

....

b. How do you understand the expression "the new black"?

....

2. Organize your ideas and make a plan.

....

3. Write an organized account in French.

....

Document 3 Video

Coca marketing campaign in Australia

Video 08
liennathan.fr/az54f9

Task 3

1. Watch the video.

a. Anticipate from the title.

....

b. Write how you consume and then compare.

....

c. Watch the whole video and collect the main ideas, the examples, and write a report.

....

2. Organize all information you have collected.

3. Write a report.

TRAINING
EXAMS
EXERCISES
INTERNSHIP

2 Background

How does marketing operate?

Marketing is a process based on multiple activities to sell a product to consumers referred to as the 4 Ps of the marketing mix: Product Place Price Promotion

– The product or service must be designed to satisfy and attract its targets audience. Audiences are not targeted at random. Marketers should know who their core targets are according to age group, gender, social background, etc.

– The place where the product will be sold to the customers must also be decided after a thorough study on how the company wants its product to be positioned. That is the reason why customers cannot find luxury brands at huge retailers' stores. If luxury goods were marketed in a superstore, it would greatly damage the brand image of the companies they belong to.

– The price has to correspond to the product's features and to the image it is supposed to convey. A too low price has the same negative impact as a too high price.

– Promotion. To make their products known to their audience, marketers generally communicate through advertising although an increasing number of high profile companies rely on word of mouth.

– Packaging is sometimes considered as the 5th P of the marketing mix in an increasingly competitive market where each brand's goal is to stand out.

I Retailing

Without retailing manufacturers would not be able to reach the customers, which makes of retailing the final but essential link between companies and consumers.

The retailing landscape has undergone tremendous changes ever since high technology has allowed customers to make their purchase in one click. Smartphones' cutting edge technology allowing their users to compare, buy, and pay in one device is aggravating the pressure on retailers. In order to fight back, traditional brick-and-mortar retailers have to wrack their brains to find how they can attract customers again and keep them loyal.

II How do retailers fight back?

Pop up stores have been multiplying ever since the first pop up store opened in Los Angeles in 2000. The aim is to offer customers an original experience where the point of sales becomes a place for short lasting events.

III Multi format stores/multi channel retail

Mainstream grocery stores such as Carrefour in France, Tesco in the UK and Walmart in the US have developed multi format stores allowing them to open small and medium sized points of sale in the center of cities and towns.

IV Click and Collect

In an effort to counter the growing power of online retailers such as Amazon, mainstream grocery stores around the world have developed a Click and Collect service. Customers are invited to shop online and drive to collect their prepaid and prepacked groceries directly delivered in their cars' boots by members of the staff.

V Conclusion: the price war

Retailers are doing their best to satisfy their customers' needs for a specific product by making it available almost instantaneously either in the point of sales or at their doorsteps. And yet, some realize they cannot compete with giants like Amazon which are able to deliver at their customers' doorstep a branded product for almost half the price they would have paid in a point of sale.

Now that Amazon has tapped the grocery market, mainstream grocery retailers find themselves threatened by two enemies: the online giant on one side and the German hard discounters on the other side. We can wonder what place will be left for them in the years to come.

Test

**Say if the following statements are true or false.
Write a sentence supporting your answer.**

1. Marketing is based on a unique activity. ❑ T ❑ F

2. The 4th p of the marketing mix is packaging. ❑ T ❑ F

3. Prices must always be as low as possible. ❑ T ❑ F

4. Products or services must be available in all types of points of sales. ❑ T ❑ F

5. It is important for marketers to define their core targets. ❑ T ❑ F

6. Advertising is not always necessary for famous companies. ❑ T ❑ F

7. Retailing has changed because of high technology. ❑ T ❑ F

8. A pop up store is a temporary online store. ❑ T ❑ F

9. Carrefour Tesco and Walmart have only one format stores. ❑ T ❑ F

10. Click and collect services try to counter the power of on line giants. ❑ T ❑ F

11. Amazon's products are more expensive because they are delivered at the customer's doorstep. ❑ T ❑ F

2 Background

What is digital marketing?

Digital marketing, also referred to as 'online marketing', 'internet marketing' or 'web marketing', uses internet and online based digital technologies such as computers, mobile phones and other digital media and platforms to promote products and services. Its ongoing spectacular development which began in the 1990s, changed the way brands and businesses use technology for marketing. Today, all retailers, large or small propose their own interactive websites where clients can browse and order their products and services online. The boom of hi tech devices such as smartphones and tablets allow an increasing number of people to visit retailers' sites wherever they are, encouraging them to compare, choose and buy their products or services in one click.

From the marketers point of view

Today's consuming trends, aggravated by the pandemic, have encouraged people to use their digital devices instead of going to physical stores. Retailers today cannot expect to survive the competition if their digital marketing is not adapted to their prospective customers needs. A brand's priority Is to create and maintain a performing commercial website where customers can easily navigate to find the best suited product or service at the best price.

A short list of the main techniques used by brands to improve their digital marketing

- Search engine optimization (SEO).
  It consists in improving the visibility of companies' websites when people browse the internet looking for a product or a service.
- Search engine marketing (SEM):
  Companies buy well positioned ads appearing on top of search results: it has a positive impact on brand awareness and conversion rates
- Social media marketing:
  Marketing through social medias such as Meta (Facebook), twitter Instagram; LinkedIn has become essential as it allows companies to promote themselves to large, diverse audiences that could not be reached through traditional marketing such as phone and email- based advertising.

Besides, marketing on most social media platforms comes at little to no cost- making it accessible to any size business. Social media can also be used to promote brand events, to engage with customers directly etc., Moreover companies can easily use social media to select the age range, location, gender, and interests of their core targets. Furthermore, based on a customer's recent search history they can be 'followed' on the internet so they see advertisements from similar brands, products, and services This enables businesses to target the specific customers that they know are more liable to be interested and to purchase their product or service, something that had limited capabilities up until the digital age.

Digital marketing weaknesses

Digital marketing means collecting and storing a huge number of data liable to be misused or hacked. Consequently data security is the top issue digital marketers are confronted to. For customers, privacy and phishing concerns can stop them from buying online.

A brand reputation can also be tainted by bad reviews, while copyright and plagiarism represent another difficulty: digital media is remarkably easy to copy and reproduce. Indeed, copyright laws are increasingly hard to enforce, as the music and movie industries have discovered to their cost.

Conclusion

Society continues to become more and more impersonal as digitized machines replace humans. People shop online, do their banking online, pay bills online, and increasingly work online. Transport is also set to become automated, which will ultimately result in taxis and delivery vehicles becoming driver free. Loneliness and a lack of human contact with a real person are becoming increasingly common. Do we really want this?

Test

Read the background carefully and answer the following questions.

1. Quote the other names given to digital marketing.

2. Quote 3 different digital technologies.

3. When did digital marketing begin?

4. What can customers do on retail websites?

5. What is the role of smartphones in digital marketing?

6. What do the initials SEO and SEM stand for?

7. Why is social media marketing attractive for businesses?

8. Give two examples of digital marketing drawbacks.

9. According to the conclusion, what will be the consequences of digitization and automation on social relationships? Do you agree?

2 PowerPoint Presentation

MACY'S SWOT

1. **Study Macy's SWOT.**
2. **Make your own SWOT for one of the following companies:**
   MARKS AND SPENCER'S • ALDI • OXFAM
   a. Prepare a PowerPoint presentation.
   b. Presente to the class.

Favourable | Unfavourable

Internal

Strengths

- One of the largest chain stores in the US operating more than 800 stores across various states.
- Excellent brand recognition.
- Wide variety of products.
- Ships products to over 100 countries across the world.
- Quality customer services.
- Excellent updated and high-profile stores.
- Strong market share.

Weaknesses

- Does not generate enough revenue.
- The company has limited global brand recognition. No international scope.
- The market share is decreasing due to fierce competition.
- The company should plan to invest and spread and operate more subsidiaries.

SWOT

External

Opportunities

- The company's reputed brand name could be marketed across the globe.
- E-commerce is another opportunity that the company has to develop
- The company should open new stores to boost sales.
- With the promotional events such as environmental causes the company can create more awareness.

Threats

- The company should focus on the competitors and counter their moves.
- Low prices offered by the major brands such as Walmart.
- Massive attacks by the giants of e-commerce.
- Slowdown of economy makes people spend less.

Act

Choose one of the following role plays to act in front of the class.

Role play 1

Student A tries to convince that traditional dairy products should be replaced.

Student B is hard to convince.

Role play 2

Student A is a spokesperson for an industrial food company. He/she is debating with student B about the dangers of processed industrialized food.

Student B is a spokesperson for an environmental group called "Forks over Knives" defending organic food.

Role play 3

Student A is a fan of e-commerce and online shopping.

Student B only buys his products in physical stores and is strongly opposed to buying online.

Notes

TRAINING
EXAMS
EXERCISES
INTERNSHIP

Companies

Why Facebook became Meta?

Word box

- revenue: *chiffre d'affaires*

Video 09
liennathan.fr/h328mp

?

1. Who presents the video?

....

....

2. Why did he decide to change facebook's brand name?

....

....

3. What is the company's new name?

....

....

4. What is the origin of the name?

....

....

3

The largest companies in the world

Questions

1. Quote the companies belonging to the following sectors:

a. Car industry: ....

b. Oil industry: ....

c. Retail: ....

d. High tech: ....

2. Which one has the largest revenue?

....

Notes

....

....

....

3 » Starters

Document 1

Only 10 companies control almost every large food and beverage brand in the world

These companies — Nestlé, PepsiCo, Coca-Cola, Unilever, Danone, General Mills, Kellogg's, Mars, Associated British Foods, and Mondelez — each employ thousands and make billions of dollars in revenue every year. Each company owns a variety of brands consumers are familiar with, but most consumers are not aware these brands they buy every day belong to multi -billion dollar corporations. For example, when you buy a box of Pringles, the money goes to Kellog's, The famous mineral water brand Evian belongs to Danone, and the Coca-Cola Company owns 200 brands worldwide, including Sprite, Fanta, Schweppes. The giant company also sells mineral water, coffee and teas.

1. Write the names of the brands you recognize.
2. What do they sell?
3. How are Danone and Evian related?
4. What about Pringles and Kellogg's?
5. What are their revenues?

Document 2

Audio 18
liennathan.fr/jvu969

Companies Facing Environmental Issues

Tick the right box.

1. Top companies in the world:
   - are aware of climate change. ❑
   - are not interested in climate change. ❑
   - will have to to change their strategy because of climate change. ❑
2. Oil companies:
   - aren't responsible for damaging the environment. ❑
   - aren't the only ones damaging the planet. ❑
   - are doing their best to reduce pollution. ❑
3. Ikea:
   - is aggravating the greenhouse effect because it uses a lot of chemical material. ❑
   - has no negative impact on the environment because it uses natural material. ❑
   - has started to make efforts to reduce its impact. ❑

4 Electronic devices:
   - are the least polluting. ❑
   - aren't considered dangerous. ❑
   - are the ones generating tons of waste. ❑

Document 3
Samsung and Apple

1. Identify the document.
2. What are these companies famous for?
3. Do they work together? Why?
4. Do they cooperate with each other?
5. What would they both like to be?
6. Which one appears as the strongest in the visual?
7. Do you think this could change? Why?

Document 4
What is a start-up ?

1. Identify the document.
2. List all the elements necessary to launch a start-up.
3. Is money the most important element?
4. Why are teamwork and innovations essential?
5. Is it true also for other types of companies?

3 Prep page

Audio 19
liennathan.fr/85ah9p

Text

Small Businesses Can Make a Big Impact on the Economy

Being a small business owner is challenging. Oftentimes they're independently owned and operated and have few employees. Despite and because of this, small businesses are vital to the future of the United States. These businesses might be small but their impact is not.

Small businesses are often eclipsed in the news by large corporations and conglomerates. They may not generate as much revenue individually as large corporations but they're vital to the success of our economy. These aren't the mom and pop stores that you'd traditionally imagine and there's more industry variety now than in the past. Nearly anything imaginable can be transformed into a small business with hard work and a little luck.

Small businesses give people the opportunity to achieve financial independence, encourage innovation, and create employment opportunities. It's that sort of desire for independence that boosted the freelance contractor economy. Being your own boss is challenging but definitely empowering.

Never forget the impact that your small business can have in your community businesses are born out of big ideas that no one else believes in yet. Massive companies starting in garages is a real thing too, and that's how we ended up with Microsoft, Apple, Amazon, Google, HP, and Disney. Each of these founders had an innovative idea that they believed in. In many cases, true innovators have to believe in themselves first and prove their ideas can be done before anyone else will believe in them.

Small businesses generate a broad variety of new employment opportunities. It's easy to underestimate their importance if you neglect to look closely at the statistics. In reality, small businesses account for between 60-80% of all U.S. jobs. Since 1995, small businesses are responsible for paying out 44% of the total U.S. private payroll. Another important advantage of small businesses is that they give money back to their community because the people who work there also live and spend there. That revenue and the resulting tax dollars are then spread around the community, enriching and supporting everyone in the process.

Our nation's stability is in part based upon a stable economy and the financial strength derived from these businesses. Small businesses are an engine of growth that allows both citizens and the government to acquire the goods and services they need to grow. At the same time it allows real people with good ideas to act upon them and make their business a reality. In turn this stimulates local (and national) economies and encourages others to take the same leap toward becoming a small business owner.

■ Adapted from *the Huffington post*, 2019.

Notes

A step-by-step approach

1 Lexical work

Find the lexical equivalents in the text:

a. Propriétaire : ....

b. Entre prise indépendante : ....

c. Entreprise familiale : ....

d. Salaires du secteur privé : ....

e. Moteur de croissance : ....

2 Read the whole text

a. Comment on the title: ....

b. Identify the source of the document (title, source, nature).

....

3 Check the facts

Underline the right statement:

a. The article is about the revenue of small companies in the world.

b. The article is about the domination of big companies.

c. The article is about the impact of small businesses on the US economy.

4 Train for the exam

Find the key ideas in each paragraph.

§1 ....

§2 ....

§3 ....

§4 ....

§5 ....

§6 ....

5 Topic debrief

Use your answers above to write a short account of the article (50 to 100 words).

Language

Les subordonnées concessives → page 198 / Le présent simple → page 190
Might **→ page 175 / Les quantifieurs → page 199**

Translate into French.

1. **Despite** this, small businesses are vital to the future.
2. Small businesses **generate** a broad variety of new employment opportunities.
3. Small companies have **fewer employees**.
4. They **might be** small but their impact is big.

TRAINING

EXAMS

EXERCISES

INTERNSHIP

Text

How Aldi is changing America's supermarket

Audio 20
liennathan.fr/33ikz2

How a cheap, brutally efficient grocery chain is changing America's supermarkets.

Running a supermarket in America has never been harder: Profits are thin and online shopping and home delivery are changing the way people buy their food. Pressures are so intense that some famous regional chains filed for bankruptcy. Large companies increasingly control the industry, which had long operated as a dispersed network of smaller, local grocers. And even Walmart—the largest player of all—faces new competition from Amazon.

But when Walmart's US CEO Greg Foran invokes words like "fierce," "good" and "clever" in speaking almost admiringly about one of his competitors, he's not referring to Amazon. Foran is describing Aldi, the no-frills German discount grocery chain that's growing aggressively in the United States and reshaping the industry along the way.In recent years, Aldi has expanded its produce and organic offers to draw in more customers.

New customers may be surprised at first by the experience of shopping at an Aldi, which expects its customers to endure a number of minor inconveniences not typical at other American grocery stores. Shoppers need 25 cents to rent a shopping cart. Plastic and paper bags are available only for a fee. And at checkout, cashiers hurry shoppers away, expecting them to bag their own groceries in a separate location away from the cash register. But customers are willing to do the extra work because the prices are so cheap that Aldi often beats Walmart at its own low-price game amazing.

Aldi has more than 1,800 stores in 35 states and is focused on growing in the Midwest, the Mid-Atlantic, Florida and California. It's on track to become America's third largest supermarket chain behind Walmart and Kroger, with 2,500 stores by the end of 2022. Its close competitor Lidl, another German grocer with a similar low-cost business model, is racing to grow in the United States, too.

The two discount chains have forced the rest of the grocery industry to make big changes to hold onto their customers. Aldi has even opened a store in Bentonville, Arkansas, just a mile from Walmart's corporate headquarters."I never underestimate them," Foran said at an industry conference in March. "I've been competing against Aldi for 20-plus years. They are fierce and they are good."

■ Adapted from, *CNN Business*, March 2020.

A step-by-step approach

1 Lexical work

a. Find the lexical equivalents in the text for:

Concurrence: ....

Concurrent: ....

Caisse (la machine): ....

Caissier/ère : ....

b. Find the French equivalents:

CEO: ....

File for bankruptcy: ....

No-frills: ....

2 Read the whole text

a. Comment on the title.

b. What is changing America's supermarkets?

3 Check the facts

Say if the following statements are true or false.

a. Nowadays, it is easier for American supermarket chains to make profits. ❑ T ❑ F

b. Aldi offers a wider number of organic products to compete with Amazon. ❑ T ❑ F

c. Walmart is the largest American grocery retailer. ❑ T ❑ F

d. Aldi is gaining ground in the US because its prices are sometimes cheaper than Walmart's. ❑ T ❑ F

e. Aldi has too many inconveniences to attract customers. ❑ T ❑ F

f. Aldi will have opened over 2000 stores in the US before 2023. ❑ T ❑ F

g. Lidl is a new American hard discounter. ❑ T ❑ F

h. Aldi's corporate headquarters are located in Akansas. ❑ T ❑ F

4 Train for the exam

Find the keys ideas in each paragraphs.

§1-2 ....

§3 ....

§4 ....

§5 ....

§6 ....

5 Topic debrief

Use the information above to write a 50 to 100 words account of the article.

Language

Les adverbes → page 170 / Les propositions infinitives → page 197
Le *present perfect* → page 192

Translate into French.

1. Large companies increasingly control the industry.
2. **Cashiers expect shoppers to bag their own groceries.**
3. Aldi has even opened a store in Bentonville.
4. **I've been competing against Aldi for 20-plus years.**

Notes

TRAINING

EXAMS

EXERCISES

INTERNSHIP

3 Video track

1 Pronunciation work

Audio 21
liennathan.fr/pa5r26

Listen, repeat the following words and record yourself.
South Korea • dust mist • carbon footprint • environment • award • harmful • automated • welding machine • waste water • eco-friendly • sustainable development.

2 Before you start watching the video

a. **Where was this video taken?**

....

....

b. **What is a green company?**

....

....

3 Watch the video

Video 10
liennathan.fr/694tur

Underline the words you hear among the following list:
Dust • Carbon footprint • emissions • profits • environment • auto parts • award • harmful • plant • automated • waste • measurement • storage • eco-friendly • decrease • sustainable development • label • responsible • benefits.

Video

S. Korean green companies adopt eco-friendly systems to protect environment

4 A step-by-step approach

1. Watch the whole video once

Underline the statement which best sums up the video.

a. This footage is about the way green companies around the world can protect the environment

b. This video is about how some eco- friendly South Korean companies manage to reduce their carbon footprint.

2. Watch the video a second time

c. What is the source of this video?

....

d. What phenomenon makes more Korean companies go green?

....

e. Does going green imply reducing productivity?

....

f. Nowadays what are companies also focusing on?

....

g. What products does the company given as an example make?

....

h. What did the government give this company and why?

....

i. How did this company innovate?

....

j. What are they able to save during the night?

....

k. What are the results on its productivity?

....

l. On its toxic emissions?

....

m. What elements are important to achieve sustainable development?

....

n. What other companies are involved in sustainable development?

....

5 Train for the exam

Oral report: put together all the information you have collected and report to the class.

3 Audio track

1 Pronunciation work

Audio 22
liennathan.fr/f6y79s

Listen the following words. Then repeat them and record yourself.
Greenwashing • whistle blowing • lure • research • honest • environmentally • commitment • out of reach • law enforcement • buzz words • time consuming.

2 Before listening

a. Comment on the visual document.

b. Find information about:

– The COP 26 ....

– Glasgow ....

c. Translate into French "Little streams make big rivers".

....

d. Explain the meaning of this proverb in English in simple words. You can give examples.

....

....

....

....

3 Listen to the audio

Audio

Are companies guilty of greenwashing?

Audio 23
liennathan.fr/33va9n

e. Anticipate the topic of the audio.

f. Listen and try to understand the following words:
Misleading • sensitive • by pass • laws • enforcement • commitment • lure • mass fashion • time consuming • out of reach • insight • issue.

g. Debrief with the other students and the teacher about their meaning.

4 A step-by-step approach

1. Listen to the whole audio once

Tick the right box.

a. The topic of the day is the COP 26 and its conclusions. ❑
b. The programme is about the oil and car industries using greenwashing to improve their image. ❑
c. The programme is about the definition of greenwashing and how it is also used by the fashion industry. ❑

2. Listen to the whole audio a second time

→ Listen to the first part

Say if the following statements are true or false. Support your answer with a sentence.

d. Greenwashing means that companies are doing their best to save the planet. ❑ T ❑ F
e. Greenwashing is illegal is some countries but the laws aren't always enforced. ❑ T ❑ F
f. Greenwashing involves only polluting industries. ❑ T ❑ F
g. The fashion industry is being honest with consumers. ❑ T ❑ F

→ Listen to the second part

Answer the questions.

h. How does the fashion industry lure its consumers?

....

i. Quote two fashion retailers involved in greenwashing

....

j. What words should raise consumers' suspicion?

....

k. How should consumers react when they hear those words?

....

l. What makes this type of research difficult for consumers?

....

m. What proverb shows that Petra Schonberg is quite optimistic?

....

n. What example does she give?

....

o. What shows that the audience is satisfied with the programme?

....

5 Train for the exam

Choose one of the two following exercises:

a. Prepare an oral report on the audio (30" to 60").
b. Prepare a written report on the audio (50 to 100 words).

3 Tasks

Document 1 Video

Getting to the bottom of Samsung's Galaxy Note 7 crisis

Video 11
liennathan.fr/9c35tk

Task 1

1. Watch the video.

a. Explain what you know about Samsung and the problem they had with their flagship product. ....

b. What do you know about the smartphone market today?

....

c. What should smatphone companies focus on to establish and keep their customers' trust?

....

2. Organize all the information you have collected.

....

3. Write a report.

Audio 24
liennathan.fr/9isp97

Document 2 Audio

Thanks to Tiwal, sailing becomes easy and cheap

Task 2

1. Listen to the whole audio.

a. Anticipate from the title.
b. Collect key words, key data, key ideas.

2. Write an organized account in English.

Notes

....

....

....

Document 3 Text

Audio 25
liennathan.fr/2vb2y3

What does it take to destroy a company's brand name?

What changes a corporate branding disaster from being a costly and damaging affair, to one with fatal consequences for the company concerned?

How is it some firms have been able to bounce back while others are unable to survive? Both the German car giant Volkswagen and South Korean mobile phone maker Samsung have been subject to controversy in recent times. VW is still dealing with its diesel emissions scandal, and Samsung has had to face overheating phone batteries. Yet both have put these corporate disasters behind them. VW has just seen its pretax profits rise 44.3%, while Samsung's operating profits have gone up by 48%. Other firms have not been so fortunate.

Emissions scandal

In 2015, it emerged that Volkswagen had fitted illegal software to its diesel vehicles allowing them to cheat on emissions tests. It meant VW's diesel vehicles were able to emit up to 40 times the legally allowable pollution level. The revelations came as a shock to many. VW has so far agreed to pay about $25bn (£19bn) to address US claims.

Yet this public relations disaster has not stopped VW from overtaking Toyota as the world's largest carmaker.

As the scandal broke, VW put together a comprehensive plan to deal with it. It has acknowledged its wrong-doing, pleading guilty in the USA. At the same time, the group has embarked on a significant cost-cutting exercise. The scandal has cost VW billions, but could have cost it even more if it had mishandled things. What VW did was clearly wrong but it has had a positive effect on the group.

Burning batteries

If you're one of the world's leading smartphone sellers, the last thing you want is to have to recall one of your flagship products.

Yet that is just what South Korea's electronics giant Samsung was forced to do amid reports of inflammable batteries. Last September, Samsung recalled 2.5 million Galaxy Note 7 smartphones after complaints of overheating and exploding batteries. The debacle cost Samsung about $5.3bn, and has been hugely damaging to its reputation. Samsung has said it takes "responsibility for our failure to ultimately identify and verify the issues arising out of the battery design and manufacturing process." That acceptance is a crucial part of its crisis management strategy, says Wayne Lam, analyst at IHS Market.

Adapted from *www.bbc.com*, 2017.

Task 3

1. Read the whole text and answer.

a. Which companies is the text about?

b. Describe the mistakes they made.

c. Do mistakes and frauds always damage a company's brand name?

Notes

2. Organise your ideas and make a plan.

3. Write an organized account of the article in English (50 to 100 words).

3

Background

What is a company today?

▶ The word **company** is a general term which can be replaced by **firm** or **corporation**, according to the context. The word **business** can also be used to refer to a company.

Companies can be small, **medium sized (SME)** or big. They can be **global**, meaning they are present in many parts of the world. A new breed of companies, called **start-ups**, are innovative and fast growing businesses generally launched by one person or a small team.

Companies **manufacture** and **market** goods and services. They are managed by an executive team headed by the **Chief Executive Officer (CEO)**, sometimes called the **chairman**.

Companies are made of several **departments** (i.e. the **sales department**, the **human resources** department, the **accounting department, the R&D → research and development department** etc.) and generally have their **headquarters** in their hometown (i.e Coca Cola in Atlanta, Georgia, USA).

Companies manufacturing products often operate their own factories, but they can also **outsource** the manufacturing process (i.e. Renault's Dacia is manufactured in Romanian factories).

The GAFAM: Google, Apple, Facebook, Amazon and Microsoft are called the "big" five or the GAFAM. They represent the most active and innovative global US companies focused on high technology and artificial intelligence (AI).

The BATX: The GAFAM's domination is being challenged by the Chinese BATX, along with the South Korean consumer electronics company Samsung. These initials stand for four Chinese companies similar to the GAFAM:

- Baidu (the Chinese Google)
- Alibaba (the equivalent of Amazon)
- Tencent (a social network like Facebook)
- Xiomi (the Chinese equivalent of Apple)

I External problems

- Companies depend on the general economic and political context which can have a disastrous impact on their bottom lines. For example, the economic downturn triggered by the subprime crisis of 2008 forced many companies of goods and services to file for bankruptcy.
- They also depend on the cost of raw materials.
- Natural disasters such as floods, earthquakes, hurricanes, tsunamis, droughts can seriously damage a company.
- Climate change and environmental change can **transform the demand for goods**: for example, if global temperatures rise, demand for cold weather products such as heating might decline.
- Massive social unrest can also pose a threat to companies. When strikes affect the transport network, employees are late or stuck at home.
- New legislation imposing new standards can force companies to abruptly change the manufacturing of their products, or their strategy. This type of changes can come with huge financial cost.

There are no real solutions to avoid external problems except being constantly on the watch to be able to prevent a disaster.

II Internal problems

Companies also have to face internal problems although they should be easier to prevent than external ones:

- Problems in the managing team may have negative consequences on a company, affecting its profitability.
- Lack of trust between the employer and the employees can constitute an obstacle for the company's growth.
- A wrong strategic move may also have long lasting consequences.
- A bad public image due to a company's mistreatments of its workforce, at home or abroad.
- A bad public image because the company has betrayed consumers' trust.
- Faulty products can also damage a company's image with consequences on its sales.

Test

I Read the background carefully and answer the following questions.

1. What are the other words for company?

2. What are the different sizes of companies?

3. Who is the CEO?

4. Where do companies generally have their headquarters? Give examples.

5. Quote two of the departments you can find in a company.

6. Do companies always operate their own factories?

7. What does the acronym GAFAM stand for?

8. What companies are referred to as the BATX?

II Give a detailed answer to each question.

9. Are pandemics and other natural disasters external or internal problems for companies?

10. Make a list of the internal problems companies may be confronted to.

3 PowerPoint Presentation

EasyJet's SWOT

1. **Study Easy Jet's SWOT closely.**
2. **Choose a company in the list below.**

RYAN AIR • TESLA • IKEA • ZARA

a. Prepare a power point presentation of their SWOT.

b. Present it to the class.

	Favourable	Unfavourable
Internal	**Strengths** • **Network:** huge network in Europe, carrying more than 73 million passengers, second biggest airline carrier in Europe by number of passengers carried • **Pricing:** average fares somewhere around 50% lower than those of the major carriers on short haul routes and 20% to 40% below those of most other lower cost competitors • **Fleet:** average fleet age is around four years, versus 9-11 years for European flag carriers, giving advantages in terms of fuel efficiency, maintenance costs and customer perception	**Weaknesses** • **Competition:** cost per seat is around 50% higher than Ryanair's, so it is vulnerable to direct competition • **Earnings:** highly seasonal hence vulnerable to any unexpected problems in the summer
External	**Opportunities** • **Market growth:** a significant market player in the growing aviation industry in years to come • **Cost cuttings:** have defined areas for cost reduction, such as airports, ground handling, engineering and fuel	**Threats** • **Brexit:** the consequences of Brexit still unknown → decided to move to Vienna after Brexit to remain in the euro zone • **Climate change:** increasing number of periods of bad weather across Europe disrupting air carriers • **Pandemics:** the latest Sars Covid-19 pandemic put all air traffic at a stop for many months generating big losses.

SWOT

Act

Choose one of the following role plays to act in front of the class.

Role play 1

Student A only buys his products from major companies and stores.

Student B prefers to trust small companies and mom and pop stores.

Imagine a dialogue in which each student develops his/her arguments to convince the other.

Role play 2

Student A has an idea for a new product: a motorbike helmet for women only.

She/ he is convinced consumers are going like it and buy it.

Student B is isn't convinced and develops her/his arguments against this innovation.

Imagine their dialogue.

Role play 3

Student A buys his/her clothes only from big retailers who advertise their commitment to the planet.

Student B believes these companies are greenwashing in order to attract customers.

Imagine the dialogue.

Notes

Work

Gender equality in the workplace by ILO
(International Labour Organisation)

Video 12
liennathan.fr/xg44w6

1. What is ILO? What does it take care of?

2. Which women is it about?

3. Why is affordable care a priority?

4. What is the impact of violence towards women?

5. What about women's salary?

■ Source : Otto Dettmer, *Automation*, illustration, XXIe siècle.

Questions

1. What does the picture by Otto Dettmer represent?
2. How do people feel about it? Why?
3. Should we also rejoice at seeing boring tasks performed by robots?
4. What do you see in the background?

Notes

4 » Starters

Document 1

Looking for your next job? Make sure your social media profiles are safe for work.

Employers look at social media accounts for an array of reasons, but many want to make sure a candidate will be a good fit with their company.

Social media channels employers check

Before you apply for a job, you should audit your social media accounts. Job seekers should assume that employers will check every social media platform. While it's important to audit every account, there are some platforms hiring managers are more likely to check, such as LinkedIn.

"The three main platforms that most employers check are LinkedIn, Facebook and Twitter,» said Matt Erhard, senior partner at Summit Search Group. «I am personally most interested in the candidate's LinkedIn profile, as it's the most relevant.»

What to avoid on social media to be hired

While they might not be searching for anything negative, more than half of the employers who were surveyed (57%) said they found something during their social screenings that led them to not hire someone.

According to the survey, these are the leading types of posts and behavior that left employers with a bad impression:

1. Job candidate posted provocative or inappropriate photographs, videos or information: 40%
2. Job candidate posted information about them drinking or using drugs: 36%
3. Job candidate had discriminatory comments related to race, gender, religion, etc.: 31%
4. Job candidate was linked to criminal behavior: 30%
5. Job candidate lied about their qualifications: 27%
6. Job candidate had poor communication skills: 27%
7. Job candidate bad-mouthed their previous company or fellow employees: 25%
8. Job candidate's screen name was unprofessional: 22%

■ Adapted from *businessnewsdaily.com*, November, 2021.

1. Identify the document.
2. Which platforms are most likely to be screened?
3. Why should job seekers "clean" their social media account?

Document 2

Audio 26
liennathan.fr/93n7cx

Metaverse

1. What is the meaning of metaverse.
2. What is a *portemanteau* word? What are the two examples provided by Joan?

Document 3

Video 13
liennathan.fr/787hhs

The World Ahead 2022: five stories to watch out for

1. What is hybrid working?
2. Who is in favour?
3. Who will lose out?

4 Prep page

Text

The Revolt of the American Worker

Audio 27
liennathan.fr/976gzb

All happy economies are alike; each unhappy economy is unhappy in its own way.

The labor situation looks like a genuine reduction in supply. Total employment is still five million below its prepandemic peak. Employment in the leisure and hospitality sector is still down more than 9 percent. Yet everything we see suggests a very tight labor market.

On one side, workers are quitting their jobs at unprecedented rates, a sign that they're confident about finding new jobs. On the other side, employers aren't just whining about labor shortages, they're trying to attract workers with pay increases. Over the past six months wages of leisure and hospitality workers have risen at an annual rate of 18 percent, and they are now well above their prepandemic trend.

The sellers' market in labor has also emboldened union members, who went on strike after receiving contract offers they consider inadequate.

Until recently conservatives blamed expanded jobless benefits, claiming that these benefits were reducing the incentive to accept jobs. But states that canceled those benefits early saw no increase in employment compared with those that didn't.

For America is a rich country that treats many of its workers remarkably badly. Wages are often low; adjusted for inflation, the typical male worker earned virtually no more in 2019 than his counterpart did 40 years earlier. Hours are long: America is a "no-vacation nation," offering far less time off than other advanced countries. Work is also unstable, with many low-wage workers – and nonwhite workers in particular – subject to unpredictable fluctuations in working hours that can wreak havoc on family life.

So although this new choosiness by workers who feel empowered is making consumers' and business owners' lives more difficult, let's be clear: overall, it's a good thing. American workers are insisting on a better deal, and it's in the nation's interest that they get it.

By Paul Krugman, *The New York Times*, December 8, 2021.

A step-by-step approach

1 Lexical work

Find the lexical equivalents in the text:

a. Le secteur de hôtellerie ....

b. Avoir confiance ....

c. Son homologue ....

Find the French equivalents:

a. A genuine reduction ....

b. At unprecended rates ....

c. To embolden ....

d. The incentive ....

2 Read the whole text

a. Comment on the title: two key words are repeated several times. What are these two words?
b. Identify the source of the document (title, source, nature).

3 Check the facts

Say if the following statements are true or false.

a. An unhappy economy is when there is a recession. ❑ T ❑ F
b. A tight labour market is when there are not enough workers looking for a job. ❑ T ❑ F
c. Workers go on strike more easily. ❑ T ❑ F
d. When workers have no job, they do not look for a new job as they get unemployment benefits. ❑ T ❑ F
e. American workers were treated badly. ❑ T ❑ F
f. With the pandemic, workers no longer want to cope with bad jobs. ❑ T ❑ F
g. Americans are right to look for better jobs. ❑ T ❑ F

4 Train for the exam

Rephrase in your own words.

a. What is the revolt of the American worker?
b. What has the pandemic triggered?

5 Topic debrief

Choose the sentence which you think corresponds best to the main topic of the document.

a. American workers are fed up with their lousy jobs so they have decided to resign in droves. ❑
b. The pandemic has enabled American workers to rethink their work-life balance and asked for better working conditions and higher pays. ❑

Notes

Language

Preterit simple → page XX / *Present perfect* → page XX

Translate into French.

1. Many Americans <u>hated</u> their jobs two years ago.
2. Conservatives <u>blamed</u> jobless benefits.
3. Over the past six months wages <u>have risen</u> at an annual rate of 18%.

TRAINING
EXAMS
EXERCISES
INTERNSHIP

4 Text track

Audio 28
liennathan.fr/9m3w8j

Text

Is the pandemic accelerating automation? Don't be so sure

As economies reopen, labour shortages are still worsening. In America the number of unfilled vacancies, at 9.3m, has never been so high. Even in Europe, a growing number of employers complain of how hard it is to find staff.

Economists have confidently asserted that a wave of job-killing robots was sweeping the labour market. In a recent co-written article Joseph Stiglitz, a Nobel prizewinner, says the extra costs of Covid-19 are "accelerating the development and adoption of new technologies to automate human work." But can pandemic-induced automation really be creating an army of surplus workers if employers are complaining of a deficit?

The economists had good reason to believe that job-killing automation would surge. Recessions often lead firms to adopt more robots, in part because labour gets more expensive as revenues but not wages decline. In a pandemic bosses have an extra incentive to automate jobs. Thanks largely to government stimulus programmes, firms have also accumulated spare cash, to deploy on robotics.

Those who believe that automation is speeding up can point to many examples. British farmers boast of using ever more machines to pick strawberries and kill weeds.

According to some research, last year automatable jobs vanished in large numbers. It is true that America's GDP is nearly at its pre-pandemic level even as the level of employment is 7m lower.

It is not only labour shortages which undermine the story. In America the wages of the worst-paid workers are rising more quickly than the average. *The Economist* has divided America's labour market into "routine" and "non-routine" roles. Routine jobs involve patterns which are easier for robots to learn. For four decades routine jobs have slowly declined, as robots have improved.

So far jobs were in relative decline before the pandemic, falling to 57% of the workforce by 2019. The trend has continued, with evidence of a Covid-19 acceleration. Automation is not, it seems depriving people of their jobs.

■ Adapted from, *The Economist*, June 19th 2021.

A step-by-step approach

1 Lexical work

Find the French equivalents:

a. Unfilled vacancies ....

b. Job-killing robots ....

c. Wages ....

d. Aftermath ....

Find the lexical equivalents in the text:

a. S'aggraver ....

b. Provoqué par la pandémie ....

c. Une raison supplémentaire ....

d. Se vanter ....

e. Provoqué par la Covid ....

2 Read the whole text

a. **Comment on the title.**

b. **Identify the source of the document (title, source, nature).**

3 Check the facts

Choose the right answer.

a. What is the problem in the US and in Europe?

– a recession ❑

– a pandemic ❑

– a labour shortage ❑

b. What do economists predict?

– the coming of robots ❑

– the end of work ❑

Answer the following questions:

c. Why are robots better?

– ....

– ....

d. What happened to wages of worst-paid workers? Has America more extra routine jobs?

e. So does it mean there are more automation investments? What has Covid-19 accelerated? More jobs? Fewer?

Notes

4 Train for the exam

a. **Write ideas that explain what automated jobs are.**

b. **Then list arguments that show labour shortages are not related to automation.**

5 Topic debrief

Choose the best recap.

a. Automation is the main focus of this article and claims that automation has no repercussion on employment, i.e. it does not reduce the number of jobs available. ❑

b. Automation is an on-going process that has not been sped up by the Covid-19 pandemic as the number of routine jobs has increased and unemployment is at its lowest. ❑

Language

Adjectifs composés → page 170 / *Present perfect* → page 192 / Comparatifs → page 179

Translate into French.

a. America's GDP is nearly at its **pre-pandemic** level.

b. For four decades, routine jobs **have slowly declined** as robots **have improved**.

c. Labour gets **more expensive** as revenues decline.

4 Video track

1 Pronunciation work

Audio 29
liennathan.fr/862vhr

Listen, repeat the following words and record yourself.
Historic • executives • lobby • unionizing • frustrated • overstaffing • striking • 9,000.

2 Before you start watching the video

a. **Anticipate on the title.**

....

b. **What do you know about Starbucks?**

....

3 Watch the video

Video 14
liennathan.fr/3rcg94

Underline the words you hear among the following list:
Particular • work • ripple effect • wages • labour shortages • upstate • tracking • rising power.

Video

Buffalo Starbucks Workers vote to form chain's 1st Union in US on ABC.

4 A step-by-step approach

1. Watch the whole video once

a. Identify the source of the document.

2. Watch the video a second time

b. Explain what Starbucks workers have voted on.

3. Watch the video a third time

c. What did Starbucks executives do as they were opposed to unionization?

d. What are the other companies where there are strikes that are mentioned?

e. What do workers want the company to improve?

5 Train for the exam

Write a report or make an oral presentation following the guidelines below.

I. Introduction: What is the topic?
Give the source.

II. Development
Problem the Starbucks workers have met

III. Conclusion

4 Audio track

1 Pronunciation work

Audio 30
liennathan.fr/9v4bc8

Listen to the following words. Then repeat them and record yourself.

Schedule • employment-to-population ratio • family circumstance • the permanent damage • devastating effect.

2 Before listening

a. Look at the visual document and say as much as you can.

....

b. Look at the title and rephrase it.

....

3 Listen to the audio

Audio

Women, Work and the Pandemic

Audio 31
liennathan.fr/7bag45

c. Anticipate the topic of the audio.

....

....

d. Who is the host?

....

....

e. Among the following words which ones do you hear?

Lockdowns • workforce • flexibility • housework/hospitality sector • to edge up • a drop-off • personal choice • educational needs • labour force • career • push back • to waste • pride • to keep up • tax laws • remote.

4 A step-by-step approach

1. Listen to the whole audio once

→ Listen to the first part

a. Collect data on the first interviewee ; her job ; the job of her husband.

2. Listen to the audio a second time

→ Listen to the second part

b. Find out how many women left their job during the lockdown.

c. Who does the household chores?

d. Why were working women hard-hit by Covid?

e. What is the name of the 2nd interviewee?

f. What has been the trend since the 1950s in terms of work?

g. What was the percentage of working women in April 2020?

h. What is the number of women who left the workforce and did not return?

i. Reasons that could explain this trend.

→ Listen to the third part

j. Is it good for the US economy if women do not go back to work?

k. What does "scarring" mean?

l. What has a devastating effect?

m. Did women go back to work when schools reopened?

n. What has become expensive?

o. What has Sarah been unable to do?

p. What is she proud of?

5 Train for the exam

Oral work: speak for at least two minutes about what you have just learned.
Put together all the information you have collected.

4 Tasks

Document 1 Video

Google execs tell employees they won't raise pay to match inflation

Video 15
liennathan.fr/h9e3v3

Task 1

1. Watch the video.

a. What are the companies that are mentioned in the video? (5)

b. Why do workers ask for a pay rise?

c. Will Google workers get a raise in salary?

d. Which company wants to unionize?

e. What do we see on the screen about Alphabet and Starbucks?

2. Organize all the information you have collected and write a report.

Document 2 Audio

Could a robot do your job?

Audio 32
liennathan.fr/m48pf7

Task 2

1. Listen to the whole audio.

a. Anticipate from the title.

2. Collect key words, key data, key ideas.

b. Inquire about the meaning of utopia and dystopia.

3. Write an organized account in English.
The following questions can help you:

– What are the jobs quoted in the audio that are being automated?

– What tasks are humanoid robots expected to perform?

– What is the difference between automation and Artificial Intelligence?

Document 3 Text

'I'm still in pain': Amazon employees say climate of fear has led to high rates of injuries

Audio 33
liennathan.fr/yi62z4

Workers say Amazon's 'excessively rapid work pace', surveillance and disciplinary systems have created a dangerous environment

In May Chloe Roberson of Chattanooga, Tennessee, injured her knee while working her shift at Amazon and she has been out of work since, while fighting with the company for workers' compensation and paid medical leave.

Roberson, 21, chose to go to the emergency room rather than Amazon's on-site medical clinic, Amcare, and was referred to a sports medicine doctor who diagnosed her with a dislocated patella (kneecap). Her initial recovery was 10 weeks of physical therapy followed by a steroid shot, but she was later scheduled for surgery on 28 October to repair her knee.

"While all of this is going on, I've been having to fight Amazon for time off and money," said Roberson. "They refused workers' compensation, as I had a dislocated patella when I was 14 years old. I'm 21 now so I don't see how it's related."

Reports of high injury rates and high turnover rates at Amazon warehouses around the US as a result of immense productivity pressures and quota rates on workers have been documented by numerous media outlets and organizations over the past several years and confirmed by OSHA logs. Amazon shareholders have recently called for an independent safety audit of the company [...].

Amazon did not comment on complaints about workers' compensation and deferred to a blog post by CEO Dave Clark on time-off task surveillance and disciplinary systems.

In regards to injury rates, a spokesperson for Amazon said in an email: "The safety and well-being of our employees is always a top priority. We recognize that helping employees stay safe in physical roles takes a lot of focus and investment, which is why we're investing hundreds of millions in safety in many different ways, from people – we now have a team of nearly 8,000 dedicated safety professionals – to training, to tools and technology."

OSHA: Occupational safety and Health Administration (Department of Labor in the USA)

Adapted from Michael Sainato, *The Guardian*, Thu 30 Dec 2021.

Task 3

1. Read the whole text and answer.

a. Who is Chloe Roberson?

....

b. What happened to her?

....

c. What was scheduled on October 28, 2021?

....

d. What does Chloe Roberson want Amazon to do? ....

e. What is Amazon known for?

....

f. What have many media outlets documented?

....

g. Why is OSHA mentioned in the text?

....

h. What is Amazon's response?

....

2. Organize your ideas and make a plan.

3. Write an organized account of the article in French (50 to 100 words).

TRAINING
EXAMS
EXERCISES
INTERNSHIP

4 Background

Hybrid work and Unionization: don't be sure

Digitization and automation are revolutionizing the workplace. The pandemic has also introduced working remotely and will change the relationship between employers and employees. So companies need to adapt to the future of work and stay competitive.

I Technology

While indeed some careers are disappearing, and certain elements of work are no longer necessary, only 5% of occupations are able to be automated in their entirety, according to McKinsey & Company. However, around 50% of work tasks worldwide are potentially automatable with existing technology. What will change is the nature of the work being done, not necessarily the entire career field.

Not to be forgotten is that technology doesn't only destroy, but it creates. This is indeed what Schumpeter has described as Creative destruction. In France, the rise of the Internet caused 500,000 jobs to be lost. But that's only one way to see it. This same trend led to the creation of 1.2 million new jobs. That's 2.4 new jobs for every one lost.

Along with this also comes new career options. The same study suggests that previously unpaid occupations, such as care and domestic work could grow from 50 million to 90 million jobs by 2030. We should not be surprised as the baby boomers have started to retire and will need looking after. Of course, this is more likely to apply to western countries that are able to pay for senior help and aid.

II Telecommuting or hybrid working

Put simply, telecommuting means using modern communication tools and technology to perform work duties from a remote location. But, bear in mind that telecommuting is not for everybody and not for every job. First, there will be jobs where telecommuting is not an option and second, telecommuters will have much less interaction with colleagues. Third, if some team members are physically closer to the boss, their promotion prospects could be better than other's. So the hybrid workplace will be unequal, unless bosses design it not to be.

So there are downsides and upsides to telecommuting but companies are already negotiating the number of days at home, financial compensations, etc.

III Labour shortages and how it brings back trade unions

Many countries are facing or will be facing labour shortages. Ireland faces shortages of lower-skilled workers and therefore there is subsequent pressure on wages. It is in care, manufacturing, agri-food, and food-processing sectors that the shortages are most acute. Therefore, when employment vacancies arose, they should be advertised domestically in the first instance and then in the EU and EEA to attract workers from these regions.

With staff shortages, the role of unions is shifting from saving jobs to boosting pay and conditions. So there is a rush of activity among union members pushing for better pay and conditions. Indeed, after decades of decline, trade union membership in the UK increased for the fourth year in a row in 2020, rising by almost 120,000 as employees sought protection from the risks of Covid-19 and redundancies. In the US unionization is back in the forefront and will reintroduce collective bargaining and better pay.

Test

Read the background carefully and answer the following questions.

1. What is "creative destruction"?

2. The workplace and work are changing. Why?

3. Should we worry that new technology is replacing the human workforce?

4. If tasks are done by robots or are automated, what does it mean for employees?

5. What figures are quoted about France?

6. Baby boomers are retiring, what does it mean for the labour market?

7. Covid-19 has brought with it new ways of working. Can it apply to everybody? Why? Why not?

8. Some people are afraid of not being promoted if they work from home. Do you agree with them?

9. Telecommuting is not for everyone. Do you see yourself working from home 2 days a week?

10. What can countries do to offset labour shortages?

11. Shall countries deal with shortages of unskilled employees in the same manner as skilled employees?

12. What about having access to the EU labour market?

13. Salaries are increasing: what are the expected consequences of an increase in pay?

14. Should we be in favour of unionization?

15. Labour stoppage has an impact on a company and on the GDP. What does it reflect?

4 PowerPoint Presentation

Trade union's SWOT

1. **Study Trade union's SWOT closely.**
2. **Choose a company in the list below:**

FORD • AMAZON • GENERAL MOTORS • GENERAL ELECTRIC

a. Prepare a PowerPoint presentation.

b. Present it to the class.

	Favourable	Unfavourable
Internal	**Strengths** • A strong political backing for trade unions • A more comfortable position & labour standards respected when labour shortage • Welfare of the employees of a company • Consistent media support • Collective bargaining	**Weaknesses** • A change in power can reverse a trend. • The growth of trade union has stagnated. • Trade unions can be political. • The trade union movement is fragmented. • Younger generation is less committed. • High union fees
External	**Opportunities** • Tightening in the labour market means more bargaining power • Abilities to unionize different industries: fast-food industry	**Threats** • Reverse of power may mean less support • Corruption is prevalent among trade unions

SWOT

Act

Choose one of the following role plays to act in front of the class.

Role play 1

Work in pairs: Student A is a spokesperson for the Real Living Wage Campaign. He/she wants to persuade the Human Resources Manager of a famous company (Student B) to adopt the Real Living Wage Programme for the company's workers.
Student B is the Human Resources Manager of a famous company, aware of its brand image. He/she wants to know what the Real Living Wage is about and needs to be convinced that he/she can adopt it for his/her workers without putting the company's profits in danger.
TIPS: Students A and B may use the arguments developed in the document in the previous pages as well as their own.

Role play 2

Student A is a reporter interviewing a young boy (Joe) who has been helped out of child labour thanks to a NGO.
Student B is the young boy answering Student A's questions about his past and present life.

Tips for Student A:
Ask questions about Joe's former work, his working conditions, salary, etc.
Ask questions about his present life, and what he plans for the future.
Use the vocabulary you have learned for the video.

Tips for Student B:
Prepare yourself to answer all the above questions and more.
Use the vocabulary you have learned from the video.

Role play 3

Student A and **Student B** are both Human Resource Managers in two different companies. They do not share the same view on workplace diversity:
Student A tries to convince Student B that diversity in the workplace is an asset for a company.
Student B doesn't believe in diversity. She/he counters Student A's arguments with her/his own.

Notes

TRAINING EXAMS EXERCISES INTERNSHIP

Transports

Why is the Tesla Semi the Future of trucks?

Video 16
liennathan.fr/7ue2i7

?

1. What do trucks transport ?

....

2. What has Tesla come up with ?

....

3. Why will Tesla Semi replace diesel trucks ?

....

Word box

- windshild: *pare-brise*
- wear: *usure*

5

Questions

1. What is the shortest route from Taiwan to Europe?
2. How long does it take a vessel around Cape of Good Hope?
3. What might be the reason for using the longest route?

Notes

5 » Starters

Document 1

Ethiopia opens new rail line to Djibouti in industrial drive

ADDIS ABABA (Reuters) - Ethiopia opened a new train line on Wednesday linking its land-locked capital to the Red Sea state of Djibouti, part of Addis Ababa's infrastructure program aimed at turning the poor, agrarian nation into an industrial hub.

Ethiopia's economy is one of the fastest growing in Africa, even though it has suffered a severe drought in 2016 and 2017. Growth has been fueled by construction of railways, roads and hydro-electric dams to power industry.

Ethiopian Railways Corporation spokesman Dereje Tefera said the $4 billion, Chinese-built 750-km (470-mile) electrified line "will minimize the cost of the transport and the transport time and it's free from pollution, it uses renewable energy."

"It's part of the trans-African railway network so it will give an opportunity for connecting Ethiopia with other neighboring countries," Dereje said.

Ethiopia's economic development has long been hampered by poor roads and an aging fleet of trucks, which ply the route between the industrial heartlands in the center of the country and Djibouti, Ethiopia's main import and export route.

■ Adapted from *Reuters staff* October 5, 2021.

1. Identify the document.
2. Why is China mentioned in the text?
3. What will the new rail track bring Ethiopia?

Document 2

The Economics of Shipping

Video 17
liennathan.fr/uc8i54

1. What do you think this video is about?
2. Why is rail good for shipping goods but not as good as maritime shipping?
3. 4 reasons for choosing sea shipping.

Document 3
Shipping & Customs

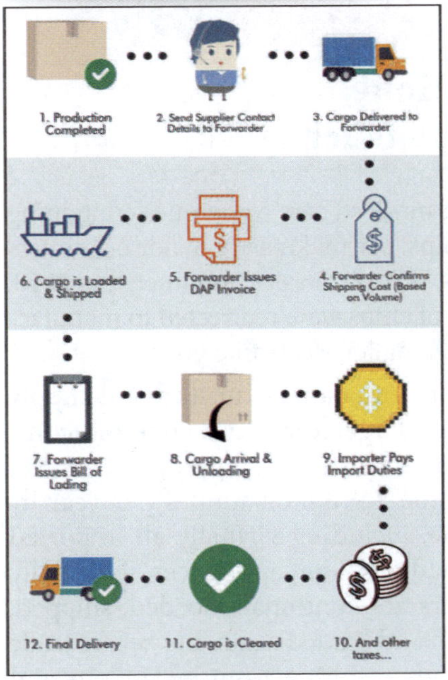

1. Identify the document.
2. How many steps are necessary before a cargo from China arrives at its final destination?
3. Which word refers to the client who ordered the cargo?
4. Explain what a transport supplier is. Do you know any transport supplier companies?
5. Apart from the price of the cargo, what are the other costs?
6. How long do you think it takes on average between the order and the delivery from China? (Look for the info on the net to check your answer.)

Document 4
Strait of Hormuz

Audio 34
liennathan.fr/r5c8b2

1. Locate the strait of Hormuz (Look at the general map).
2. Why is the Strait of Hormuz so busy?
3. Which countries need to ship oil and gas through the Strait of Hormuz?
4. What are the three countries mentioned on the map.
5. Look up each country and find out its population and its size.

5 Prep page

Audio 35
liennathan.fr/n7nt32

Text

Supply chains in 2022: shortages will continue, but for some sellers the problem will be too much stock

Everything was about shortages in 2021. COVID vaccine shortages at the start of the year were replaced by fears that we would struggle to buy turkeys and toys. Some shortages were resolved quickly, others linger.

It's worth reflecting that the shortages have happened for many reasons. During the early 2020 lockdowns, a sudden run on essentials such as toilet paper and pasta left shelves around the world bare. Singapore ran out of eggs. Retailers ordered more eggs, desperate to satisfy demand. But once the demand had been satisfied, there was suddenly an oversupply. In June 2021, distributors threw away 250,000 eggs.

This is what happens when demand temporarily changes. The effect magnifies with each tier of the supply chain as every supplier adds an extra buffer to their order to be on the safe side. Minute changes in customer demand can therefore result in huge extra demand for raw materials. This is called the bullwhip effect. As with a whip, a small flick of the wrist can lead to a big crack at the other end. The bullwhip effect can be from demand suddenly falling as well as rising. For instance, a combination of the crash in demand for new cars and higher demand for devices like laptops and games consoles for lockdown entertainment contributed to the semiconductor-chip shortage.

With modern cars sometimes containing 3,000 chips, car makers are major customers for chips. But as car sales plummeted in 2020, supplies of chips were redirected to manufacturers of smaller electronic goods.

Other imbalances in today's supply chains are larger than in competing companies or industries. Shipping containers move some 1.9 billion tonnes per year by sea alone, including virtually all imported fruits, gadgets and appliances. Normally containers are continually loaded, shipped, unloaded and loaded again, but severe trade disruptions resulting from lockdowns and border closures broke that cycle. Containers were left in wrong locations, shipping capacity was reduced and vessels couldn't land. Coupled with congested ports and problems with timely unloading and onward transportation, a typical container now spends 20% longer in transit than before the pandemic. Shipping rates have soared in this environment. Prices on major east-west trade routes have increased by 80% year on year, which is bad news for economic recovery. […]

Worker shortages were particularly evident with lorry drivers in the UK and other countries.

In sum, it is likely that different industries will experience both shortages and over-supply problems throughout 2022.

■ Adapted from *The Conversation*, January 2022.

Notes

A step-by-step approach

1 Lexical work

a. Find the lexical equivalents in the text:
Une pénurie de vaccins • échelon • surapprovisionnement • faire des réserves • augmenter.

b. Find the French equivalents:
To ease • yet.

2 Read the whole text

a. Identify the source of the document (title, source, nature).

....

b. Two words are opposed in the title.
What are these two words? What are the two ideas that are repeated in the first and second paragraphs?

....

....

3 Check the facts

Say if the following statements are true or false.

a. Shortages were all solved. ❑ T ❑ F
b. Shelves were left empty in 2020. ❑ T ❑ F
c. Demand is always the same. ❑ T ❑ F
d. The bullwhip effect can be defined as a small change causing a major disruption. ❑ T ❑ F
e. Car manufacturers were short of chips. ❑ T ❑ F
f. 1.9 billion tonnes of merchandise are shipped by cargo containers yearly. ❑ T ❑ F
g. Shortages of goods are doubled with shortage of labour. ❑ T ❑ F

4 Train for the exam

Rephrase in your own words.

a. Shortages are due to the Covid-19 pandemic and the lockdown worldwide.

....

b. Consumers have become erratic consumers.

....

5 Topic debrief

Choose the sentence which you think corresponds best to the main topic of the document.

a. Shortages are not the only problems. Oversupply is also a major disruption for retailers especially. ❑

b. Shortages are not only shortages of goods but also of workers because of local policies to prevent Covid from spreading among other reasons. ❑

Language

Questions ouvertes → page 201 / Discours rapporté → page 181 / *Pluperfect* → page 188

Translate into French.

1 **Are we facing** another year of shortages?
2. Experts ask **if the supply chain crisis will decrease soon**
3. Once the demand **had been satisfied**, there was suddenly an oversupply

TRAINING
EXAMS
EXERCISES
INTERNSHIP

Text

Kazakhstan unrest: how will China's economic interests be affected by the protests?

Audio 36
liennathan.fr/cj549q

The world's attention has been drawn to Kazakhstan in recent days after dozens of people were killed in clashes on the streets and protesters torched and ransacked public buildings in several cities. The violence is the worst seen in the Central Asian state since it gained independence 30 years ago. The unrest has stirred concerns about the impact on Chinese companies operating in the country, which has been showered with investment under President Xi Jinping's Belt and Road Initiative.

But where is Kazakhstan and why is it "where China's global dream began"? Kazakhstan is located on China's northwest border and is the largest landlocked country in the world, sitting on rich reserves of oil and minerals. Positioned between China and Europe, it is a crucial link in the Belt and Road Initiative and was where Xi announced the globe spanning infrastructure project in 2013.

Commerce between Kazakhstan and China can be dated back to ancient times, when businesspeople from the Han dynasty traversed the old Silk Road with troops and camels on their way to Europe. China wonders if the unrest will affect Chinese companies and investment.

The Chinese embassy in Kazakhstan has sent out a security risk alert to Chinese companies advising them to pay close attention to how the situation develops. State media, however, have cited industry insiders saying so far the unrest has not had a great impact on Chinese businesses, and that gas pipelines running between the two countries should be safe because they are located in remote areas far from cities where the protests are occurring. The Kazakh government is taking measures to ensure the safety of Chinese companies.

Kazakhstan counts on China as its second largest trading partner, and its number one export destination. Total bilateral trade was US$22.94 billion in the first 11 months of 2021, according to data from Chinese customs, up 14.7 per cent from 2020.

Trade has been bolstered by the Belt and Road Initiative and has not been hindered by the pandemic. In 2021, China Railway Express that travels from the mainland and Europe sent 15,000 container freight trains through Kazakhstan, and 1.46 million twenty-foot equivalent units.

China invested US$19.2 billion in the country between 2005-20. Some 56 China-backed projects worth nearly US$24.5 billion are due to finish by 2023.

Other infrastructure projects include solar panel factories, logistics parks and wind farms.

The China-Central Asia Gas Pipeline, which began operating in 2009, starts in Turkmenistan and Uzbekistan, runs through southern Kazakhstan and ends in Khorgas in China's northwest Xinjiang Uygur autonomous region.

Adapted from Luna Sun, *scmp.com*, January 2022.

A step-by-step approach

1 Lexical work

a. Find the French equivalents for:
Ransack • stir • shower • landlock • spanning.

b. Find the lexical equivalents in the text:
Conseiller/expert/professionnel du secteur d'activité • échauffourée/émeute • lointain/éloigné • soutenir/appuyer.

2 Read the whole text

a. Comment on the title.

b. Identify the source of the document (title, source, nature).

3 Check the facts

Choose the right answer or answer.

a. What is the problem in Kazakhstan?
- a recession ❑
- an unrest ❑
- a labour shortage ❑

b. Where is Kazakhstan? What have Chinese merchants been used to doing?

c. What are Chinese leaders afraid of?
- attacks against Chinese companies ❑
- a major influence in China ❑

d. What did Kazaks government ensure?

....

e. Kazakhstan is one of China's trading partners: give figures

....

f. What is traded?

....

g. What are the other projects China invested in?

....

4 Train for the exam

a. Write ideas that explain how trade between China and Kazakhstan has increased and why.

....

b. Then list arguments that could slow down trade between two countries.

....

5 Topic debrief

Choose the best recap.

a. This article is about the Chinese-Kazakh trading relationship and how unrest may damage Chinese companies. ❑

b. This article is about trading partners that export and import goods thanks to the Belt and Road Initiative. ❑

Language

Forme passive → page 184 / *Should* → page 177 / Propositions infinitives → page 197

Translate the sentences.

a. Dozens of people <u>**were killed**</u> in clashes.

....

b. The gas pipeline running between the two countries <u>**should be**</u> safe.

....

c. The government is taking measures <u>**to ensure**</u> the safety of Chinese companies.

....

TRAINING
EXAMS
EXERCISES
INTERNSHIP

1 Pronunciation work

Audio 37
liennathan.fr/42xvc7

Listen, repeat the following words and record yourself:
Environment • luxury liner • powered • harmful • diesel • hazard waste • harmful substances • huge • container ship • emit • cruises.

2 Before you start watching the video

a. Explain what cruise ships are and why they attract so many tourists.

....

b. Anticipate the topic of video.

....

c. Look at the title and think about the ways in which cruise ships have an impact on the environment.

....

3 Watch the video

Underline the words you hear among the following list:
Ocean liners • disaster fuel oil • diesel • hazardous • waste • emit • incinerator • harmful • average • demands • amount • ports • pollution • particles • spread • increase • container • rise • levels • sulphur • suppliers • greener.

Video

How bad for the environment are cruise ships?

Video 18
liennathan.fr/35xi3y

4 A step-by-step approach

1. Watch the whole video once

a. Write in French what it is about.

2. Watch the video a second time

b. How many people per year spend their holidays on a cruise ship?

c. Give the reasons why cruise ships are considered a "disaster."

d. Quote facts and figures.

e. Explain why cruise ships continue to pollute when they are at ports.

f. Explain what means of transport is the most polluting.

g. Compare by quoting figures.

h. Explain the solutions that could be adopted and their impacts on the consumers.

5 Train for the exam

Oral report: put together all the information you have collected and report to the class.

5 Audio track

1 Pronunciation work

Audio 38
liennathan.fr/r99e5m

Listen to the following words. Then repeat them and record yourself.
Containers • container ships • supply • chains • crisis.

2 Before listening

a. Look at the title and imagine what the topic will deal with.

....

3 Listen to the audio

b. Anticipate the topic of the audio.

....

c. Reasons for the world's crisis.

....

d. Listen and try to understand the following words:
Shipping container • refilled • supply • chain • crisis • loaded • disruption • unloaded • stolen • avoid • vessel • trade route • makeshift • affordable • amenities • inland • depots • ports.

Audio

Shipping and the pandemic

Audio 39
liennathan.fr/d2ng39

4 A step-by-step approach

1. Listen to the whole audio once

a. Who is the host?

....

2. Listen to the audio a second time

→ Listen to the first part

b. Collect data on the interviewer and interviewee : ....

– Name the news media that he mentions : ....

– Name the event that he refers to : ....

– What are the two figures mentionned : ....

→ Listen to the second part

c. Name of the historian; name of the entrepreneur.

....

d. With the coming of the container, what problems were solved?

....

e. Two sizes are given: which ones?

....

f. How were goods transported before the coming of the container?

....

→ Listen to the third part

g. What changes were introduced with shipping containers?

....

h. Which two canals are mentioned?

....

i. How many containers were carried at first?

....

j. And later on?

....

k. What are shipping containers used for?

....

l. How is the crisis explained?

....

m. What happened in Germany in 2015?

....

n. Who manufactured containers?

....

5 Train for the exam

Oral work: speak for at least two minutes about what you have just learned.
Put together all the information you have collected.

TRAINING

EXAMS

EXERCISES

INTERNSHIP

Document 1 Audio

Audio 40
liennathan.fr/7vdn96

The rail freight

Notes

Task 1

1. Listen to the whole audio.

a. What is the difference between Europe and the US in terms of rail?

b. Why has rail freight been able to develop?

c. What is the problem when combining high-speed passenger trains and freight trains?

d. How has global warming impacted the trucking industry?

e. What else has introduced its demise?

2. Write an organized account in English.

Document 2 Text

Audio 41
liennathan.fr/7c6c2a

Coal emissions: a step backwards

The US is even further from hitting its 2030 climate goals as coal emissions increased for the first time in 7 years in 2021, a new preliminary analysis found. According to a report from researchers at Rhodium Group, greenhouse emissions increased more than 6% from 2020 to 2021, in part due to a 17% increase in coal-fired power.

Coal emissions had been dropping since 2014, but rebounded as the economy shook off a slowdown caused by the coronavirus pandemic. "We are doing exactly the opposite of what we need to be doing", said a spokes person from Rhodium group.

The sector with the largest increase in emissions year-over-year was the transportation sector, fueled by diesel consumption, according to the report. Overall, greenhouse emissions in 2021 were still 5% lower than 2019 levels. But the US greenhouse gas emissions were only 17% below 2005 levels in 2021, putting the US further behind its targets as part of the Paris Agreement Climate Agreement. The US had agreed to reduce emissions to 50-52%

below 2005 levels by 2030. The Rhodium researchers said Congress, the federal government, and individual states "all must act quickly" to get the US back on track.

The Build Back Better package — which stalled in the US Senate — was expected to cut US emissions to between 45-51% of 2005 levels, according to a separate Rhodium Group report. President Joe Biden said his goal is to cut emissions to net-zero by 2050, which climate scientists said will require closing all coal-fired power stations across the country by 2025. "It means that by 2025 we will have to have closed down all coal-fired power stations across the planet," Potsdam Institute for Climate Impact Research director John Schellnhuber told The Guardian. "And by 2030, you will have to get rid of the combustion engine entirely. That decarbonization will not guarantee a rise of no more than 1.5 Celsius, but it will give us a chance. But even that is a tremendous task."

Adapted from DeArbea WalkerJan, *Business Insider Australia*, October 2022

Task 2

1. Read the whole text and answer.

a. What is revealed in the title? ....

b. What happened from 2020 and 2021? ....

c. Why has coal consumption increased? ....

d. Which sector is known for its high polluting impact? ....

e. What do the Rodium researchers say must act now? ....

f. What is the aim of the "Build Back Better" package? ....

2. Organize your ideas and make a plan.

3. Write an organized account of the article in English (50 to 100 words).

Video 19
liennathan.fr/h7c86n

Document 3 Video

Inside Elon Musk's underground loop tunnels in Las Vegas

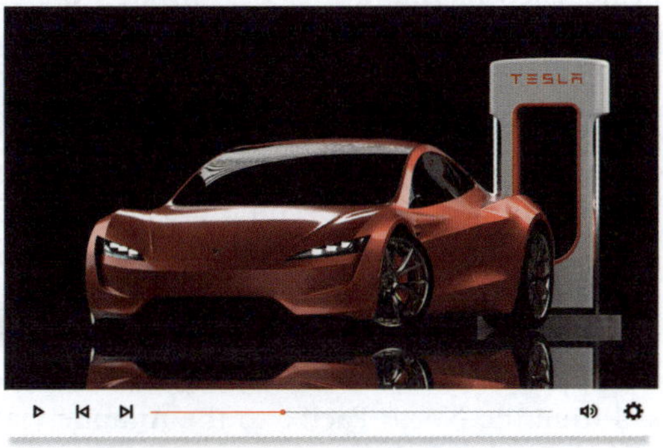

Task 3

1. Watch the video.

2. Anticipate from the title of the video.

....

....

3. Organize all the information you have collected and write a report.

Notes

....

....

....

....

5 Background

Trading ships plied the Silk Road again

Transporting goods around the world has been slowed down with the pandemic and many countries no longer want to rely on China for manufacturing goods. By the same token, shipping has to be cheap and green. So what is happening to shipping goods at a low price without endangering the health of the planet?

I Shipping goods by sea: the Suez Canal, the Bering Strait and the sea routes

Container vessels navigate the ocean like trucks on busy highways, following specific shipping routes to and from the world's busiest seaports. What are these routes that support international trade by offering the fastest sailing times?

A trip through the 120-mile-long Suez Canal takes about 16 hours, with an average of 100 vessels completing the crossing each day. In March 2021, the Ever Given, a huge container ship that blocked the Suez Canal - disrupting global trade was loaded with about 18,300 containers. The Suez Canal is responsible for about 12% of global trade, around one million barrels of oil and roughly 8% of liquefied natural gas passes through the canal each day. It takes more time if you go around the Cape of Good Hope.

The Bering Strait is located between Russia and Alaska. With the sea melting, the passage through the Bering Strait has become easier for vessels, and commercial shipping interest is increasing. However, ship traffic and oil drilling are posing a threat to Arctic wildlife — the perfect recipe for disaster. Recently, a luxury cruise ship was able to sail from the North Pacific to the Atlantic via the fabled Northwest Passage.

II The Silk Road Belt Initiative

There is an overland economic belt of 6 corridors that serve as new route to get goods in and out of China. The railroad that links China to London will enable trade to move even faster. But this multi-billion dollar Belt and Road Initiative (BRI) also consists of gas pipelines, high speed train network, oil refineries, industrial parks and power plants. China has invested heavily abroad to strengthen its power.

III Amazon: a new player in the shipping industry

Even Amazon is trying to break into the cargo shipping business now. Amazon arranges shipping for much of the cargo that it owns and sells directly, but it also can arrange shipping for other parties, like, for example, companies that sell on Amazon Marketplace. In some cases, these vendors are competing with Amazon. They sell the same products that Amazon itself sells. Handling the shipping may give Amazon insight into the businesses of its competitors. This relationship between Amazon and sellers on Amazon Marketplace has been something that has been looked at by antitrust authorities and others.

IV Transporting people: shipping cruises

Before the Covid 19 pandemic, an increasing number of holiday makers were opting for a cruise holiday. From 2005 to 2018, the demand for cruising increased by more than 60%. The offer of cruise operators followed, and gigantic cruise ships such as the Harmony of the Sea or the Symphony of the Sea with a capacity of more than 6000 passengers were launched. The rise in demand generated more affordable prices, attracting a middle class clientele from all over the world, especially from China.

Although the cruise industry has been on hold since the pandemic, cruise operators remain optimistic for the future. But beyond the pandemic, the environmental issues still need to be addressed as these sea giants and their passengers are causing terrible damage to the eco system, on land and on sea.

Test

I Read the background carefully and answer the following questions.

1. Why has transporting goods become more difficult in the last two years?

2. Which sea routes are mentioned?

3. Why has shipping goods by sea become the new normal?

4. What happened to the Ever Green in March 2021?

5. Why do companies like it better to transit through the Suez canal than the Cape of Good Hope?

6. Is the Bering Strait a new sea route?

7. Say what the Silk Road Belt initiative means.

8. What did the big online company do to avoid delays?

II Give a detailed answer to each question

9. What effect did the Covid-19 pandemic have on the cruise industry?

10. What problems does the cruise industry generate?

Training
Exams
Exercises
Internship

5 PowerPoint Presentation

Port of Singapore's SWOT

1. **Study Port of Singapour's SWOT closely.**
2. **Choose a company in the list below:**
   BOMBARDIER • ALSTOM • AIRBUS • SNCF.
   a. Prepare a PowerPoint presentation.
   b. Present it to the class.

Favourable | Unfavourable
Internal | External

Strengths

- Maritime industry is supported by a secure and pro-business government
- Conducive tax environment for businesses: tax incentives such as Scheme and tax benefits for ship registration
- Tax benefits for ship registration to keep up a workforce of well-trained, qualified and committed English speaking personnel
- Singapore provides a Maritime Business Development Programme
- The city state's maritime community is resilient and adaptable
- The port offers quality, efficiency and competitiveness

Weaknesses

- China's economy and competition from developing ports in Singapore's nearest neighbours, Malaysia and Indonesia, which are beefing up their own port facilities.
- The dependence of Singapore's port on external demand.
- Singapore must keep investing in port infrastructure to accommodate the future needs of the maritime industry in order to stay competitive and draw more container ships.
- Singapore's weather is pretty unpredictable, it rains without warning and the sun is also always temperamental and scorching hot.
- It has a small local market.

SWOT

Opportunities

- Investments have already been voted on to expand the facilities: Singapore has made bold decisions to remain ahead and to handle the envisaged growth in trade volumes.
- Cargo services will keep increasing.
- Singapore's located at the crossroads of important trade lines.

Threats

- Much competition from many other ports and the Silk & Road Belt Initiative from China that will take some shipping away from Singapore.
- Affordability needs to be closely taken into account.
- Singapore must develop both its regional operations and its international ones.

Act

Choose one of the following role plays to act in front of the class.

Role play 1

Work in pairs or in group:
Student A has goods manufactured in China that need to be shipped to London.
Student B should provide answers to the best way to ship goods either by land or by sea.

Student A tips
List questions you need to have an answer to (price, time, dangers, containers, types of goods, etc.).

Student B tips
Use the visual document in the Starter section. Find out more about prices by going on the net.

Role play 2

Student A is a customer doing his/her Christmas shopping at his/her usual shopping mall.
Student A is surprised and concerned not to be able to find the toys he/she had planned to buy.

Student B is another angry shopper who cannot find the products he/she expected to buy at the mall.

Student C is the mall customer relationship manager who explains his/her customers that because of the bankruptcy of a South Korean shipping company, many products are still waiting to be shipped.

Imagine the exchange between the three people using information you remember from the video.

(N.B.: other students can join their voices to the complaining customers.)

Role play 3

Group A
Students from group A are against the increasing restrictions on flights. They argue that the ban on liquids, food, even electronic devices for some destinations, are useless, and prevent air travelling from being efficient.

Group B
Students from group B argue that restrictions have to be as strict as possible, and even stricter, they argue that it is the only way to ensure passengers' safety.

Each group prepares their arguments, using examples from their own experience or from their imagination.
A student from each group distributes speaking and listening roles equally.

Notes

World challenges: sustainability and AI

Four ways AI can help tackle climate change

Video 20
liennathan.fr/b2by97

1. Take notes of the four ways AI can help to reduce climate change.

....

....

....

....

Word box

AI (Artificial Intelligence): *intelligence artificielle*

6

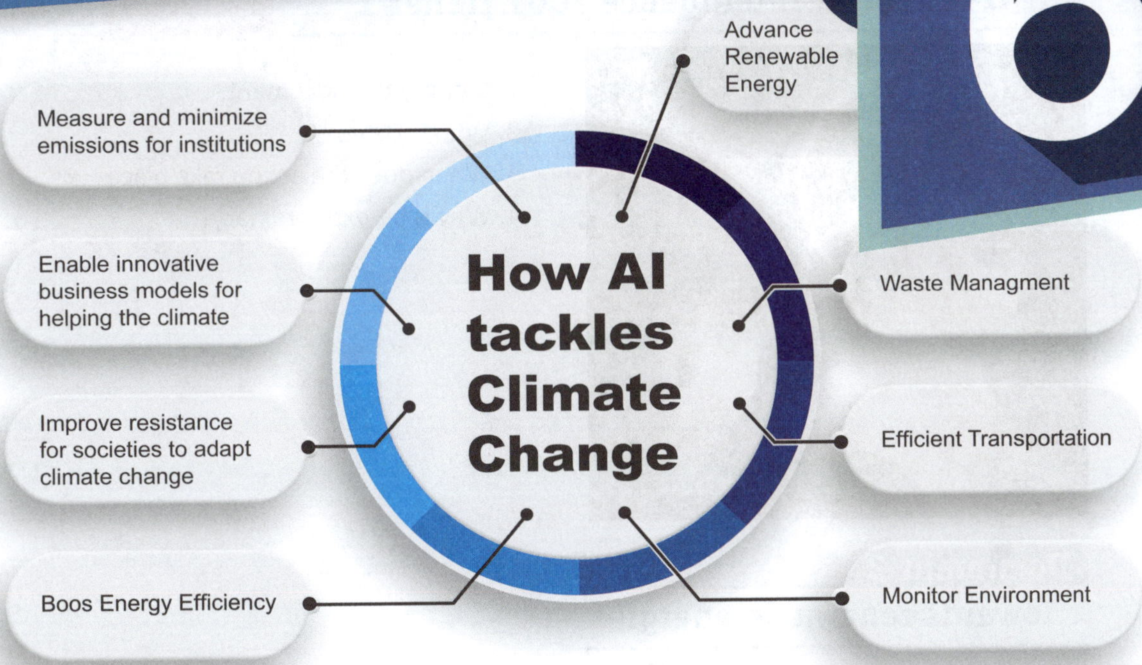

Questions

1. What do you know about AI ? Give examples.
2. Look at the picture and quote three sectors in which AI can help reduce climate change.

Notes

....

....

....

....

....

....

....

....

....

TRAINING EXAMS EXERCISES INTERNSHIP

6 » Starters

Document 1

AI–Artificial Intelligence 2001 trailer 1

Video 21
liennathan.fr/s9q73p

1. Identify the document.
2. Who is David?
3. When does the action take place?
4. Why is he extraordinary?

Document 2

Towards renewable energies

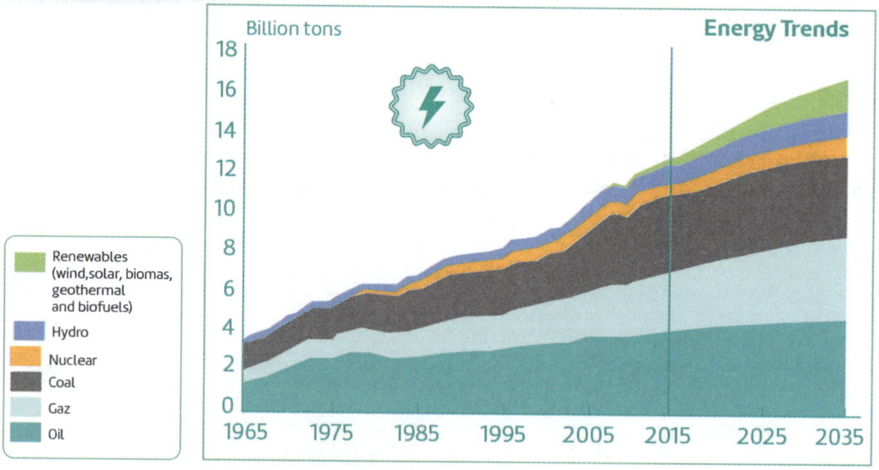

Source: From *www.ogj.com*

1. Identify the document.
2. What does this document represent?
3. When did renewables start being used?
4. Is oil consumption decreasing?
5. What about coal?

Document 3

The impact of climate change: a mind map

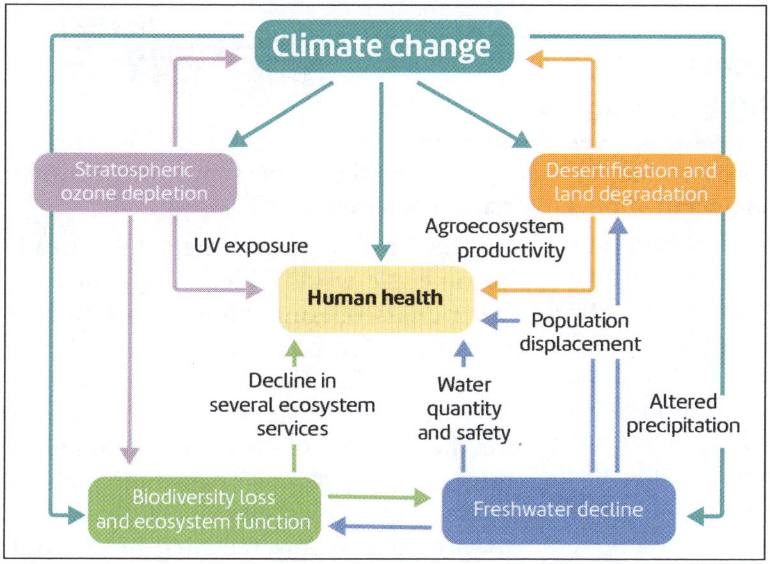

■ Source: From *www.elementshealthspace.com*

1. Identify the document.
2. Focus on the mind map and comment on the major effects of climate change.
3. Express your point of view (give examples).

Document 4

Is Artificial Intelligence compatible with a sustainable environment?

Some studies suggest that the environmental benefits from self-driving cars may turn out to be overrated. Machines driving our cars, for example, may lead to people making more trips, which could lead to increases in emissions, not decreases. Another major risk for the planet is that large-scale implementation of artificial intelligence may destroy all of our jobs, leading to widespread unemployment. A recent report estimated that automation will replace 6 percent of US jobs by 2021, with further job reductions coming in the medium term. A world without jobs presents a host of new, uncharted challenges for sustainability, few of which we can predict.

■ Adapted from *www.greenbiz.com*

1. Identify the document.
2. What are the possible downsides of Artificial Intelligence on sustainability? Give your point of view.

6 Prep page

Text

China, moving to cut emissions, halts production of 500 car models

Audio 42
liennathan.fr/yq939s

China is suspending the production of more than 500 car models and model versions that do not meet its fuel economy standards, several automakers confirmed Tuesday. It is the latest move by Beijing to reduce emissions in the world's largest auto market and take the lead in battling climate change. The government-affiliated China Vehicle Technology Service Center said that the suspension, effective Jan. 1, would affect both domestic carmakers and foreign companies.

Cui Dongshu, the secretary general of the China Passenger Car Association, said that the ban would affect at most 1 percent of the Chinese market. But the government's decision to cite fuel economy in the deregistration of so many versions at the same time is nonetheless a signal of the government's commitment to fuel economy. The country, which for years prioritised economic growth over environmental protection and now produces more than a quarter of the world's human-caused greenhouse gases, has become an unlikely defender of climate action after President Trump's rejection of the Paris Climate Agreement.

Chinese leaders are under intense pressure to cut in dangerous air pollution, a hot-button issue in China, where thick smog has at times forced schools and businesses to temporarily shut down. Late last month, China said it was going ahead with plans to create the world's largest carbon market, giving Chinese power companies a financial incentive to operate more cleanly. "They are sending a signal to everybody that this is for real," said Michael Dunne, president of Dunne Automotive, a Hong Kong-based consultancy on China's clean car market. "This shows their emission standards have teeth*."

The Chinese government has already become the world's biggest supporter of electric cars, offering automakers numerous incentives for producing so-called new energy vehicles. Those incentives are set to decrease by 2020, to be replaced by quotas for the number of clean cars automakers must sell. That has encouraged global automakers to accelerate in their shift toward battery-powered cars. By contrast, the United States is considering relaxing tailpipe* emissions standards and very nearly killed off a tax credit for electric vehicles during its latest tax overhaul.

The Chinese government had long held back from aggressive emissions standards to allow its own automakers to catch up with the latest clean car technology. But that is changing, with the government setting increasingly stringent tailpipe rules. The latest development "is a testimony to how quickly their own automakers have evolved," Mr. Dunne said. "They're saying: We are ready to play this game."

Global automakers will have no choice but to meet the increasingly strict government policies in China, said Michelle Krebs, an analyst at the Auto Trader Group. "The simple fact that China is the biggest market means automakers will be accommodating," she said.

Adapted from *The New York Times*, January 2, 2018.

* to have teeth: expression idiomatique qui signifie avoir du pouvoir, de l'influence

* tailpipe: pot d'échappement

A step-by-step approach

1 Lexical work

Find the meanings of the following expressions:
To meet standards • fuel economy • latest move • ban • deregistration • greenhouse gas • a hot button issue • smog • incentive • tax overhaul • to hold back from • testimony • accommodating.

2 Read the whole text

a. **Comment on the title.**
b. **What industry is concerned by China's decision?**

3 Check the facts

a. Give the key ideas in each of the six paragraphs in one or two sentences.
b. Focus on the last paragraph and explain why foreign automakers will have to adapt.

4 Train for the exam

Go further:
a. Why is it important for a country to cut out its CO_2 emissions?
b. In what way has China's government's attitude towards pollution radically changed?
c. Why did the US step out from the Paris Agreement in 2017?

5 Topic debrief

Use your answers above to write a short account of the article (50 to 100 words).

Notes

TRAINING
EXAMS
EXERCISES
INTERNSHIP

Language

Adjectifs et noms composés → page 170 / Superlatif → page 202
Proposition infinitive → page 197 / Préfixes et suffixes → page 189

Translate into French.

1. China produces over a quarter of **human-caused greenhouse gases**.
2. Those measures are taken **to decrease and to be replaced** by **clean car** quotas.
3. China plans to become **the world's largest carbon market**.
4. China has become an **unlikely** defender of the environment.

Text

How Artificial Intelligence helps sustainability

Audio 43
liennathan.fr/mh9x85

A study conducted in May 2020 in France showed that a brand's positive contribution to social issues is the main criterion of brand loyalty for 57% of people in France.

Although awareness is important today and has been increasing year after year (seven out of ten people in France consume organic foods at least once a month) when it comes to sustainability, the market and expectations are still difficult to estimate. Organic, carbon neutral, recycling, recycled, zero-plastic, circular economy, green, vegan, natural products, etc.: the list of characteristics is often long and complicates the notion of eco-responsibility.

But today, there are many measures that companies can take to support their eco-responsible approach. The good news is that a brand, by pursuing sustainable development, also improves its economic gains. Nearly 80% of brands say that doing so increases customer loyalty and 63% report that it directly contributes to an increase in revenues.

Artificial intelligence (AI) has already reduced greenhouse gases by about 13% among manufacturers and retailers and can help brands reach 45% of their carbon reduction target by 2030. Thus, how concretely can it help brands accelerate their eco-responsible initiatives? AI is involved in many stages in the value chain, from supplying materials to shipping products. Once the units are produced, the right products must be sent to the right stores while avoiding error and optimizing distribution.

Inventory management, logistics, and overall processes are improved through algorithms. At the warehouse level, AI solutions have helped Amazon reduce packaging requirements by 33%, saving more than 915,000 tons of packaging materials, which is equivalent to the elimination of 1.6 billion shipping cartons. As far as shipping is concerned, information technology companies are now able to deploy tools that generate a complete cost-benefit analysis, which details estimated fuel consumption, fuel costs, and $CO2$ emissions and identifies different scenarios to optimize delivery strategies.

Manufacturing only the number of products sold is the dream of any organization. In addition to the economic gains associated with reducing the number of unsold items, it is also a great way to lower the carbon footprint (fewer raw materials used, less energy consumed, etc.). Carrefour, with the help of the information technology sector, is using AI to optimize inventory management and reduce waste. By collecting and processing data from stores, warehouses, and e-commerce sites, Carrefour can better anticipate demand and adjust orders from suppliers. Thanks to a smarter management of its supply chain, Carrefour has reduced the number of shortage and overstock in stores as well as warehouses.

We can no longer afford to evaluate companies based solely on traditional criteria. Instead, the carbon standard must be integrated into the entire value chain to allow consumers to choose the most respectful product on the planet.

Adapted from *capgemini.com*, Paris, France 2021.

A step-by-step approach

1 Lexical work

a. Translate the following words:
Organic • carbon neutral • recycling • recycled • zero-plastic • circular economy • green • vegan.

b. Find two verbs in the article meaning the opposite of "increase".

2 Read the whole text

a. Comment on the title.

b. Write all the words and expressions you know related to Artificial Intelligence and sustainability.

3 Check the facts

Answer the questions for the following paragraphs.

§1 What do we learn about French consumers?
§2 Why is the notion of eco responsibility complicated?
§3 Why is it positive for brands to support sustainable development?
§5 What famous company did AI help? How? How is shipping optimized?
§6 What was Carrefour able to do thanks to AI?
§7 What essential standard must be integrated to the chain of value?

Notes

4 Train for the exam

Find the keys ideas of each paragraphs.

§1 ....
§2 ....
§3 ....
§4 ....
§5 ....
§6 ....
§7 ....

5 Topic debrief

Use the information above to write a 50 to 100 words account of the article.

Language

Proposition subordonnées → page 198 / Indénombrables → page 187
Expression de la fréquence → page 183 / Auxiliaire modal *must* → page 176

Translate into French.

1. **Although** awareness is important today the market is still difficult to estimate.
2. The good **news** is that a brand, by pursuing sustainable development, also improves **its** economic gains.
3. Seven out of ten people in France consume organic foods at least **once a month**.
4. The carbon standard **must** be integrated into the entire value chain.

6 Video track

1 Pronunciation work

Audio 44
liennathan.fr/4p5av6

Listen, repeat the following words and record yourself.
Scientists • temperature • sea level rise • to fuel • heat wave • vulnerable • pollutant • throat • hurricane.

2 Before you start watching the video

Find out more about:

a. NRDC. ....

b. Countries the most exposed to climate change. ....

c. The different weather phenomena induced by climate change. ....

d. Pollution related diseases. ....

3 Watch the video

Video 22
liennathan.fr/39tt5j

Underline the words you hear among the following list:
sea level • health • concern • heat wave • vulnerable • pollutants • smog • throat • lungs • pollens • allergies • asthma • insects • illnesses • virus • disease • events • fire • hurricane • energised • demand • secure • children.

Video

Climate change will impact health (from NRDC)

4 A step-by-step approach

1. Watch the whole video once

a. Write in French what it is about.

2. Watch the video a second time

→ 1'47 – Watch the first part

b. Is climate change a new topic for scientists?

c. What is today's big concern?

d. What are the consequences of successive heat waves?

e. What parts of the population are most at risk?

f. How many people are concerned in the USA?

g. What is the second most important pollution factor?

h. How are pollution and temperatures related?

i. What parts of the body can be damaged?

j. When can pollen be dangerous?

k. What symptoms can it generate?

l. What is the third consequence of global warming?

m. What viruses can insects carry?

→ 1'47 → end – Watch the second part

n. What is the cost of climate change?

o. What recent disasters are quoted?

p. How much did they cost?

q. What kind of reaction from the people do scientists hope for?

5 Train for the exam

Oral report: put together all the information you have collected and report to the class.

6 Audio track

1 Pronunciation work

Audio 45
liennathan.fr/285ftm

Listen to the following words. Then repeat them and record yourself.
Launch • breeder • processor • insect-based • drastically • resources • nutrients • sustainable scale.

2 Before listening

a. Comment on the visual document.

b. Write in french what the audio is about.

....

....

3 Listen to the audio

a. Anticipate the topic of the audio.

b. Underline the right sentence.

– This audio is about an innovating US company which produces insects for animal food.

– The guest is the co-founder of a recent start up specialized in insect-based food.

– All types of insects can be bred and processed to produce animal food.

c. Debrief with the other students and the teacher about their meaning.

Audio

Can insects save the world?

Audio 46
liennathan.fr/9iex93

4 A step-by-step approach

1. Listen to the whole audio

a. Collect information on:

- the guest: ....

....

- the company: ....

....

2. Listen to the audio a second time

b. What is the breed of insect used by Innova feed?

....

....

....

c. What are its qualities?

....

....

....

d. What is the main part of agriculture dedicated to?

....

....

....

e. How does Innova Feed contribute to decrease the environmental impact of agriculture?

....

....

....

f. In what parts of the world can insect-based food be the most efficient?

....

....

....

g. Where does Innova Feed intend to operate soon?

....

....

....

5 Train for the exam

a. Write a short account of the audio (100 words).
b. Prepare an oral report about the audio (1minute) and record it.

6 Tasks

Document 1 Video

Watch Sophia the robot walk for the first time

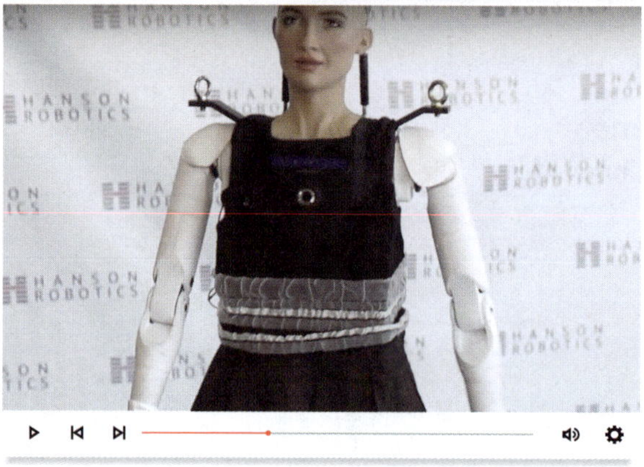

Video 23
liennathan.fr/44jn9v

Word box

- Frubber: *a new substance*
- DRC Hueber: *another type of robot which won the DARPA Robotics Challenge in 2015*
- Hanson Robotics: *the company that created Sophia*

Task 1

1. Watch the video.

a. Explain the video's title.

b. What is the specificity of "Frubber"?

c. List the movements and facial expressions the robot can perform.

d. Describe what the robot's legs allow it to do.

e. In what sectors can this robot be used?

f. What can Sophia also do?

2. Organize all the information you have collected.

3. Write a report.

Notes

Document 2 Text

Life-like robots meant to win over humans

Audio 47
liennathan.fr/6p8sf8

Founder David Hanson envisions a future in which AI-powered robots evolve to become 'super-intelligent genius machines' that might help solve some of mankind's most challenging problems."

The Texas-born former sculptor at Walt Disney Imagineering and his Hong Kong-based start-up Hanson Robotics are combining AI with southern China's expertise in toy design, electronics and manufacturing to craft humanoid "social robots" with faces designed to be lifelike and appealing enough to win trust from humans who interact with them. Hanson, 49, is perhaps best known as the creator of Sophia, that he calls his "masterpiece."

Hanson Robotics has made about a dozen copies of Sophia. A multinational team of scientists and engineers are fine-tuning her appearance and the algorithms that enable her to smile, blink and refine her understanding and communication. Sophia has moving 3-D-printed arms and, with the help of a South Korean robotics company, she is now going mobile Her skin is made of a nanotech material that Hanson invented and dubbed "Frubber," short for fleshrubber, that has a flesh-like, texture. Cameras in her eyes and a 3-D sensor in her chest help her to "see," while the processor that serves as her brain combines facial and speech recognition, and natural language processing. Global market revenue for service robotics is forecast to grow from $3.7 billion in 2015 to $15 billion in 2020.

Adapted from *Voice of America*, January 16, 2018.

Task 2

1. Read the whole text and answer.

a. What is the purpose of making robots?

b. Who created Sophia?

c. List all the features Sophia has and what it allows it/her to perform.

d. Give figures on the robotics markets.

e. Explain the title and rephrase it.

2. Organize your ideas and make a plan.

3. Write an organized account of the article in English (50 to 100 words).

Notes

Audio 48
liennathan.fr/q57ma7

Document 3 Audio

Some of the biggest Artificial Intelligence (AI) trends in 2022

Task 3

1. Listen to the whole audio.

a. Anticipate from the title.

b. Make a list of the three fields quoted by the reporter.

Say how each of these fields will be impacted by AI.

–

–

–

2. Prepare an oral account of the audio.

Can you think of other sectors or industries impacted by AI?

3. Write an organized account in English.

6 Background

Will AI help the planet become sustainable ?

Under the threat of global warming's effects, sustainability is an utmost priority. Warnings about climate change have been on the agenda since the 1970s. But today, the effects of human activities' impact on climate change have reached an overall consensus.

The rise in carbon emissions and other toxic exhausts have disrupted the climate in almost every region of the world. Droughts, floods, storms, hurricanes and wild fires combined with the rising of sea levels have transformed the most economically vulnerable parts of the world into regions where food and water shortage have become endemic. The only solutions seem to lie in a radical shift towards clean energies, powered by natural and renewable elements such as sun, water and wind.

I Towards sustainable corporate policies

An increasing number of companies are turning to Artificial Intelligence to help them become more sustainable. Some companies have already been able to reduce their carbon footprint by turning to green energy and adopting environmentally friendly infrastructures thanks to AI 's growing impact on technological progress.

II Reversing deforestation

Around 70% of deforestation is linked to the production of agricultural commodities that end up in food products eaten around the world. And deforestation accounts for around 12% of global manmade greenhouse gas emissions. As a consequence, the recent COP 26 has promised to halt and reverse deforestation by 2030.

Meanwhile a growing number of companies from McDonald's to Ikea are also voluntarily committing to eliminate deforestation from their supply chains, both in their individual sustainability policies and through participation in larger initiatives.

III Fair trade: a win-win situation

Fair trade promotes sustainable development by offering better trading conditions to small producers and workers in developing countries. Buying products from producers in these countries at a fair price is an efficient way of promoting sustainable development. For example, 60 % of the products sold by the famous British retailer Marks and Spencer are sustainable. In 2022 the British retailer launched a programme aimed at rewarding their customers for making more sustainable choices.

IV AI in the transport industry

The willingness of vehicle manufacturers to develop automated cars, transfer trucks, and other vehicles opens a wealth of new opportunities. Companies that can innovate in this new market are bound to find a lot of investors.

V Can too much AI generate dehumanization?

Some branches of Artificial Intelligence are specialized in "human enhancement". Although nobody would protest against the medical progress made possible by Ai, some people fear that the concept of "human enhancement" may find no limit. Thanks to AI's progress, will genetic engineering allow mankind to generate "perfect" human beings in a near future? Will carers in hospitals be replaced by high performing robots? Are we on our way to a dehumanized future? The question remains unanswered today.

Test

Read the background carefully and answer the following questions.

1. Quote the disasters generated by global warming.

2. What solution is proposed?

3. What do some companies resort to in order to become more sustainable?

4. What did the COP 26 promise?

5. What measures did Ikea and Mac Donald's take?

6. Why is fair trade a "win win" situation?

7. Why is Marks and Spencer's remarkable?

8. What industry will also be positively impacted by AI?

9. What do some people fear about the progress of AI?

10. What could happen in hospitals and other institutions?

PowerPoint Presentation

What should we think of Artificial Intelligence?

1. **Study AI's SWOT closely.**
2. **Choose a company in the list below**
   INNOVA FEED • SIEMENS • MARKS AND SPENCER • MAC DONALD'S • BODY SHOP
   a. Prepare a PowerPoint presentation of their SWOT.
   b. Present it to the class.

SWOT

	Favourable	Unfavourable
Internal	**Strengths** • Has allowed progress in all sectors, from health care to finance • A lot of money invested • A good return on investment so far	**Weaknesses** • Lack of available data • Amount of energy required to process the data • A threat for many jobs
External	**Opportunities** • Gaining all types of industries • Create new needs, new companies, niches, new markets, new jobs	**Threats** • Domination of some countries • Unethical use • Loss of control • Dehumanisation

Act

Choose one of the following role plays to act in front of the class. Prepare your arguments.

Role play 1

Work in pairs or in group

Student A is a spokesperson for the Chinese government. He/she is informing foreign automakers of the newemission standards China has just adopted.

Student B is the CEO of a foreign car brand (European, Japanese, American etc). He/she explains Student A that it is impossible to respect the standards immediately.

Student A and B negotiate to find an agreement

Role play 2

Student A is worried about the consequences of climate change and tries to convince.

Student B that it is high time for people to adopt a new lifestyle by giving examples.

Student B is not really aware of the threat and thinks mankind will be saved sooner or later thanks to new technologies.

Role play 3

Group A

Students from group A believe AI is going to disrupt mankind's lifestyle in a negative way: it will replace many human jobs by machines without creating other jobs, which will leave millions of people on the side of the road.

Group B

Students from group B believe AI is the future of mankind, and will help us live better and longer.

Notes

TRAINING
EXAMS
EXERCISES
INTERNSHIP

Global issues

As U.S.-Taiwan Trade Strengthens, Tensions With China Complicates Business

Video 24
liennathan.fr/cg9p92

?

1. What types of goods are traded from Taiwan to the US? How much does it represent?

This vidéo is from Wall street "journal.
Taiwan produces roofing screws to construct
fasteners, hardware, furniture and toys.
Taiwan controls 92% of the moste advance
chips

7

Questions

1. Which border is represented ~~on~~ in the picture?
2. What is required to come across the border?

Notes

1- This is the US southern border between Mexico and the USA. It is 3,145 km long.

2- One knows that goods at least until 2025 from Mexico cross the border more illegal immigrants. We also remember the wall that Donald Trump, president of the US from 2016 and 2020 wanted to build.

7 » Starters

Document 1

A plot to challenge Beijing's growing clout in manufacturing

Owing to a slew of economic reforms since the late 1970s, which saw China open up its market to global trade and the abundant availability of cheap labour, the world's most populous country became the global manufacturing hub that it is today. As of 2020, China was the largest exporter in the world, with an approximately 15% share of global trade, according to UNCTAD statistics.

Right from iron & steel used in buildings, to apparels, electronics, and even children's toys, there is hardly any tangible product around the world that doesn't have a little bit of China in it. In the process, China has emerged as the second largest economy in the world, with a GDP size of $14.72 trillion in 2020, with an over 18% of the world GDP.

As we enter into a new year, the world that we inhabit has become significantly more complicated. Supply chains faced many disruptions and the winds of change have been blowing. China's geopolitical tensions around the South China Sea, trade wars with countries such as the US, rising wage rates and escalating environmental costs have somewhat dented the relative competitive advantage that Chinese manufacturing enjoyed over the decades. So what should we expect?

■ Adapted from *The Economic Times*, January 19, 2022.

1. Identify the document.
2. Why is China a world's power?
3. Explain why China may face challenges.

Document 2

A more connected planet

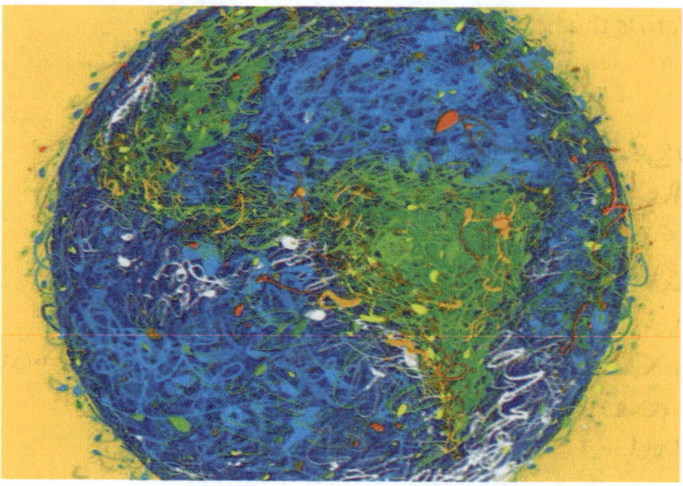

1. Identify the continents on the globe.
2. What is your reaction to this document?
3. Why do we feel that we live in a village?
4. Give reasons that can explain why we feel the earth is a smaller place.

Document 3

Audio 49
liennathan.fr/446nqs

Oil companies want to keep oil supplies from growing too fast even as global demand has increased. Credit... Brandon Thibodeaux for The New York Times

1. Is energy a paramount asset?
2. Why can we say that energy like oil, natural gas, nuclear power, renewables are global goods?
3. Does it impact oil-importing countries when an oil barrel is more expensive?
4. To eradicate global warming, we are slowing doing with less fossil fuel, which global players will disappear?

Document 4

Global trade and logistics overview

Video 25
liennathan.fr/3a6zc9

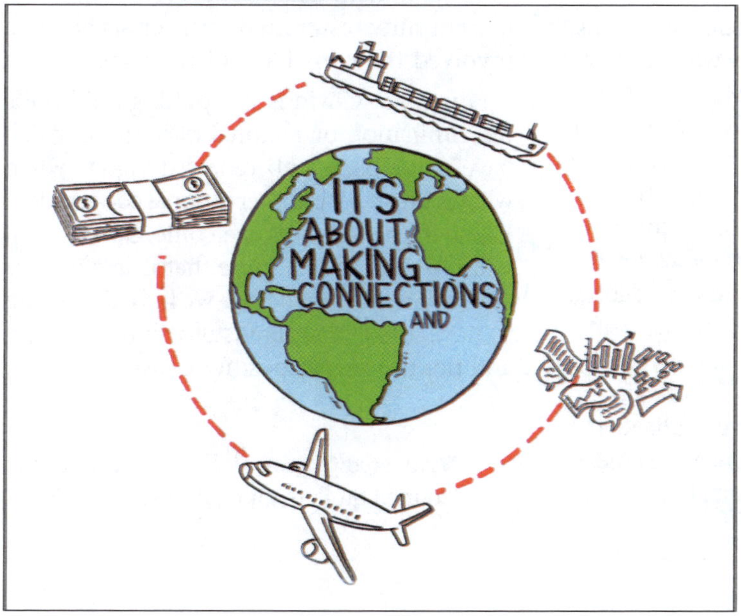

1. Identify the document.
2. What does global trade and logistics mean?
3. What type of transactions does global trade and logistics involve?

TRAINING
EXAMS
EXERCISES
INTERNSHIP

Text

The deglobalisation virus

Audio 50
liennathan.fr/z3z8f9

Covid-19 comes at a time when the world's governments have fewer tools for fighting against its effects than they once did. The coronavirus is bringing the world to a standstill. It is not that the coronavirus has put in train a process of deglobalisation. This originated earlier, in the reactions to the 2008 crisis.

Covid-19, the contagion that has been so widespread largely because of human hyper-interconnection, is dramatically accelerating the process, with profound effects. Combating the virus involves keeping people apart. Borders – on land, at sea, and in the air – are staging a comeback, sometimes unilaterally, even in the European Union.

The Covid-19 crisis has become the third great shock of the century (the 9/11 attacks and the September 2008 financial crisis). This is simultaneously a human shock, a supply-side shock and a demand-side shock.

Increasing numbers of supply chains, much more complex than they were in 2008, are seizing up or stalling. Many factories making machinery, cars, toys, and other products have had to cut or cease production for lack of vital components originating in, for example, China, Air and other forms of travel are in abeyance; the same goes for the movement of shipping containers. Global tourism has taken a massive hit. The pandemic has laid bare our mutual dependence. And there is no shortage of people advocating retreat. Many companies have realised the risks of this over-interdependence, and mean to curb it. Multinationals investigated plans to repatriate part of their production, known as re-shoring.

The virus is going to lead to greater national emphasis, or regional emphasis at least, on production. This includes the field of medical supplies, where the crisis is revealing, for instance, Europe's dependence on medicines manufactured in China and India. Europeans depend on such countries for one-third of their (mainly generic) medicines, and their production should be brought to Europe to ensure supply.

Covid-19 is slowing physical globalisation down, it is also promoting an ever more digital, online form of globalisation. Systems using drones and other autonomous systems have made headway. The same applies to digital services for detecting illnesses using artificial intelligence.

The World Health Organisation, and the multilateralism that it represents, has had its centrality restored. But the crisis has also involved the comeback of the state.

But what Covid is not putting a lid on is discrimination or national narratives, which have come back with renewed vigour when what is imperative is international cooperation. When the pandemic is overcome, globalisation will resume but in a guise that is less intense and different from the one we have known up to now. The global standstill will have lasting and not necessarily positive consequences.

■ Adapted from Andrés Ortega, European Council on Foreign relations, March 2020.

A step-by-step approach

Notes

1 Lexical work

Find the French equivalents.

Put a lid on • abeyance • make headway • emphasis • supply chain • re-shoring • borders • a standstill

2 Read the whole text

a. Identify the source of the document (title, source, nature).

b. Comment on the title by giving a definition of "deglobalisation". Then, explain why the term "virus" is used.

3 Check the facts

Answer the following questions.

a. What started deglobalisation?

b. What has Covid-19 done to deglobalisation?

c. How is Covid-19 described?

d. What has Covid-19 lockdown revealed?

e. What should we understand by "greater national emphasis"?

f. Physical globalization is opposed to digital globalization. What is working well?

g. What does a pandemic require countries to do?

h. What will Covid-19 leave behind?

4 Train for the exam

Choose the best summary.

a. The 21st century will be known for focusing on national and regional economies: production will be relocated at home so as to avoid shortages. ❑

b. The 21st century has drawn the lessons from the Covid-19 pandemic and each country will bring back production to its shores so as not to depend on faraway countries that deliver late and at a cost. ❑

5 Topic debrief

Finish each sentence.

a. **Part 1.** The pandemic is responsible for speeding up ....

b. **Part 2.** Digital globalization has replaced ....

Language

Gérondif → page 186 / Comparatif → page 179
Quantifieurs → page 199

Translate the sentences.

1. <u>Combating</u> the virus involves <u>keeping</u> people apart.
2. This originated <u>earlier</u>.
3. The world's governments have <u>fewer tools</u>.

TRAINING EXAMS EXERCISES INTERNSHIP

Text

Misguided U.S. Trade Policy

Audio 51
liennathan.fr/h6v6h3

The Trump administration's initial mistake in launching a trade war was to assume that U.S. trade deficits were inherently bad and that China was to blame. However, trade deficits are not a good indicator of the state of the economy but have little to do with China. The irony is that bilateral trade between the United States and China has now rebounded to all-time highs, China's trade surplus has increased, and the U.S. deficit has gotten worse.

Trump also echoed popular but misguided sentiments that U.S. firms had been overinvesting in China, resulting in a loss in competitiveness. But over the past two decades, only 1–2 percent of annual U.S. foreign investment has gone to China. By contrast, the EU has invested roughly twice as much as the United States has annually.

China's alleged failure to protect intellectual property rights is also mischaracterized. At the extreme, China is accused of stealing foreign intellectual property, especially technology. But such events may not occur unusually often or are possibly exaggerated.

Further, China's patent courts have matured in dealing with this problem—foreign plaintiffs are now more likely to win their cases than domestic firms.

The reality is that it takes generations to develop a sound regime for intellectual property rights, as was the case for the United States. The foundation of China's system was laid only two decades ago with reforms that accompanied China's 2001 accession to the World Trade Organization.

But there are also credible concerns that China's investment policies treat foreign firms unfairly. One complaint is China's use of subsidies. All countries provide subsidies to domestic companies and households, such as U.S. support to farmers, tax deductions to households to encourage clean energy use, and incentives to companies like Amazon to relocate.

China's protectionist tendencies are also evident from the requirement that foreign firms form joint ventures with domestic Chinese firms as a condition for market entry in some economic sectors. But these Chinese requirements, too, have seemed to get less stringent in recent years, as exemplified by major foreign investments in chemical manufacturing (BASF), auto manufacturing (Tesla), and finance (BlackRock). These foreign companies have been allowed for the first time to enter key sectors without a Chinese partner.

China's willingness to drop the joint venture requirement featured prominently in the EU-China Comprehensive Agreement on Investment negotiated in December 2020 (which has not yet been ratified). This experience suggests that policy differences can be addressed.

Adapted from Yukon Huang, a senior fellow in the Carnegie Asia Program, 16 September 2021.

A step-by-step approach

1 Lexical work

a. Find the French equivalents:
Misguided • mistake • mischaracterized • blame • foreign plaintiffs • trade war • trade policy.

b. Now try to rephrase the title in your own words.

2 Read the whole text

a. **Comment on the title:** "Misguided" and "mischaracterized" do mean almost the same thing. What is the point of view expressed by the journalist?

b. **Identify the source of the document** (title, source, nature).

3 Check the facts

Say if the following statements are true or false.

a. China is responsible for US trade deficits. ❑ T ❑ F

b. Trade deficits imply an economic recession. ❑ T ❑ F

c. The US invest more in China than Europe. ❑ T ❑ F

d. China is accused of stealing American technology. ❑ T ❑ F

e. China has improved its legislation regarding patents. ❑ T ❑ F

f. China joined the WTO in 2001. ❑ T ❑ F

g. China required foreign firms to find a Chinese partner in the past. ❑ T ❑ F

4 Train for the exam

a. **Complete the following sentences to get a full summary of the article.**

Introduction

This article was published ....

This article deals with the trade relationship between ....

Development

First, China is not responsible for ....

Second, China has reviewed its policy about foreign companies such as ....

Third, the US is also to blame especially ....

Conclusion

Trade can improve between ....

5 Topic debrief

Finish each sentence.

a. The US have accused China of ....

b. China has improved ....

Notes

Language

Forme passive → page 184 / Cas possessif → page 179

Translate the sentences.

1. The foundation of China's system was laid only two decades ago.
2. These foreign companies have been allowed for the first time to enter key sectors.
3. China's protectionist tendencies are also evident.

TRAINING EXAMS EXERCISES INTERNSHIP

7 Video track

1 Pronunciation work

Audio 52
liennathan.fr/37sm5n

Listen, repeat the following words and record yourself.

China • Russia • vaccines • require • although • vaccinated • much needed shopping time.

2 Before you start watching the video

a. Look at the visual document and the title and say as much as you can. ....

b. Find out more about Mexico and the USA: their area, their population. ....

c. Look at the title and rephrase it. ....

3 Watch the video

Underline the words you hear among the following list:

Non-essential • along the border • unable • some employ • in retail sales • vendors • magnified • southern • dynamic.

Video 26
liennathan.fr/923mik

Video

Border Reopening Brings Business Boom

4 A step-by-step approach

1. Watch the whole video once

a. Write in French what it is about.

....

2. Watch the video a second time

→ Watch the first part

b. Who is allowed to cross the border?

....

c. What did the first interviewee buy?

....

d. When was it the last time she enters the US?

....

e. When were Covid-restrictions put in place?

....

→ 1'10 – Watch the second part

f. How much was lost in the San Diego region?

....

g. Where did the 200 businesses close?

....

h. How many million fewer crosses were there between the US and Mexico?

....

i. How is the region described?

....

→ 2'03 – Watch the third part

j. What is the vaccination protocol?

....

k. How many vaccines are there in Mexico?

....

l. Which 2 vaccines will prevent Mexicans from crossing the border?

....

5 Train for the exam

Oral report: put together all the information you have collected and report to the class.

7 Audio track

1 Pronunciation work

Audio 53
liennathan.fr/5ai32d

Listen to the following words. Then repeat them and record yourself.
Alliances • billion • nationalistic • obviously • migration • Marshal program • to violate • undisguised protectionism • thorny • asylum seekers • hemisphere.

2 Before listening

a. **What do you know about Canada, Mexico?**

b. **Look at the title and think about what might have been discussed at the Washington summit?**

3 Listen to the audio

c. **Anticipate the topic of the audio.**

Audio

Audio 54
liennathan.fr/95szf7

Summit with leaders of Canada and Mexico at the White House, Washington

From left to right: Mexican President Lopez Obrador, US President Joe Biden and Canadian Prime Minister Justin Trudeau.

4 A step-by-step approach

1. Listen to the whole audio once

a. Write what the interview is about.

2. Listen to the audio a second time

→ Listen to the first part

b. What is the nickname of the summit?

c. When was the last meeting between the three countries?

d. Name of the president of Mexico and the Prime Minister in Canada.

e. Reasons for this summit.

f. When did the first meeting occur?

→ Listen to second part

g. Who has never attended this meeting?

h. How long has the Mexican president been in office?

i. How often has he been abroad since the beginning of his term?

j. Give three adjectives to describe the Mexican president.

k. Trade: how much does trade represent?

l. Why is the tax credit seen as undisguised protectionism.

→ Listen to the third part

m. Why is Mexico a key country regarding immigration?

n. What is "Remain in Mexico"?

o. Who introduced it?

p. What must asylum seekers do?

q. Where will the economic development program be introduced?

5 Train for the exam

Oral work: speak for at least two minutes about you have just learned. Put together all the information you have collected.

7 Tasks

Document 1 Audio

The India - UK free trade agreement

Audio 55
liennathan.fr/5yb73c

Task 1

1. Listen to the whole audio.

a. Explain why a FTA is negotiated between India and the UK.

b. When did the negotiations start?

c. What are the reasons for the UK to negotiate FTAs?

d. What has the Northern Ireland protocol provoked?

e. What has the Brexit triggered?

2. Write an organized account in English.

Notes

Document 2 Text

Who benefits from China-Africa relations?

Audio 56
liennathan.fr/v9d89s

China's donation of one billion doses of its Covid-19 vaccines to Africa was among the first things Chinese President Xi Jinping promised at the 8th Forum on China-Africa Cooperation (Focac) in Dakar, Senegal, which started on Sunday and closes today. According to Xi, 400 million doses are to be produced in the continent.

The announcement could be seen as part of China's efforts to burnish its image.

A spokesman for the ministry in Beijing cited a survey published in November 2021 by the pan-African institute Afrobarometer, which states 63% of Africans believe China has had a positive influence in their country.

"I see the influence of the Chinese," admitted Bamidele Adekunle, adjunct professor at the Canadian University of Guelph, to Deutsche Welle, DW, "When I was in Dar es Salaam, I saw lots of things done by the Chinese. And it has really transformed Dar es Salaam."

But analyst Asche scoffed at the notion. "I sincerely doubt that it is a conscious policy. China has no interest to see African countries caught in a trap," even if the Chinese strategy of swapping infrastructure projects for mineral resources, known as the 'Angola-mode', has resulted in financial troubles for many African countries.

Adapted from DW, November 2021.

Task 2

1. Read the whole text and answer.

a. What has China given African countries ?

b. What does China hope to achieve in doing so ?

c. Why can we say trade imbalance is what characterized trade between China and Africa ?

d. What is being swapped between China and some African countries ?

e. What needs to be more transparent ?

2. Write an organized account of the article in English (50 to 100 words).

Notes

Video 27
liennathan.fr/45hc7j

Document 3 Video

Amazing' New Beans Could Save Coffee from Climate Change

Task 3

1. Watch the video.

a. Where is coffee from?

b. What about new species of coffee?

c. What are the two African countires mentioned in the video.

2. Organize all the information you have collected.

3. Write a report.

Notes

TRAINING EXAMS EXERCISES INTERNSHIP

7

Background

Globalisation during and after the pandemic

I Deglobalisation is key.

The Pandemic started on January 11, 2020 and since then much has changed. We have been in lockdown and have realized that masks were made in China and that we were waiting in line to get them. But masks were one commodity among others. So relocation seems to be the solution to supply chain shortages. Then shipping containers that move some 1.9 billion tonnes per year by sea alone were delayed, blocked and could not deliver toys, microprocessor chips, etc.

The pandemic had disrupted trade as borders had closed. Offshoring manufacturing to Europe, the US is the new mantra. Why is it a good idea? Or is it?

Joseph Stiglitz mentioned that concerns have been voiced about the loss of know-how that comes from excessive offshoring to countries like China. Indeed, manufacturing medicines in China was seen as the wrong move as Europe had to stop being dependent on Chinese output. Others think that a stop in Sino-American trade relations would be too costly as the two economies are too interlinked. Yet, reintroducing manufacturing instead of relying on China's powerhouse might bring more competition. And globalisation has been reassessed and seems to bring smaller benefits.

One might see President Biden's Build Back Better scheme as a step toward relocating industries to the US.

II Sustainability and globalisation.

Globalisation has an environmental cost as goods must be shipped to factories or consumers. So to reduce global warming and energy consumption, goods could be made closer to their end-users. Would it reduce traffic by sea? To some extent, but we also know that if it is not manufactured merchandise or car parts or else that is exported, raw materials will be exported: wood to make Ikea furniture, rare earth elements to make smart phones. So there is not one easy solution to solve it all.

So what is to be done? Companies could decide to work with green companies in China and elsewhere. In fact, an NGO, "China's Top 100 Green Companies", from China released a list of 100 Chinese companies that promote green companies.

But what we have to keep in mind is that, as the American economist Jeffrey Sachs says, sustainable development embraces three goals, not only one: economic development, social inclusion, and environmental sustainability within a coherent framework.

III To conclude.

What sounded good yesterday is questioned today. What was viewed as a response to the well-being of the people is now much criticized. But certainly the way forward is to keep trying. Trial and error experience is part of the path to get there.

Climate catastrophes, abusive corporate behavior such as the encroachment of oil companies into Amazonia, chronic public underinvestment in care, housing, and renewable energy infrastructure. every single one of these issues should be tackled. Approach to energy costs would quicken transition away from fossil fuels, making the types of big investments in electric heat pumps and electric vehicles (both charged by solar) that will over time drastically bring down energy prices.

Test

Read the background carefully and answer the following questions.

1. What has the pandemic triggered?

2. What did countries realize had been happening?

3. How did they react to the shortage of goods?

4. Economists do not agree: What are the viewpoints of these two schools of thought?

5. So what is "deglobalization"?

6. What is the name of President Joe Biden's policy?

7. What about the environmental cost of shipping goods around the world?

8. What is Jeffrey Sachs's point?

9. Why is it we do not get it right?

10. What is social inclusion?

TRAINING

EXAMS

EXERCISES

INTERNSHIP

7 PowerPoint Presentation

Brexit's SWOT

1. Study Brexit's SWOT closely.

2. Choose a company in the list below :

EXXON MOBIL • TATA MOTORS • PFIZER

a. Prepare a PowerPoint presentation of their SWOT.

b. Present it to the class.

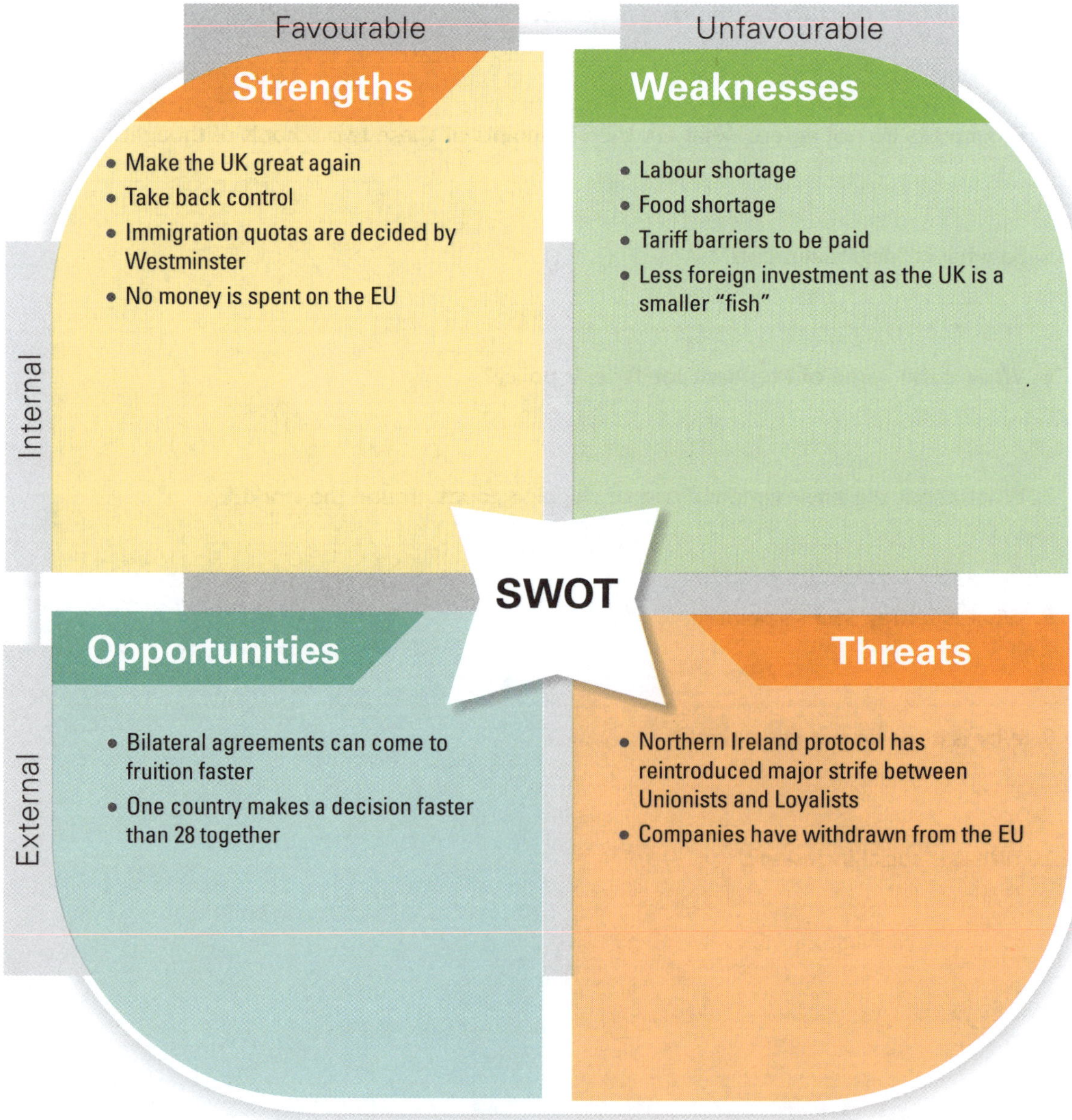

Act

Choose one of the following role plays to act in front of the class.

Role play 1

Work in pairs:

Student A tries to list arguments in favour of European spending in remote areas of European member states.

Student B is hard to convince and thinks it prevents farmers from being dynamic and self-reliant.

Student A tips:

List arguments; use link words such as: first, second, third, unlike, etc.

And start with: if we are to believe the article...; we can clearly see that...; there is not the shadow of a doubt that... without any doubt.

Role play 2

Group A supports free trade and is strongly against protectionism and tariffs.

Group B is in favour of protectionism, against free trade.

Each group prepares its arguments.

The debate is launched under the supervision of a student from each group whose role is to distribute speaking and listening roles equally.

Role play 3

Student A and B are British expats living and working in the Irish Republic (Dublin).

Student A is worried about his post-Brexit situation whereas Student B is optimistic about the outcome of Brexit.

Each student prepares his/her arguments before playing the situation.

Record the scene.

Notes

EXAMS

1 Faire un compte rendu oral ou écrit en anglais à partir d'un document écrit en anglais

→ Modèle

How should firms deal with a "toxic employee"?

When Simon realised he had to deal with a "toxic employee", he knew he needed to act fast. Simon, the boss of a small firm in New York, says the man in question had been wrongly trying to claim credit for other new business wins, and was deliberately ignoring members of his team. At the same time the employee was said to be rebelling against the company by forming a clique, and threatening to start his own business.

"We needed to show our company that one person does not stand above the team," says Simon. And so the alleged rabble-rouser was sacked.

Simon adds: "The money and time we spent handling this situation... well, it could have been a lot worse if he had stayed on. The internal politics would have been terrible. I don't know if we'd even have a company now."

Most of us have had to endure a corrosive fellow member of staff on one or more occasions during our working lives, whose bad behaviour – everything from selfishness, bullying, rudeness, being overtly-domineering, or even just being constantly too loud and opinionated – can have a devastating impact on staff morale. In academic circles, such a problem employee is now more often described as "toxic". Numerous studies have shown that they cost a business or government department money, due to the productivity of other workers plummeting, or people taking sick leave or even resigning.

One 2015 report by Harvard Business School estimated that keeping a toxic worker on the payroll can cost an average firm more than $12,000 (£9,400) a year. This is more than double the £5,000 of increased annual productivity it says a good employee can provide. A separate study said that the annual financial impact of a toxic employee could be even more onerous. The 2012 survey of 2,700 firms by jobs website Career Builder found that a quarter of respondents put the figure at more than $50,000, while 41% said the number was around $25,000.

Prof Dylan Minor, co-author of the Harvard report, says that what can be frustrating for managers is that toxic employees "are usually very productive, because overconfident workers can be successful." He adds: "But employers have to think about the other dimensions, the toxicity." Still with employment law in many countries making it far from easy to get rid of a damaging worker, how can companies best deal with the problem without necessarily seeking the termination of the toxic employee? And how can firms best avoid such people in the first place? Also, could the existence of toxic employees be blamed on the company itself and a bad working culture that enables such people to behave the way they do in the first place?

Bruce Tulgan, a US management expert, says that company leaders need to be clear about what is permissible within the firm, and identify "low performers", which is what he calls toxic employees. He suggests meeting with the difficult employee to "make the behaviour explicit, and break it down, monitor and measure it, and offer course-corrected feedback." Mr. Tulgan adds: "A lot of time that can correct the [bad] behaviour."

But if those corrected measures don't improve the employee's conduct, he recommends firing them "since you are paying them and they aren't following instructions, and that is insubordination."

Adapted from *BBC Business*, December 8, 2016.

I Introduction

Comme l'épreuve est orale, le niveau de stress peut être élevé. Pour vous donner de l'assurance, rédigez votre introduction et donnez votre plan.

Vous devez obtenir une introduction semblable à celle-ci :

The text is from BBC Business posted on BBC website on 8 December 2016. The main idea is toxic employee. So clearly we shall start by defining what a "the toxic employee" is and how to solve the problem.

II Plan

Le temps est compté : vous n'avez que 20 minutes pour préparer votre plan en trois parties.

A. Faire la liste des arguments qui définissent "the toxic employee".
B. Faire la liste des conséquences à l'intérieur de l'entreprise.
C. Faire la liste des solutions.

III Reformuler et expliciter

Une fois les listes faites, il faut apprendre à reformuler. Voici quelques exemples :

Selfishness: a toxic employee is selfish or acts selfishly. The other members of the team do not count in his eye.
Rudeness: a toxic employee is rude. He or she might not say hello or thank you. He or she considers he/she deserves the help of his/her co-workers.
Overly domineering: he or she wants to be right all the time. He or she is bossy.

The company loses money. Employees are sick so they are absent on leave more often. Employees resign, which means that they leave the company for a job elsewhere.
Productivity is down: employees are less productive.

The company needs to say what is permissible. A set of rules or a code of conduct must be defined by the company.
The company must meet the toxic employee.

IV Citer le texte

Vous pouvez citer le texte pour asseoir vos arguments.

Exemple : He suggests meeting with the difficult employee "and speak frankly". This sentence shows that a way to find a solution is to talk to the toxic employee.

V Conclusion

Ne pas oublier la conclusion ; ici, savoir qui est responsable du "*toxic employee*" :

L'entreprise qui a embauché le mauvais salarié ou une situation de travail qui génère ce comportement ?

VI *Branching out*

- **Comment enrichir le sujet à partir de vos connaissances ?**
  L'approfondissement du sujet dépend des connaissances que vous avez acquises sur la problématique présentée dans l'article. Ici, il s'agit du monde du travail. Vous pouvez donc partir de la problématique de l'employé(e) toxique pour vous exprimer plus largement sur la thématique du travail.

  Deux exemples d'enrichissements possibles :
  – Today the work place has changed thanks to new technologies; the possibility to work from home may preserve employees from the bad impact of a toxic atmosphere at work.
  – Managers should be able to anticipate tensions in a team by separating people who cannot work together. They should treat every employee equally and try to highlight their qualities rather than insist on their flaws. Although competitiveness can be encouraged, it mustn't turn into a counterproductive confrontation of egos.
- **Votre examinateur peut également vous emmener vers des problématiques plus larges en vous demandant par exemple d'exprimer votre opinion sur :**
  – le télétravail ;
  – l'open-space ;
  – la discrimination au travail ;
  – les droits des salariés (avantages sociaux, etc.).

→ Application

Amazon's rising air shipments fly in the face of climate plan

The company's use of airplanes – the most climate-damaging mode of transportation – is on the rise, according to data provided to Reuters. Amazon Air's U.S. volume has risen steadily since its 2016 launch. In July, Amazon Air flew 136 million lbs[1] of goods in the United States, according to the data. That was up 29 % from the year earlier and just 9 million lbs short of December 2018, when the peak holiday shipping season was in full swing. Bezos has said Amazon will cut its use of airplanes as it builds more local warehouses and fills them with goods that it can deliver to customer doorsteps in one day, or even one hour.

But for the time being, Amazon's air shipments are climbing as it speeds up deliveries to lure customers and pressure rivals like Walmart Inc and Target Corp. In April, Amazon started offering no-minimum purchase, one-day free shipping to members of its Prime subscription service.

Last month, Amazon said its CO2 emissions in 2018 were 44.4 million metric tons and set a goal to be net carbon neutral by 2040. "We expect the percent of total shipments to customers utilizing air transportation to reduce from year to year as we significantly increase one and same day shipments," Amazon spokesman Sam Kennedy said. A standard package flown on a plane in the United States creates an estimated 6-10 times more CO2 emissions than one traveling by truck, said Jacques Leonardi, a senior research fellow at the University of Westminster in London. Amazon Air leases 47 planes and is expected have 50 by the end of the year. It operates roughly 110 daily flights in the United States and around 20 per day in Europe. In June, shortly after FedEx Corp said its planes would stop shuttling packages for the online retailer, Amazon Air announced plans to have 70 planes on lease by 2021.

But Amazon says it is getting closer to customers with an expanding network of well-stocked warehouses. Those local fulfillment centers underpin the company's one-day and same-day delivery services. Amazon said those options were "better for the planet" because there aren't many miles in the trip to customer doorsteps. Because those time windows are so tight, "you are eliminating the possibility of air transportation," Amazon's Bezos said in September. "Even though it's counterintuitive, the fact of the matter is that shorter delivery times end up being less carbon-intensive than longer delivery times."

■ Adapted from *Reuters*, November 6th, 2019.

I Rédigez votre introduction

Introduction

....

....

....

II Plan

A : ....

....

B : ....

....

C : ....

....

III Reformulez

A : ....

....

B : ....

....

C : ....

....

IV Citez le texte

....

....

....

V Conclusion

....

....

....

VI Enrichissez/allez plus loin.

....

....

....

TRAINING

EXAMS

EXERCISES

INTERNSHIP

2 Faire un compte rendu écrit en français à partir d'un texte anglais

→ Modèle

State of play: Toymakers bounce back in the land of adult nappies

They have become pioneers in how to adapt to a rapidly ageing society.

WILLIAM ELLIOT GRIFFIS, an American educator who travelled to Japan in the 1870s, noted that in the previous two and a half centuries, "the main business of this nation was play." He described toyshops filled as full as Christmas stockings and plenty of grown-ups.

Griffis would have found it familiar walking today around Hakuhinkan Toy Park, one of the largest toy stores in Tokyo. Teens, office workers and grandparents are mostly to be seen perusing its 200,000-odd knick-knacks across five floors. Its director, Hiroyuki Itoh, says he wants the store to be a place where everyone can play. After work, suited salarymen come to spend ¥200 (under $2) for a five-minute whizz around a 36-metre slot-car racetrack. In another corner a group of university students fiddle with displays of toys from their childhoods.

Playthings aimed at the over-20s make up 27% of Japan's domestic toy sales, according to figures from Euromonitor, a market-research firm. That grown-up portion of the market has been crucial for Japan's three biggest players, Bandai Namco, Takara Tomy and Sanrio, as the country's birth rate has slumped. Since the 1970s the proportion of under-15s has halved, to 12% of the population. By 2060 it is likely to be 9%.

Fumiaki Ibuki of Toy Journal, a 114-year-old trade magazine, says Japanese toy companies are pioneers in adapting to ageing. Despite a slow economy, the sector has, in the past two years, done its best in a decade: in the fiscal year ending in 2015, sales in core categories (excluding video games) rose by a tenth on the previous year, to over ¥800bn. Mr Ibuki says toymakers are taking a "borderless" approach: selling to a wider age range, and teaming up with trend-driven sectors like tech and fashion.

When Bandai's Tamagotchi, virtual pets housed in an egg-shaped toy, were booming in the mid-1990s, women in their 20s and 30s were big buyers. The same age-group snapped up Licca-chan, Japan's answer to Barbie, made by Takara Tomy. The firm now has an adult range: its "Cappuccino One-Piece" doll, sells for ¥12,000.

A stigma against adults having fun, strong in the aftermath of the second world war, has faded. Many want to recapture their youth, not so much by playing, but by collecting and displaying toys, says Harold Meij, the boss of Takara Tomy—so, for its premium Tomica model-car range, the company uses vintage designs that adults admired as boys. Having only one child later in life, as more Japanese now do, means that parents have more to spend on their offspring. Children are said to have "six pockets": two from their parents, and four from their grandparents.

During the global financial crisis of 2008, cheap impulse-buy toys took off, such as trading cards and coin-operated machines that dispense capsules of small toys—usually of well-known characters from Japanese comic books and television series.

The big themes in the toy industry are collectability and intellectual property (IP). A recent hit was a watch branded "Yo-kai", after the word in Japanese for supernatural spirits, by Bandai. It exemplifies a popular strategy: Yo-kai, whose hero wears the watch, began as a cartoon series in 2013, was adapted for TV and made into a hit video game.

The model is known as "media mix" in the industry. Bandai has partnered with Dentsu, an advertising giant, to promote anime, a word defining Japanese animation.

But when the story of a character catches on, toy- and film-makers end up splitting fat profits. It all makes for a sizzling recipe.

Adapted from *The Economist*, Feb. 23, 2017.

En général, il vous est demandé de faire en français la synthèse d'un texte en anglais, c'est-à-dire que votre compte-rendu doit être plus court, et faire en général le tiers du texte initial.
Comment procéder en temps limité ? Il vous faudra quatre ou cinq paragraphes distincts : introduction (source, date, idée principale), développement en deux ou trois parties et conclusion.

I Introduction

Vous devez obtenir une introduction semblable à celle-ci.

L'article de *The Economist* du 23 février 2017 relate le succès des entreprises japonaises de jouets dans une société vieillissante. Quelles sont les raisons de ce succès ?

II Développement

Voici le modèle pour ce texte.

I. Un paradoxe : les entreprises de jouet japonaises sont prospères dans une société avec de moins en moins d'enfants.

- Noms des entreprises mentionnées dans le texte : Hakuhinkan Toy Park à Tokyo sur cinq étages, Bandai Namco, Takara Tomy et Sanrio.
- Les clients sont des adultes de plus de 20 ans et leurs achats représentent 27 % des ventes sur le marché national.
- Les acheteurs collectionnent et exposent.
- La plupart des Japonais n'ont qu'un enfant, souvent assez tard.
- Parents et grands-parents contribuent à maintenir les ventes de jouets pour enfants.

II. Des sociétés ont adapté leur stratégie

- Une population vieillissante.
- Des jouets qui rappellent l'enfance.
- Des partenariats avec des secteurs de la mode et du Hi-Tech.
- Pendant la crise, des jouets peu chers sont proposés.
- Acquisition de droits de marchandisage, un modèle dit « media mix ».

III Conclusion

La culture du jouet liée à des partenariats avec les médias génère des profits. Le ralentissement économique général au Japon n'a pas de prise sur les industries du jouet qui ont augmenté leurs ventes de 10 % en 2015 par rapport à l'année précédente.

LES PIÈGES

- Évitez les mots anglais.
- Ne pas prendre en compte le paragraphe anecdotique en début d'un article, accroche pour le lecteur.
- Ne pas citer tous les exemples. Ils ne sont là que pour illustrer un propos.
- Pensez en termes abstraits : ainsi « adult nappies » est relancé dans le sous-titre par « ageing society ».

→ Application

Would you let your child become a 'kid influencer'?

Social media "influencers" - people who promote goods and services for money online - are getting younger and younger it seems. And services are springing up to teach parents and kids just how to do it.

Ralphie Waplington is just two-and-a-half years old, yet he has almost 20,000 followers on Instagram. His page features pictures of him wearing clothes sponsored by brands such as Peppa Pig and McDonald's. His parents set up the account in 2017 when he was just a couple of weeks old. Initially, this was simply to "document pictures of him for friends and family", they say.

Stacey, the baby's mother, says his mini-stardom has led to incredible opportunities. "It is giving us an unbelievable experience as a family and it's great if we can create some kind of media CV for him, put money away in the bank and build memories for us."

From babies appearing on accounts set up by their parents, to teenagers creating their own channels on YouTube, more kids are becoming social media "influencers".

A survey found that 34 % of six-to-17-year-old children would like to be a YouTuber when they grow up. And almost 18 % said they would like to be a blogger or vlogger [video blogger].

Fire Tech Camp, a computer training school, offers a five-day "Creating for YouTube – Become a YouTube influencer" training, which costs from £425. "Last year it was one of our bestselling courses," says Jill Hodges, Fire Tech chief executive.

But should parents be encouraging their child to become an influencer at such a young age? "While it is true that a small minority of children and families have found financial success, parents should be cautious before encouraging their children to become kid influencers," advises Dr Elizabeth Milovidov, an eSafety consultant. "Parents need to be aware of the effects that constant photo snapping can have on a child's mental, physical and emotional well-being. We are hearing more and more about children and young people who do not want to have an online presence or who are faced with an online identity created by their parents." She also highlights issues such as bullying and identity theft and advises parents to control the accounts and guide their children in responsible and safe use in the digital world.

But for now it looks like there's no stopping the rise of young social media stars.

But what if Ralphie decides when he's older that he doesn't want his pictures being shared with thousands of people? "Then that's the day it stops," Stacey says.

Adapted from *BBC.com*, August 2019.

I Introduction

II Développement

1.

2.

III Conclusion

3 Rédiger une lettre ou un courriel commercial

→ Modèle

Vous rédigerez un courriel en anglais en respectant les consignes suivantes :

Vous êtes Camille Germain, assistant/e de gestion dans l'entreprise « Des antennes au Plafond », 21 rue Pierre Brosolette, 33000 Toulouse.
Email : camillegermain@gmail.com

Vous répondez à votre cliente Jamie Tackle, directrice des achats chez « Genuine Bookstore for kids » par courriel à l'adresse : jamietackle@gmail.com.

I Vous la priez d'accepter vos excuses pour le retard dans la livraison en utilisant les formules d'usage.

Formulations possibles :
Ex: We wish to apologise/We are very sorry etc

II Vous rappelez les circonstances de la transaction.

En effet, Genuine Bookstore for kids, 22 Winston Street Birmingham C342970, vous a passé une commande de jeux pour enfants (de 3 ans à 13 ans) le 27 mars 2018.

Formulation également possible :
Ex: You placed an order on behalf of Genuine Book store for kids on 27 March 2021.

III Vous expliquez les raisons de ce retard.

Vous n'avez pas pu respecter les délais de livraison car votre entrepôt a été inondé et la marchandise (jeux de cartes, jeux de société, jeux de construction, puzzles) a été abîmée.

Formulation possible :
Ex: We were unable to meet the April 10 deadline because...

IV Vous donnez une nouvelle échéance.

Formulation possible :
Ex: I'm afraid we will be able to deliver your order within two weeks only.

V Vous faites un geste commercial : une réduction ou autre.

Formulation possible :
Ex: As a commercial gesture, we propose to exempt you from the post and packaging fees/from the shipping fees.

VI Vous espérez que la relation commerciale ne sera pas modifiée.

Formulation possible :

Ex: We do hope our business relationship will remain on good terms despite this incident.

VII Vous vous excusez à nouveau pour la gêne occasionnée.

Formulation possible :

Ex : We apologise once again for the inconvenience.

VIII Vous terminez votre courriel par une formule de politesse.

Autres formulations possibles :

Ex: Yours truly/Yours faithfully/Best regards

New Message

From: camillegermain@gmail.com

To: jamietackle@gmail.com Cc Bcc

Subject: Apologising for a late delivery

Date: 10 April 2018

Dear Mrs Tackle,

We really would like to apologise for not delivering the games on time. Genuine Bookstore for Kids placed an order for board games, construction sets, and decks of cards on 27 March 2018.
However, we were unable to deliver the goods on 10 April 2018 because our warehouse where we stock our merchandise was flooded. Board games, decks of cards, jigsaw puzzles, etc. were damaged.
We will be able to deliver your order in two weeks' time only. We do hope that it will not cause too much inconvenience.
As a gesture of goodwill, we would like to offer you 10 units of our new board game Dixit.
We hope our business relationship will not suffer from this incident.
Once again accept our apologies for the inconvenience caused.

Yours sincerely,
Camille Germain
Personal Assistant

Send

Tips

1. Ne confondez pas destinataire et expéditeur.
2. Vérifiez que vous connaissez les termes administratifs et usuels. La gêne occasionnée : *inconvenience caused* ; un geste commercial : *a goodwill gesture* ; livrer : *to deliver* ; la relation commerciale : *the business relationship* ; être abîmé : *to be damaged*.
3. Faites des paragraphes en fonction des idées qui vont ensemble.
4. Vous connaissez par cœur les deux formules de politesse, même si les courriels sont souvent moins formels.

Tools for the exam

→ Application

Écrivez un courriel à une entreprise qui est à la recherche d'une assistante de gestion. L'entreprise s'appelle Look at Beauty. Elle est située à Londres.

La responsable est Ms Jennifer Soro. Son adresse courriel : jennifer.soro@lookatbeauty

La date est le 6 juin 2023.

Collecter des informations pour présenter votre expérience, votre personnalité et votre intérêt pour l'entreprise. Votre parcours académique est en pièce jointe sur le CV.

Quelques pistes :

– I worked for ...... for 2 years.
– I am currently working as a personal assistant at (name of the company).
– I am responsible for (tasks you carry out).
– I am also in charge of (other tasks you do).
– Adjectives: well-organised; hard-working; efficient; etc.
– I take initiatives; I upgrade customer files; I send reminder letters.
– Please, find attached my CV.

New Message

From:

To: Cc Bcc

Subject: job application

Date:

Dear Ms Smith,

....

....

....

....

....

....

....

Send

I 1er paragraphe :

Indiquez que vous avez vu que l'entreprise est à la recherche d'un/e assistant/e de gestion.

II 2e paragraphe :

Signifiez votre intérêt. Présentez votre expérience professionnelle et vos qualités. Indiquez que le CV en pièce jointe permettra à l'entreprise de connaître le parcours professionnel du candidat ou de la candidate.

....

....

....

....

....

....

....

....

III 3e paragraphe :

Indiquez que vous allez venir habiter à Londres. C'est la raison pour laquelle vous allez quitter votre entreprise.

....

....

....

IV 4e paragraphe :

Il est possible de faire un entretien d'embauche par Skype. Une lettre de recommandation est possible.

V 5e paragraphe :

N'oubliez pas les salutations.

VI 6e paragraphe :

Signez le mail avec votre nom ou votre titre.

....

....

....

....

....

....

....

4 Négocier

→ Modèle

– **Il y a deux grandes phases de négociation :**
- **Première phase : prise de contact et découverte des besoins.**
- **Seconde phase : récapitulation des besoins et vérification, traitement des objections, conclusion avec la commande et ses modalités, et enfin, prise de congé.**

– Vous aurez la première ou la seconde partie à jouer. Il est entendu que vous saurez qui est votre prospect, les produits que vous voulez lui vendre, l'entreprise et l'activité de votre prospect.
– Le prospect est classé selon le profil SONCASE. En fonction des raisons pour lesquelles il/elle désire ce produit, ou encore en fonction de la relation commerciale qu'il/elle veut instaurer. Ainsi, le prospect est perçu comme à la recherche d'un produit de prestige, d'un produit nouveau, ou encore pour une relation commerciale simple et donc, le qualificatif «confort» peut décrire ce qu'il/elle recherche.

Info

SONCAS
- **Sécurité:** *security*
- **Nouveau :** *novelty*
- **Confort :** *comfort*
- **Argent :** *money*
- **Sympathie :** *sympathy*

Phase 1 : Rencontre avec le prospect + découverte des besoins

- **Prise de contact :** I am Mrs NAME, the Sales Manager from COMPANY. And I have an appointment with Mr/s NAME at 1 o'clock. Could you, please, let her/him know that I have arrived?
- ***Small talk*:** Mr/s NAME, nice to meet you. I hope you had a good trip to London. Is it your first time?
- **Découverte des besoins (*needs appraisal*) :** I met with a colleague of yours at the Fair in Hannover last November. That's right and and I was told that you were interested in some of our products. Could I ask you a few questions to find out what your needs are? *Vous avez besoin de bien comprendre les besoins de votre prospect en lui posant des questions.*

Phase 2 : 2e rencontre avec le prospect pour finaliser la vente

Récapitulation des besoins : Last time we met, you told me that you were interested in having 100 bottles of a specific fragrance. You had not yet decided the size of the bottles you wanted. You were not quite sure if you only wanted 100 ml bottles or also 50 ml bottles.
Vous vérifiez que votre négociation redémarre bien sur les mêmes bases. Il est clair que le prospect peut revenir sur des choix préalables.

Traitement des objections :
Can you ensure me that the delivery will be two weeks after placing the order?
Votre prospect, s'il ne vous connaît pas, a besoin d'être rassuré sur le bien-fondé de son achat. Vous devez le rassurer sur les conditions de livraison, etc. Vous aurez prévu les objections.

Conditions de paiement et transport :
I guess you would like to pay in pounds, that is fine with us. As for the shipping of the fresh produce, we will start every other day and if you feel it should be every day, we will organise it to be a daily delivery.
Les Incoterms auront été évoqués, choisis, et la vente doit se conclure sur le sentiment que les deux partis ont obtenu un contrat équitable.

Conclusion et prise de congé :
It was a delight to do business with you. If you have any questions, please, do not hesitate to contact me. You have my business card. Good bye.

→ Application

Situation

Mrs Johnson is the CEO of a restaurant chain.
She wishes to equip some of her upscale restaurants with a state of the art sound system.
You are the sales representative from the cutting edge French sound system brand Devialet.
Find information on the brand online and follow the different phases of the negotiation (1st and second meeting).

I Phase 1

Rencontre avec le prospect et découverte des besoins

- Prise de contact

....

....

- Small talk

....

....

- Découverte des besoins

....

....

II Phase 2

2e rencontre avec le prospect pour finaliser la vente :

- Récapitulation des besoins (reformulation)

....

....

- Traitement des objections

....

....

- Conditions de paiement et de transport

....

....

- Conclusion et prise de congé

....

....

TRAINING EXAMS EXERCISES INTERNSHIP

5 Préparer un entretien d'embauche

→ Modèle

La préparation permet de limiter le stress et de se sentir plus à l'aise. Préparer, c'est anticiper les questions qui vont vous être posées. Savoir mettre en avant vos qualités et les points positifs (imaginaires) de l'entreprise auprès de laquelle vous postulez. Vous saurez être réactif(ve), et montrer de l'enthousiasme et de l'intérêt. Présentez vous en tenue professionnelle. **Attention, vous devez faire preuve de réactivité et ne pas vous laisser déstabiliser par l'offre d'emploi car votre examinateur ne connaît pas non plus l'entreprise qui recrute. Vous avez le droit d'imaginer vos questions/réponses de toute pièce, à condition de ne pas être en contradiction avec ce que dit le document.**

Gordon Food Service
Are looking for a Sales representative

Location: Houston, Texas

Job: permanent

Salary $40 *OTE + bonus

Benefits: health and dental care, low-cost benefit options for your family, health, and future.

Perks: company car, laptop and cell phone.

We are looking for a **Food Sales Representative** with Gordon Food Service.
You will have the opportunity to **cultivate relationships, develop new business, and provide innovative solutions** to our customers, helping them to achieve their goals and, in return, yours. An internal support system.

The ideal candidate should have:

A qualification in sales and management.

You should have at least 1 year of prior **sales, business, or food service experience**.

You must maintain a valid state driver's license and a safe driving record.

*OTE: On Target Earnings: basic salary + commissions

Word box

- update a customer data base: *mettre à jour des données client;*
- door-to-door prospection: *prospection en porte à porte;*
- answer customers' complaints: *répondre aux réclamations des clients;*
- take appointments/arrange meetings: *prendre des rendez-vous;*
- use professional softwares: *utiliser des logiciels professionnels;*
- be hardworking: *travailler beaucoup;*
- have good interpersonal skills: *avoir un bon relationnel;*
- team spirit: *esprit d'équipe;*
- establish and maintain customer loyalty: *fidéliser la clientèle et maintenir la fidélisation;*
- enrich the portofolio: *enrichir le portefeuille (clients);*
- carry out missions/tasks: *entreprendre des missions/effectuer des tâches;*
- writing skills: *aisance rédactionnelle.*

Pendant la préparation, vous veillerez à noter et à récapituler l'essentiel des informations présentes dans le document afin de les reformuler lors de l'entretien avec votre examinateur/recruteur.

I Formule de prise de contact :

Job interviewer: Good morning/afternoon, I'm NAME the Human Resource Mmanager for Gordon Food Service. First, could you introduce yourself, and tell me about your qualifications and work experience?

Brève présentation du candidat et de son parcours.

You: Good morning/afternoon. Pleased to meet you. Thank you for having me.
I am NAME. I am here for the position of sales representative advertised on your website.
I was able to secure a job interview after my phone call with your assistant, Mr/s NAME.
I have just graduated from my school where I prepared a two-year post-baccalaureate degree specialised in marketing. During my studies, I had to carry out two internships: the first one was at Whole Foods, NYC, and the second one was at Cyril Lignac Cuisine Attitude.

II Détail sur la situation actuelle du candidat

Vous pouvez au cours de l'entretien également vous inventer un parcours professionnel fictif afin de vous valoriser en montrant un profil dynamique de quelqu'un qui souhaite enrichir son expérience professionnelle.

You: I'm currently working for another food company as a sales rep, but I would like to join your company because it is much larger and I would appreciate a new challenge.

→ *En ce moment, je travaille en tant que commercial(e) au sein d'une autre entreprise spécialisée dans l'alimentaire, mais je souhaiterais rejoindre votre équipe car elle est beaucoup plus importante et que je suis à la recherche de nouveaux défis.*

III Questions à l'employeur

Comme pour les autres jeux de rôle, vous pouvez anticiper ou inventer ce qui n'est pas précisé dans le document de départ, du moment que vous ne faites pas de contresens. D'autre part, l'entretien d'embauche vous demande de savoir formuler les questions, puisque vous serez amené à en poser au recruteur du type :

You: What salary can I expect? What are the working hours? Do you offer any benefits *(avantages sociaux)* and perks? *(avantages en nature)* When will you give me your answer? etc.

IV Détails des expériences professionnelles

Ensuite vous décrirez vos missions qui doivent révéler vos compétences commerciales, en vous aidant du vocabulaire ci-contre. En fin d'entretien, n'oubliez pas de demander quand vous aurez une réponse, de remercier et de prendre congé.

V Fin d'entretien

→ Application

Sales Representative
Furniture – job post
8340 Delta Shores Circle South, Sacramento, CA 95832
$50,000 a year – Full-time

Job details
Salary : $50,000 a year
Job Type : Full-time
Location : Sacramento (California)

Benefits
Disability insurance
Health insurance
Dental insurance
Paid time off
Employee discount

Full Job Description
Start your career as a sales associate at RC Willey !
RC Willey Home Furnishings has been in business for nearly 90 years. With a foundation built on trust, our employees get more than just a paycheck.

We are searching for enthusiastic, career-minded sales associates to assist our customers in the Furniture department. Our sales professionals earn lucrative incentives with a sales guarantee of $19.24 per hour for the first three months, but we expect that sales associates will be able to earn at least $50,000 annually.

What you will get :
- Paid Time Off Starting your first day.
- Paid Holidays.
- Incredible employee discounts !
- Annual Company Profit Sharing.

What you will be doing :
- Greet customers, determine customer needs and address any related concerns.
- Ensure customer needs and expectations are taken care of.
- Follow-up with customers through callbacks, client cards and/or thank-you notes.
- Perform other reasonable job functions as assigned by an immediate supervisor and/or other management.

What you will bring along :
- Self-motivated and enthusiastic, with a strong desire to accomplish specific goals.
- Strong customer-service orientation.
- Exceptional interpersonal skills.
- Previous sales experience is a plus.

What will help you succeed :
RC Willey provides extensive sales training and coaching in order to enhance your ability to assist customers, increase your earning potential, and teach you what you need to succeed.

Étudiez l'offre ci- contre et préparez votre entretien d'embauche en vous aidant des étapes suivantes

I Formule de prise de contact

....

....

II Brève présentation du candidat et de son parcours

....

....

III Détails sur la situation actuelle du candidat

....

....

IV Détails sur son expérience professionnelle :

– Entreprise/service/emplacement/durée : ....

....

....

– Liste des responsabilités, tâches, missions menées à bien en entreprise : ....

....

....

– Liste des compétences acquises : ....

....

....

V Motivation de la candidature

....

....

VI Questions à l'employeur à propos de :

– l'entreprise : ....

– les conditions et modalités de travail : ....

– le salaire, les avantages sociaux, les avantages en nature, les primes : ....

VII Conclusion de l'entretien

– s'informer sur le délai de réponse à la candidature : ....

– prendre congé avec les formules d'usage : ....

TRAINING

EXAMS

EXERCISES

INTERNSHIP

6 Préparer un entretien de vente

→ Modèle

I La situation

You work in a Home Appliances store and have a meeting with a potential customer who is hesitating to buy a top quality espresso coffee machine.
Prepare your arguments to convince him/her and satisfy his/her needs :
- List the assets of the product ;
- Anticipate the customer's needs ;
- Focus on the quality of the product, the price and means of payment.

BARISTA EXPRESSO MACHINE
RRP: £599
Price: £449
You save: £150

Key Features
- Compatible with coffee beans or ground coffee
- Milk frother gives your drinks a perfect creamy finish
- Cup warmer gently heats your cups for the perfect drink
- Perfect water temperature preserves flavour of the bean
- Water tank is removable for easy refilling
- Dimensions :(H)40.0x(W)33.0x(D)31.0
  - Bar Pressure : 15 bar
  - Water Tank Capacity : 2 Litres
  - Power : 1700 Watt
  - Integrated Grinder
  - Variable Grinding
  - Manufacturer Warranty : 2 Years

II Préparer les arguments

Rassembler et organiser tous les arguments indispensables pour réussir un entretien de vente.

- **Situation** : la situation est présentée avec le≈document support en anglais, les consignes sont également en anglais
- **Rôle du candidat** : Ici il s'agit de préparer un argumentaire pour convaincre un client potentiel d'acheter une machine à express.
- **Rôle de l'examinateur** : l'examinateur <u>**ne joue pas le rôle du client**</u> mais il doit échanger avec le candidat pour **évaluer la pertinence de ses arguments.** Il pourra également guider le candidat en lui posant des questions.

Remarque importante : le candidat est libre d'inventer toutes les informations concernant le produit à partir du moment où ces informations ne sont pas connues c'est-à-dire qu'elles ne figurent pas dans le document.
(Par exemple les modalités et délais de livraisons, la couleur du produit etc.).

III Les étapes

→ Étape 1

Il est indispensable de bien étudier en détail les caractéristiques du produit en répondant pendant la préparation aux questions suivantes :

- De quel produit s'agit il ? *It is an upper range espresso machine manufactured by a famous brand.*
- Quelles sont ses caractéristiques principales ? *This machine presents all sorts of state of the art features such as an integrated grinder, different temperatures, plus a two year full guarantee.*
- Quel est son prix ? *The Recommended retail price is £599 but you are offering your client a £150 discount. The client can pay in 12 instalments with zero interest.*

Attention : il ne faut pas se perdre dans les détails du produit mais en retenir les qualités essentielles compréhensibles pas tous les clients qui ne sont pas nécessairement des spécialistes.

→ Étape 2

Le candidat a réfléchi en amont à différents profils de clients. Il se sert de sa préparation pour présenter les avantages comparatifs du produit.

Suivant le type de client, les besoins vont varier, donc il faut préparer des arguments compatibles avec les différentes catégories de client. (voir la méthode SONCAS par exemple).

La liste qui suit n'est pas exhaustive.

- *This machine is perfect for a family who loves coffee and who entertains a lot.*
- *The machine's design is so elegant that it can be used outside the kitchen, in the living room for example.*
- *The Barista express is easy to maintain and to clean. It needs to de descaled (détartré) only once a year and the descaling process is very easy.*
- *The Barista express is the ideal device for coffee amateurs : the integrated grinder allows you to choose the ideal grinding for each type of coffee beans.*
- *It is a state of the art device integrating both a sophisticated technology and design.*

→ Étape 3

Traitement des objections

Le candidat doit avoir anticipé les objections du client.

La liste des objections n'est pas exhaustive :

- *This product has an excellent value for money : the high quality of the product, its reliability, its smart design explains the recommended retail price.*
- *This is a short term discount offer and it represents a good opportunity to purchase this state of the art product.*
- *The client has the possibility to pay in 12 £37.41 monthly instalments.*
- *The shipping is included in the price and the delivery times are short.*
- *If the client fills in his/her order today, the product will be delivered at his/her doorstep within a week.*
- *Our after sales service operates 7 days a week from 7 am to 10 pm.*
- *We have an extremely good feedback from our customers.*
- *We have excellent reviews on the social media.*

IV Conclusion

À la fin de l'échange avec l'examinateur le candidat peut conclure avec une phrase du type : *I think the client should seize this opportunity to purchase the Barista espresso machine before the discount offer comes to an end.*

TRAINING EXAMS EXERCISES INTERNSHIP

Tools for the exam

→ Application

Situation :

You represent the Stress away company and have an appointment with the sales manager of a furniture store.
Get prepared for this meeting :
- Present the product and the situation ;
- List the assets ;
- Anticipate the customer's needs ;
- Focus on the comfort and the practicality of the product ;
- Anticipate different means of payment.

Stress Away Luxury Massage Reclining Chair and Foot Stool

Price: £239.99
Specifications :
Max user weight: 120kg
Chair dimensions: H98 × W76 × L76cm
Seat measures: L53 × W55cm
Backrest measures: L72 × W60cm
Foot stool dimensions: H41 × W49 × L44cm
Material: leather
Weight: 19kg
*padded: *rembouré*

- Targeted massage; Pick the massage level you need to really relax your back, thighs and lumbar; 5 different massage modes give you a personalised choice
- 360-degree rotation; With the ability to fully rotate, you can find the exact spot that's right for you
- Foot stool; With a padded* foot stool included, putting your feet up has never been so comfortable
- Guarantee; 12-month

I Introduction

Description de la situation :

....

....

....

Rôle du candidat :

....

....

....

II Les étapes

→ Étape 1

De quel produit s'agit-il ?

....

....

Quelles sont les caractéristiques du produit ?

....

....

Quel est son prix ?

....

....

→ Étape 2

Avantages comparatifs

– .... – ....

– .... – ....

– .... – ....

→ Étape 3

Traitement des objections

– .... – ....

– .... – ....

– .... – ....

III Conclusion

....

....

....

....

TRAINING EXAMS EXERCISES INTERNSHIP

Mock test

Retrouvez le sujet d'examen qui vous concerne. Flashez le QR Code !

NDRC
liennathan.fr/n85ip2

MCO
liennathan.fr/y2ih46

CI
liennathan.fr/dq8p78

GTLA
liennathan.fr/3x2ej2

COMM
liennathan.fr/h456wg

MHR
liennathan.fr/7r2tu9

Mock test

AG PME-PMI
liennathan.fr/d79g7b

SAM
liennathan.fr/y27cy2

AG PME-PMI
liennathan.fr/8mg97p

CGO
liennathan.fr/724rns

TOURISME
liennathan.fr/4zt6i4

BANQUE
liennathan.fr/xa272x

EXERCISES

1 Grammar

2 Vocabulary

Grammar

1 • Adjectifs et noms composés

- **Les noms composés sont très fréquents en anglais.**
  Ils se construisent de plusieurs façons : **nom + nom** *(air fresheners)*, **adjectif + nom** *(bottled water)*, **verbe + nom** *(cooking oil), mais aussi* **nom + particule adverbiale** *(a take-off)*, **participe passé + particule adverbiale ou verbe + particule adverbiale**.

a) Ils prennent parfois un tiret entre les deux termes (*name-brand*). La marque du pluriel se porte sur le dernier élément, quelle que soit sa nature grammaticale.

b) Le dernier élément est celui qui porte le sens principal, le premier ayant valeur d'adjectif. Il est d'ailleurs invariable (*a ten-dollar-bill*) → pas de *s* de pluriel → *a dollar*, car il a valeur d'adjectif.

c) Les adjectifs composés se forment sur les schémas suivants : **nom / adv + V-*ing*** *(an air conditioning device)*, **nom / adv + V-*ed*.** *(politically-involved activitist; electrically-powered spacecraft)*.

d) Les adjectifs composés d'un **nom + V-*ed*** *(battery-powered aircraft; sun-powered house; water-powered factory)*.

2 • Adverbes

a) **Les adverbes sont des mots invariables** qui sont utilisés pour modifier le sens d'un verbe, d'un adjectif, d'un autre verbe ; ils peuvent également servir à nuancer une phrase entière. Il existe une grande variété d'adverbes : **de manière, de temps, de lieu, de degré, etc.** Leur place peut varier suivant leur nature.

b) Certains adverbes sont formés à partir de l'adjectif auquel on rajoute la terminaison ***-ly*** : ***financial* → *financially; increasing* → *increasingly; angry* → *angrily*.**
→ *They can't make ends meet* ***financially***…
Attention aux adjectifs en ***-ly*** qui, eux, ne sont pas des adverbes : ***lovely***.

Rappel :
Les adverbes dits de fréquence (***often, sometimes, always, never***) sont toujours placés entre le sujet et le verbe ou entre l'auxiliaire et le verbe.
Les adverbes de temps (***yesterday, tomorrow***…) sont généralement placés en fin ou début de phrase.
Attention aux faux amis : ***actually*** → en réalité ; ***hardly*** → à peine ; ***eventually*** → pour finir, finalement ; ***currently*** → en ce moment.

1 Adjectifs et noms composés

1 Voici 5 adjectifs composés : associez l'adjectif au nom qui convient.

Hour-long • blue-eyed • red-haired • left-handed • power-driven.

a. A ……….. boy
b. An ……….. speech
c. A ……….. man
d. A ……….. baker
e. A ……….. president

2 Associez l'adjectif composé avec le nom qui convient, n'oubliez pas l'article indéfini a/an ou ø.

Large-scale • environmentally friendly • user-friendly • solar-generated • hybrid powered • oil-exporting • Covid-induced.

a. cars
b. countries
c. crisis
d. device
e. energy
f. factories
g. measures
h. strategy

❸ Complétez par un adjectif composé ci-dessous.

Foreign-born • dark-skinned • work visa-holding • non-white • steam-hauled.

a. .... Elves and hobbits are the topic of Amazon's new series.

b. .... populations in the UK are decreasing with Brexit.

c. .... Europeans go to the Uk to become seasonal workers.

d. .... Actors are chosen for Amazon's new adaptation.

e. Enjoy some of the UK's most scenic rail journeys including a .... trip.

❹ Traduisez les phrases suivantes en utilisant un nom composé.

a. Ces producteurs de boissons sont la preuve que nécessité est source d'invention.

b. Le jeu en ligne, Wordle, développe votre vocabulaire.

c. Pour bon nombre d'hommes de la classe ouvrière à New York, ce fut une révolution.

2 Adverbes

❶ Trouvez l'adjectif ou l'adverbe ou le nom qui correspond à la définition.

Ex: A person with no child is a childless person.

a. A tobacco that does not produce smoke is a .... tobacco.

b. An actress that does not look her age is an .... beauty.

c. An institution that has no power is a .... institution.

d. A person who has skills is a .... person.

e. A person who never tires of doing things is a .... person.

❷ Trouvez l'adverbe à partir de la racine.

Ex: She operated skillfully (skill).

a. The old man looked at me .... (wary).

b. Yours .... (faith).

c. They did it .... (reluctance).

d. Members are used .... to echo their leaders' choice (mere).

e. The crowd .... welcomed the new president (heart).

❸ Placez l'adverbe dans la phrase.

Ex: She usually goes to the swimming pool on Sundays and she has always walked there.

a. She used to visit every single exhibition. Today she goes there. (hardly)

....

....

b. They had purchased any goods online. (never)

....

....

c. Prime Minister, Boris Johnson, opposed the Northern Ireland protocol. (strongly)

....

....

d. Unaffordable housing has triggered the coming of many Californians to Austin. (clearly)

....

....

e. The CEO had visited the factories of her company. (often)

....

....

TRAINING EXAMS EXERCISES INTERNSHIP

Grammar

3 • Article défini : *the* ou ø ?

Quand on emploie un nom dans son sens général, on n'utilise pas d'article en anglais, au singulier comme au pluriel. Par contre, si on veut parler d'une notion en particulier, ou si l'on connaît précisément la personne ou l'objet dont il est question, on utilise ***the***.

→ *People work more today than a decade ago.*
≠ *All **the** people I saw in this company work a lot.*

Remarques :

– Certains noms sont presque toujours employés avec ***the*** car ils sont uniques : *the Sun; the Earth...*

– Les noms de pays ne prennent pas d'article, à quelques exceptions près :
→ ***The** USA; **the** UK.*

– Pour les titres, si l'on donne le nom de la personne, on supprime le ***the*** :
→ ***The** President of the United States / ø President Trump.*

4 • Article indéfini a/an

a) ***a/an*** → un/une au singulier
On utilise ***a*** devant une consonne :
a good job → un bon emploi
an devant une voyelle :
an interesting topic → un sujet intéressant

Au pluriel ***a/an*** disparaissent
Ex: ***a good job*** → ***good jobs***
an interesting topic → ***interesting topics***

Remarque :
On utilise l'article indéfini a /an devant les noms de profession, contrairement au français.
Ex: ***my sister is an engineer*** → **ma sœur est ingénieure**

b) ***adjectif épithète***
Les adjectifs épithètes en anglais sont toujours placés avant le nom qu'ils qualifient.
Ils sont invariables donc toujours au singulier.
*A **red** alert* → une alerte rouge/ *An **expensive** item* → un article onéreux/coûteux/cher

3 - 4 Les articles

1 Décidez s'il faut ou non un article défini.

a. .... President Biden.
b. .... Queen of the United Kingdom.
c. .... Queen Elizabeth II.
d. .... France.
e. .... Netherlands.
f. She was sent .... evidence of his guilt.
g. She received .... good news.
h. Do not forget to take .... luggage.
i. .... press freedom is a right.
j. .... Obama Administration.
k. .... 2022 Chinese Olympic games.

2 Article indéfini ? A ou AN ou aucun.

a. .... work is time-consuming.
b. .... good job is for some .... well-paid job.
c. .... politics is being able to compromise.
d. .... domestic politics is different from .... international politics.
e. Pat made .... politic reply.
f. Tim is good at .... art.
g. .... interesting topics are tackled by the news.

3 Complétez par un article défini ou indéfini ou rien.

a. .... world's biggest corporations have found .... agreement to take .... measures against .... rise of .... sea level.

b. Pankaj Mishra will talk to .... Guardian columnist Aditya Chakrabortty about .... India, ... globalisation and his new novel, Run and Hide.

c. .... expert in economic affairs writes that .... major conflict could seriously derail .... global economy.

d. .... world can count on .... highly motivated young generation to adress .... human rights issues.

4 Que faites-vous ? Avec ou sans article ?

a. .... Brexit.

b. .... people with attention deficit/hyperactivity disorder (ADHD).

c. .... hoarding disorder leads to .... major distress.

d. .... evidence does indicate that people experience .... greater problems.

e. There is .... link between distress and illness.

5 Décidez s'il faut un article ou non. Puis décidez si c'est un article défini ou indéfini.

a. Lino Marrenro was leaving ....cello practice one day when he noticed .... blisters on his fingers.

b. When .... freak winter storm in .... Texas caused .... massive power outages in early 2021, Marrero got to test his invention during .... time of need, and it worked.

c. « No one in my family is .... engineer or anything like that, » Marrero says. « So I went to .... library, I went online. »

d. We need to get .... chain going, where I inspire someone and they inspire someone.

e. He came up with .... idea for his latest invention.

6 Dites si la phrase est correcte et corrigez s'il y a une erreur.

a. She has solved global problems. True or False

b. Vice President Kamala Harris fights for a justice alongside journalist Helen Zia. True or False

c. Youth can make a difference. True or False

d. Her materrnal great-grandmother, political activist in Korea, is her personal hero. True or False

e. Asian American history is American history. True or False

f. You should treat everyone with a respect and kindness. True or False

g. He believes that a real change is in legislative action. True or False

h. She is adamant that social change also happens with small actions. True or False

i. He launched collective of middle-school activists. True or False

j. An education bill would require high school students to take an ethnic-studies course in California. True or False

7 Traduisez en français et notez si les articles sont traduits de la même façon.

a. Like most teens, she has a knack for social media.

b. I have talked on the future of education.

c. She wants to monitor cyberbullying.

d. What is next for the year ahead ?

e. It has been an absolute whirlwind of emotions.

5 • Auxiliaire modal can/could

a) ***Can/could*** sont suivis du verbe sans to.

- ***Can*** **exprime : la possibilité ou la capacité**
  Ex*: **I can come tomorrow*** → Je peux venir demain.
  I can drive → Je sais conduire.
- Forme négative contractée : ***can't*** / non contractée : ***cannot***

b) ***Could*** peut correspondre :
– soit à un prétérit : ***He couldn't attend the meeting*** → Il n'a pas pu assister à la réunion.
– soit à un conditionnel : ***If I didn't have so much work, I could spend more time with my friends***
→ *Si je n'avais pas autant de travail je pourrais passer plus de temps avec les amis.*

- ***Be able to*** remplace ***can*** à tous les autres temps ex: ***In the near future, people will be able to buy self- driving vehicles*** → Dans un futur proche, les gens pourront acheter des véhicules autonomes.

6 • Auxiliaire modal may/might

- **Construction**
  May obéit aux particularités de tous les auxiliaires modaux : ni suivi ni précédé de ***to***, pas de ***-s*** à la 3e personne du présent simple, prend la marque de la négation et se place à la 1re place dans une phrase interrogative.
- **Emploi**
  Comme de nombreux autres modaux, ***may*** peut être utilisé de deux façons différentes (comme ***must***) :

a) Avec ***may***, on marque l'autorisation, dans une langue soutenue. On peut également utiliser le modal ***can*** pour la permission.

b) Pour parler des chances de réalisation d'une action.
Avec ***may***, la probabilité est moyenne. Dans ce type d'utilisation, on peut marquer que l'action a des chances de se réaliser (***may*** + BV), qu'elle est peut-être en train de se réaliser (***may*** + V ***-ing***), ou bien qu'elle s'est probablement réalisée dans le passé (***may*** + ***have*** + ***ed***).
Si l'action n'a que peu de chances de se réaliser, on utilisera l'auxiliaire modal ***might***.
→ *It **may/might boost** the sales/**may/might be boosting** the sales/**may/might have boosted** the sales.*

Remarque :
May + BV peut se remplacer par : ***is likely*** + ***to*** + verbe.
→ ***It's likely to boost*** *the sales.*

5 Auxiliaire modal *can/could*

1 Complétez les phrases suivantes avec le modal qui convient *(may/might/can/could)* à la forme qui convient (affirmative/négative).

a. I'm sorry, I .... attend yesterday's meeting.

b. The delivery .... have been delayed because of the transport strike.

c. .... I ask you a question?

d. I'm sorry, I .... drive, I haven't got a driving license.

e. The CEO .... decide to raise the salaries, but it's quite unlikely.

2 Complétez les phrases en choisissant la forme qui convient en la conjuguant au temps approprié.

a. Unsatisfied employees (can/be able to) ask their trade unions for advice.

....

....

b. Because of the metro strike, many people (can/be able to) go to work tomorrow.

....

....

c. The customs (can/be able to) seize one thousand counterfeit watches.

....

....

d. I'm afraid I (can/be able to) travel to the USA.

....

....

e. If you have reached your targets, you (can/be able to) get a pay raise.

....

....

3 Traduisez les phrases de l'exercice 2 en français.

a. ....

....

b. ....

....

c. ....

....

d. ....

....

e. ....

....

6 Auxiliaire modal *may/might*

1 Mettez les phrases dans l'ordre.

a. Go/employees/may/the/on strike/protest/conditions/against/working/their/to

....

....

b. Wasn't/CEO/questions/journalist's/able/the/answer/able/the/to

....

....

c. Reduce/warming/we/be/to/global/before/century/the/won't/next/able

....

....

d. ?/you/here/may/for/minutes/a few/wait/ask/I/to

....

....

e. Predicted/ice cap/more/the/had/melted/might/more/than/what/the/experts/have

....

....

2 Trouvez des phrases synonymes des phrases suivantes en utilisant à chaque fois le modal ou la forme verbale indiquée. Les mots soulignés doivent vous aider.

a. Customers will perhaps change their behaviour after the pandemic. (may)

....

....

b. It isn't possible for children to own a credit card. (can't)

....

c. It was not possible for this deal to be fairer. (could'nt)

....

d. We will ask the cashier for the permission to pay with a check. (may)

....

....

e. He is sitting too far away, it will be impossible for him to hear the speaker. (won't be able to)

....

....

7 • Auxiliaire modal *must*

- **Construction**
  Must obéit aux particularités de tous les auxiliaires modaux : pas de ***to*** à l'infinitif, pas de ***s*** à la 3e personne du présent simple, prend la marque de la négation et se place à la 1re place dans une phrase interrogative.
- **Emploi**
  Comme de nombreux autres modaux, (***may***) ***must*** peut être utilisé de deux façons différentes :

a) Quand le locuteur veut faire pression sur celui dont il parle. Avec ***must***, on marque une obligation.
Attention :
– ***Mustn't*** marque l'interdiction. Pour dire : « Je ne suis pas obligé de... », on utilisera l'expression ***I don't have to...***
– ***Must*** n'existe pas au prétérit (on utilise alors ***had to***) ni au futur (on utilise alors ***will have to***).

b) Pour parler des chances de réalisation d'une action.
Avec ***must***, la probabilité est très forte.
→ *They **must** have changed something in their programme, it doesn't run any longer.*
Dans ce type d'utilisation, on peut marquer que l'action a de grandes chances de se réaliser (***must*** + **BV**), qu'elle est certainement en train de se réaliser (***must*** + **verbe *-ing***), ou bien qu'elle s'est certainement réalisée dans le passé (***must*** + ***have*** + **participe passé**).

8 • Auxiliaire modal *should*

a) ***Should*** + **verbe**
Le modal ***should*** s'utilise pour donner un conseil, pour exprimer une projection probable dans le futur qui n'engage que la personne qui le donne ou qui l'exprime.
→ *We **should** listen to our employees.*
Should est comme les autres modaux : il est suivi du verbe sans ***to***. Il se traduit en français par la forme conditionnelle du verbe **devoir** : devrais (-ait, -ions, -iez, -aient).

b) ***Ought to*** + **verbe**
Ought to permet d'exprimer un conseil davantage fondé sur un usage général, admis, qu'il convient de respecter.
C'est en cela qu'il se distingue dans l'usage de ***should***.
→ *Citizens **ought to** respect their countries' institutions :* c'est la bienséance, la morale qui le prescrit.

c) ***Had better*** + **verbe** / ***'d better*** + **verbe**
Une autre manière de donner un conseil :
→ *You **had better find** a solution quickly.*
→ Vous feriez mieux de trouver une solution rapidement.

d) ***Advise*** + **COD** + ***to*** + **verbe**
Pour conseiller à quelqu'un de faire quelque chose.
→ *Governments **advise people to get** ready for further sacrifices.*

Remarque :
Changement d'orthographe entre le nom *advice* et le verbe ***advise*** (conseiller).

7 Auxiliaire modal *must*

1 Traduisez en anglais en utilisant "must" ou un equivalent.

a. Je dois aller chez la dentiste.

....

b. La réunion n'a pas commencé. Il a dû se produire quelque chose.

....

c. Quand je travaillais à Tesco, je devais arriver 30 minutes avant l'ouverture du magasin.

....

d. Je ne dois pas porter de masque au cinema maintenant.

....

e. Il faudra que j'arrive à l'aéroport deux heures à l'avance.

....

2 Choisissez *must* ou *should* ou un équivalent.

a. They .... not smoke in that building.

b. British people .... have known that Brexit would make their life harder.

c. With a Republican Senate, President Biden .... know his bill won't pass.

d. Schools .... to be peaceful places.

8 Auxiliaire modal *should* et expression du conseil

1 Transformez les phrases suivantes d'abord en utilisant *should*, puis en utilisant *had better*.

a. Online buyers ought to beware of credit card phishing.

....

b. Packaging ought to respect environmental standards.

....

c. Companies are advised to pay their employees a living wage.

....

d. If they want to restore their brand image, they ought to change their advertising campaign.

....

e. If you want to make profits I advise you to invest in AI companies.

....

2 Imaginez quatre manières de conseiller à quelqu'un :

a. De travailler moins.

....

b. D'arriver à l'heure à vos rendez-vous.

....

c. De savoir répondre aux attentes des clients.

....

d. De connaître les produits disponibles en magasin.

....

e. De venir plus souvent au bureau.

....

f. De vérifier son emploi du temps plusieurs fois par jour.

....

3 Traduisez les phrases suivantes en utilisant le modal « should » ou un équivalent

a. Il devrait arrêter de fumer.

....

b. Elle ferait mieux d'être à l'heure.

....

c. La cheffe d'établissement conseille aux parents de discuter avec leurs enfants.

....

d. Il est conseillé de ne pas être en retard.

....

e. Elle aurait dû s'en apercevoir.

....

4 Créez des phrases avec « should » ou un équivalent

Ex: She has a toothache. She should go to the dentist.

a. His mother is quite sick.

....

b. Their marks at school are not good.

....

c. We have not seen our mother for ages.

....

d. He is going to fail his exam.

....

e. You have been invited to a formal dinner.

....

9 • Comparatifs

a) Les comparatifs dits de « supériorité » = plus ... que

- **Les adjectifs courts + *-er ... than***
→ *Europe is **smaller than** America.*
- **Les adjectifs en *y* + *-ier ... than***
→ *London is **rainier than** Paris.*
- **Les adjectifs longs : *more* + adjectifs longs + *than***
→ *Cars are **more** expensive in France **than** in Germany.*
- **Les adjectifs irréguliers (à connaître) :**
→ *good / well → better ... than;*
→ *bad → worse than...*
→ *than far → further / farther ... than.*
→ *Roads are **better** now **than** 50 years ago. Los Angeles is **farther / further than** Chicago.*
→ *Pollution is **worse** today **than** in the last century.*

Remarques :

Pour indiquer un accroissement progressif, on utilise :

→ *Prices are **higher and higher** / goods are **more and more** expensive.*
→ Les prix sont de plus en plus élevés / les produits sont de plus en plus chers.

Ces formes peuvent être remplacées par l'adverbe ***increasingly*** : *Prices are **increasingly** high / goods are **increasingly** expensive.*

Pour indiquer un accroissement parallèle :

→ *Some consumers think that the more expensive an item is, the better it is.*
→ Certains consommateurs pensent que plus un article est cher, meilleur il est.

Attention à l'ordre des mots qui diffère dans les deux langues.

b) Les comparatifs dits d'infériorité = moins ... que *less* + adjectif + *than* : quelle que soit la longueur de l'adjectif. C'est la même construction pour les adjectifs irréguliers :
→ *Silver is **less expensive than** gold.*

Remarque :
Le comparatif d'infériorité est moins utilisé en anglais qu'en français. On préfère en anglais dire ***smaller*** (plus petit) que ***less tall*** (moins grand).

c) Les comparatifs dits d'égalité = aussi ... que *as* + adjectif + *as* : la forme est identique pour tous les adjectifs, irréguliers compris. Par contre, ***as*** se substitue à ***than***: → *India will soon become **as** rich **as** China.*

Remarque :
→ *Prices are **the same** (as before).*
→ Les prix sont **les mêmes** (qu'auparavant).

10 • Complément du nom et cas possessif

a) Le cas possessif ou génitif

→ *The government's response.*
→ La réponse du gouvernement.

Cette forme de complément du nom, **appelée génitif ou cas possessif**, marque ce qu'il est convenu d'appeler la possession. Le « possesseur » peut-être un nom propre ou un nom commun. Attention à la place des mots dans cette structure. Au pluriel, le ***s*** disparaît, seule l'apostrophe demeure.
→ *Governements' difficult choices.*
→ Les choix difficiles des gouvernements.

b) Nom + *of* + nom

On évite le cas possessif lorsque le nom du possesseur est trop long ou quand on veut créer un effet (insistance, suspens...) :
→ *And the name of the winner is...*
→ Et le nom du gagnant est...

Remarque :
Le ***'s*** du génitif disparaît parfois avec l'usage en formant des noms composés. Le premier nom jouant alors un rôle de déterminant par rapport au second :
→ *air quality* → la qualité de l'air
→ *unemployment rate* → taux de chômage
→ *staff turnover* → rotation du personnel
→ *football match* → match de football.

9 Comparatifs

❶ Utilisez le comparatif.

a. The Covid-19 pandemic has had/an Impact on the world's economy/the 2008 great recession.

....

....

b. Wind farms produce/energy/when the wind blows (much).

....

....

c. Trading with the UK/slow/is/when the UK/was/a EU member state.

....

....

d. High/demand for natural gas/will impact energy prices.

....

....

e. Nuclear power plants/will be built/rapidly/now that energy prices have gone up.

....

....

❷ Complétez chaque phrase par un comparatif dans certains cas il exprime l'accroissement progressif.

Ex: He told everyone that he had done better this time at the test so his score was higher than anybody else.

a. Electric vehicles are (polluting) but (autonomous) than regular cars.

....

....

b. Employees have been on strike to earn (good) salaries.

....

....

c. Sweatshops in Dacca are known for being (exploitative) than factories in the western world.

....

....

d. California is experiencing (much and much) wildfires and (high and high) housing prices so Californians are leaving.

....

....

e. Austin in Texas has attracted (many) people as renting is (low) than in California.

....

....

10 Complément du nom et cas possessif

❶ Traduisez.

a. La Saint Valentin : ....

b. Le journal d'hier : ....

c. Dans deux jours : ....

d. Une licence en droit : ....

e. Le pullover rouge de la petite sœur : ....

f. Le roman de Jane Austen : ....

g. La Saint Patrick : ....

h. La décision de toutes les écoles : ....

❷ Nom composé ? cas possessif ? À vous de jouer. Dites si c'est vrai ou faux.

Ex: it is a good football team but football club owners do not always acknowledge it.

a. A company's reputation relies on its talented CEO. R or W

b. A three-month work placement enables a student to learn a lot. R or W

c. The garment industry is mostly located in Asia. R or W

d. Bill Clinton's administration was very effective. R or W

e. London's Olympic games were a real success in 2012. R or W

11 • Conditionnel *if* clauses

- **Le conditionnel présent et passé**

a) ***If*** **+présent simple + principale au futur :**
→ *If they* ***drive*** *slowly, they* ***will consume*** *less gasoline.*
→ S'ils conduisent lentement, ils consommeront moins d'essence.
Les conducteurs ont le choix, et on ne sait pas pour quelle solution ils opteront.

b) ***If*** **+ prétérit + principale au conditionnel présent :**
→ *If she* ***had*** *an electric car, she* ***would drive*** *to Geneva.*
→ Si elle avait une voiture électrique, elle irait jusqu'à Genève.
Elle n'a pas de voiture électrique pour l'instant, mais peut-être que quelqu'un lui en prêtera une. On appelle ce conditionnel **irréel du présent**.

c) ***If*** **+ *past perfect* + principale au conditionnel passé :**
→ *If she* ***had had*** *an electric car, she* ***would have driven to*** *Geneva.*
→ Si elle avait eu une voiture électrique, elle serait allée jusqu'à Genève.
→ Elle n'a pas pu se rendre à Genève faute de voiture électrique.
Cette phrase exprime un regret, que l'on appelle aussi **irréel du passé**.

Remarque :
On notera que proposition introduite par ***if*** est suivie de ***had*** + participe passé (*pluperfect/past perfect*) et que le conditionnel passé se forme avec un modal *(**would/should/could** …)* + ***have*** + participe passé.

12 • Discours rapporté

- **Emploi :** le discours rapporté s'emploie pour rapporter les propos d'un tiers.
- **Construction :**

a) Lors du passage du **discours direct au discours rapporté,** il faut faire attention **aux pronoms susceptibles de changer et à la concordance des temps.**
→ **Discours direct :** *The manager said: "We don't see it as necessary to change our policy."*
→ **Discours rapporté :** *The manager said they* ***didn't*** *see it as necessary to change* ***their*** *policy.*

b) **Pour les phrases interrogatives**, l'ordre des mots n'est pas celui de la question directe : le point d'interrogation disparaît.
→ *"When will they recover from the disaster?" experts asked.*
→ *Experts asked when they* ***would*** *recover from the disaster.*

11 Condionnel *if* clauses

1 Traduisez en français.

a. If she had time, she would visit California.

....

b. Had they had the know-how, they would have produced this new device.

....

c. If it rains, I will take my umbrella.

....

d. She would have been unable to go to Geneva, had she not borrowed the car of her best friend.

....

e. She would be unable to go to Geneva, if she did not borrow her best friend's car.

....

❷ Utilisez le temps adéquat : conditionnel présent ou passé.

a. If demand was lower, energy prices .... (not increase).

b. Consumers would have consumed more during covid-19 if they .... (not be) in lockdown.

c. If Nord-Stream 2 operated, Germany .... (meet) its demand.

d. Re-locating manufacturing will be implemented if it means that it .... (be) less costly.

e. Remote working will be considered a good solution especially if employees .... (have) a long commute.

❸ Complétez les phrases avec un conditionnel présent ou passé.

Ex: If she had a degree in finance, she ***would work*** *for KPMG. If she had had a grandmother in the countryside, she* ***would have become*** *a sherperdess.*

a. If Lucie was broke, she (take) any job available.

b. If Tony had not broken his leg, he (be) part of the football tournament.

c. They (visit) Japan if the pandemic had not broken out.

d. Nord Stream 2 (deliver) natural gas if the regulators signed the contract.

12 Discours rapporté

❶ Traduisez ces phrases au discours rapporté.

a. Elle a demandé à quelle heure son entretien d'embauche était fixé.

....

b. Ils ont assuré que tout irait bien.

....

c. Elles ont répondu qu'elles seraient prêtes en temps.

....

d. Elle lui a demandé comment elle se rendait à son rendez-vous.

....

e. Les médias ont rapporté que les industries ne respectaient pas la législation.

....

❷ Transformez ces phrases à l'impératif au discours rapporté.

Ex: Do not come tomorrow. She asks her not to come tomorrow.

a. Don't be late. She told her ....

b. Be on time. She asked her ....

c. Bring your resume at your job interview. They ask him...............

d. Let's go now. She suggested...............

e. Do it now. She ordered him ....

❸ Transformez ces phrases au discours direct au discours indirect.

Ex: I am not going because I have too much work.

She said that ***she was*** *not going because* ***she had*** *too much work.*

a. She does not want to have a salary below £50,000.

Yesterday she said that ....

b. You are now the boss of the company.

She said that ....

c. You are worried for your job.

He said that ....

d. I've already maxed out my hours.

Two days ago Laura said that ....

❹ Utilisez le discours rapporté pour des phrases interrogatives.

Ex: "What are you doing?"

She asked him what he was doing.

a. Why did you decide to change job?

She asked her ....

b. Where are you going for the interview?

His colleague asked him ....

c. How long is your commute?

Her boss asked her......................................

TRAINING

EXAMS

EXERCISES

INTERNSHIP

13 • Ever et ses composés

Les pronoms composés en ***-ever*** se construisent à partir des mots en ***wh-*** et siginifient « peu importe, qui que / quoi que… » Un équivalent en anglais moins formel serait : ***no matter what / who / where***…

whoever : peu importe qui, qui que ce soit
whatever / whichever : quoi que ce soit
whenever : n'importe quand
wherever : n'importe où, quel que soit l'endroit
however : quelle que soit la façon dont…

→ *You can do **whatever** you want with a machine like this!*

Remarque :
Ne pas confondre ***however*** + adjectif ou ***however*** + proposition avec l'adverbe ***however*** qui signifie « cependant ».

14 • Expression de la fréquence

a) Pour connaître la fréquence à laquelle un tiers pratique une activité, l'anglais utilise ***how often*** :
→ ***How often** do you visit your family?*
→ ***How often** do you watch tv/entertain your friends/go to the doctor's?*

b) Les réponses à ce type de questions vont exprimer la fréquence à laquelle l'activité est pratiquée.
→ *Once / twice / three times a year / a week / a month…*
→ une fois / deux fois / trois fois par an / par semaine / par mois…

c) Pour donner plus de détails sur la durée de cette activité, on utilisera des expressions telles que :
→ *one hour a week / two hours a month…*
→ une heure par semaine / deux heures par mois…

d) Pour exprimer une action qui se répète à intervalle régulier, on utilise ***every*** :
→ *They visit their family **every** two weeks.*
→ Ils rendent visite à leur famille toutes les deux semaines.
→ ***Every** second, a new child is born.*
→ Un enfant naît toutes les secondes / chaque seconde.

Rappel :
Pour dire tous les jours / mois / ans, etc., on emploie ***every*** : *everyday / every Christmas / every evening.*
Pour dire à chaque fois, on utilise ***every time*** :
→ ***Every time** someone is one minute late, he's fined.*
→ Chaque fois que quelqu'un est en retard d'une minute, il est mis à l'amende.
Pour dire n'importe quand, on emploie ***whenever***.

13 *Ever* et ses composés

1 Complétez les phrases suivantes avec le composé de *ever* qui convient *(who/which/what/when/where)*.

a. CCTVs are supposed to see customers .... they are in the store.

b. With online shopping, you can place your order .... you want and .... you are.

c. .... the company recruits, she or he will have to possess the required skills.

d. We can meet at 10 AM or at 2 PM, ... time best suits you.

e. .... you go, your smartphone will track you.

f. .... hard you hit, this material won't break.

2 Traduisez les phrases suivantes en anglais. Chaque phrase doit contenir un composé de *ever*.

a. Appelez-moi quand vous voulez.

....

....

b. Quel que soit l'endroit où vous êtes, votre ordinateur doit être connecté.

....

....

c. Quel que soit ce que vous en pensez, vous devez faire le travail.

....

....

d. Peu importe qui est présent, il doit répondre au téléphone.

....

....

e. Ne croyez pas que vous pouvez faire ce que vous voulez !

....

....

14 Expression de la fréquence

1 Imaginez les questions à partir des réponses suivantes.

a. The head of department must write a report every two weeks.

....

....

b. The company organises a trip for its staff once a year.

....

....

c. Many employees telework several times a month.

....

....

d. Trains are delayed every week.

....

....

e. Staff members clock in and out four times a day.

....

....

f. She starts at 9 twice a week.

....

....

g. Co-workers organise a get-together once a month.

....

....

2 Remettez les mots dans l'ordre pour en faire des phrases correctes.

a. Get/pay raise/years/two/generally/employees/a/every

....

....

b. People /most/pay/taxes/a/once/year/must/their

....

....

c. Depends/often/how/on/travel/price/you/the

....

....

d. TV shows/by/interrupted/commercials/twenty/the/USA/minutes/are/every/in

....

....

e. Hurricanes/more/twice/year/happen/nowadays/than/a

....

....

f. 965 tons/from Mexico/are sent/of avocados/to the US/every year

....

....

g. Sea levels/on average/along the US coast/will rise/by 2050/by about a foot

....

TRAINING EXAMS EXERCISES INTERNSHIP

Grammar

15 • Forme passive

a) **La voix passive** permet de **mettre en valeur les actions subies par le sujet** alors que la forme active sert à mettre en valeur ce qui est à l'origine de l'action.
→ *The new look was inspired by global research. (forme passive) Global research inspired the new look. (forme active)*

b) La forme passive est reconnaissable en anglais par la présence de ***be*** suivi du participe passé du verbe.
Attention : il n'existe aucune exception à cette règle.

c) Le complément d'agent, quand il est exprimé, est introduit par la préposition ***by***. Le passif est rarement suivi d'un complément d'agent car, lorsqu'il s'agit de préciser qui fait l'action, on a recours à la voix active.

d) **La forme passive s'utilise à tous les temps :** présent, passé, futur, etc. C'est ***be***, et lui seul, qui marque le temps.
→ *Coffee is exported / will be exported / was exported / has been exported / had been exported / would be exported, etc.*
→ Le café est exporté / sera exporté / a été exporté, etc.

Rappel :
Le passif n'est pas un temps, c'est une forme, une manière d'exprimer une action (comme en français).

e) L'anglais ne possédant pas de pronom indéfini « on » à proprement parler, les tournures impersonnelles en anglais sont exprimées par le passif.
→ *I was given a day off to take my driving licence.*
→ On m'a donné un jour de congé pour que je passe mon permis de conduire.

16 • Futur en *will*

a) **Le futur se construit en général avec l'auxiliaire *will* :** sujet + ***will*** + base verbale.
→ *The market **will** double by 2025.*
Il peut aussi se construire avec ***be going to*** (le locuteur est sûr que quelque chose va arriver).

b) **Plusieurs expressions sont utilisées dans un contexte futur :** *in the next year, in the years to come, in the long run… when, as soon as, as long as, until/till, unless…* (conjonctions de temps pour introduire une subordonnée temporelle)
Attention : à la concordance des temps dans les propositions subordonnées temporelles : ***when*** + présent simple (proposition subordonnée) → ***will*** (proposition principale).

15 Forme passive

1 Traduisez en Français la voix passive.

Ex: English is spoken here. On parle anglais.

a. The article is entitled « The Pandemic ».

....

b. We are told that 20 people died in a road accident.

....

c. Three robbers were arrested at the station yesterday at 3 o'clock in the morning.

....

d. The birth of the royal baby was covered by every media outlet.

....

e. I was sent a letter of apologies.

....

2 Traduisez en anglais en utilisant la voix passive.

a. On m'a donné deux livres.

....

b. Deux ordinateurs ont été volés.

....

c. On dit que les Français vont souffrir de l'inflation.

....

d. On cherche un garçon de café.

....

e. On estime que le pouvoir d'achat va être atteint.

....

3 Utilisez la voix passive.

Ex: the article was published on December 26, 2021.

a. Containers .... (to offload) with container cranes as soon as container ships reach their final destination.

b. Container ships .... (to meet) by tugs.

c. Proper preparations .... (should/make) so that the cargo loading procedure .... (can/carry out) in a quick and safe manner.

d. In case any defective lashing equipment .... (to find), it .... immediately .... (should/replace).

e. Containers .... (to lift off) the ship two at a time by quay cranes.

4 Passez de la voix active à la voix passive.

Ex: They always publish articles about new films on Thursdays.
Articles about new films are always published on Thurdays

a. You should send your CV by email.

....

b. Ben obtained a promotion.

....

c. They told me there was a training in the first month.

....

d. One of your employees requests days off all the time.

....

e. You will turn down the offer.

....

16 Futur en *will*

1 Complétez les phrases par *is going to* ou *will*.

a. When I am 18, I (take) my driving license.

....

b. It (cost) much. ....

c. As long as you are safe, they (not ask) questions.

....

d. They (host) the next olympic games. ....

e. You (be) on time unless there is a strike. ....

2 Utilisez le futur avec *will* ou avec *be going to*.

Ex: When I am 18, I will take my driving license.

a. As soon as he is hired, he (move) to a new apartment.

b. If demand keeps going up, prices (rise).

c. Emma (double check) the report.

d. In Britain the purchasing power (decline) as prices increase.

e. As long as there are people of good will, wars and conflicts (be avoided).

3 Complétez les phrases suivantes avec une forme verbale qui exprime le futur soit avec *will* soit avec *going to*.

Ex: If it trains, I will take my umbrella.

a. Unless we come to an agreement, there (be) a solution.

b. They (write) a cv and a cover letter as they are applying to business schools.

c. The American working class (suffer) from not having access to affordable housing.

d. The Great Resign movement in the US (impact) the labour market.

e. The pandemic in the US (reveal) that child care centers are very expensive.

Grammar

17 • Gérondif

On utilise la forme en *-ing* (gérondif) :

a) **Pour remplacer une subordonnée relative ou traduire un participe présent (français).**
→ *The biggest factor* ***deterring*** *customers from refill is cost.*
→ Le facteur le plus important qui dissuade/ dissuadant les clients de réutiliser les emballages est le coût.

b) **Après les verbes indiquant un début, une fin, une continuité :** *start, begin, stop, continue, keep on, go on, etc.*
→ *This supermarket chain has* ***begun selling*** *new products.*

c) **Après les verbes dits d'appréciation :** *like, love, enjoy, prefer, hate, dislike, can't bear, can't stand, etc.*
→ *Before, customers* ***didn't like buying*** *that product. They* ***preferred buying*** *another brand.*

d) **Après les prépositions :** *in, by, with, without, after, before, etc.*
→ *We have a challenge finding a solution. They have made profit* ***by changing*** *targets.*

e) **Pour transformer un verbe en nom :**
→ ***Paying*** *a premium has become necessary.*

Remarque :
– Certains noms se terminent par ***-ing*** : *packaging, advertising, marketing, etc.*
– Un grand nombre d'adjectifs également : *tiring, surprising, shocking, interesting*, etc. On notera qu'ils se traduisent en français par la terminaison **-ant** *:* fatigant, surprenant, choquant, intéressant, etc.

18 • Indénombrables

a) **Les noms indénombrables** sont généralement les mots que l'on ne peut pas compter : liquides (***water***, ***milk***...), aliments, matières (***iron***, ***air***...), certains noms abstraits (***love***, ***happiness***...) ou concrets (***equipment***, ***fruit***...). Ils ne prennent jamais de ***s***, ni d'article ***a / an***, et le verbe est toujours au singulier.
→ **Retenez bien :** voici quelques noms indénombrables usuels à bien connaître : ***abuse, advice, business, equipment, furniture, garbage, hair, information, luggage, news, progress, weather...***

b) **L'article utilisé est :** ***some*** (phrases positives), ***any*** (phrases négatives / interrogatives) or ***no***.
→ *They don't do* ***any*** *publicity. He wants* ***no*** *advertising for his product. Can I give you* ***some*** *news about the teaser campaign?*

c) **Vous pouvez rendre dénombrable un nom indénombrable en lui donnant une quantité :**
→ *The market information is interesting.*
→ *He's got a* ***new piece of information***.
Ou en utilisant un nom composé :
→ *The* ***product placement software*** *is efficient.*
→ *Can we buy a* ***new software program***?
Dénombreurs usuels : *a piece of (advice), a glass of (water), a pair of (jeans, scissors)...*

17 Gérondif

1 Utilisez le gérondif.

Ex: I am fond of swimming.

a. (read) is much more pleasant than (watch) TV.

....

....

b. She is committed to (hire) a diverse labour force.

....

....

c. Before (take) the train, I must double check that there is no strike.

....

....

d. Instead of (go) on holiday abroad, I have made the decision of (go) hiking.

....

....

e. By (change) its one-child policy to a three-child policy, China wanted the Chinese to have bigger families.

....

....

2 Les phrases suivantes sont-elles correctes ? Cochez la case qui convient.

a. I am committed to binge watching series.

❑ Right ❑ Wrong

b. Advertising is part of marketing.

❑ Right ❑ Wrong

c. Corporate America decided to sharing dividends to shareholders.

❑ Right ❑ Wrong

d. You should continue working hard if you want to succeed.

❑ Right ❑ Wrong

e. Buying online is easier but will impact retailers.

❑ Right ❑ Wrong

18 Indénombrables

1 Complétez les phrases suivantes avec *some/any/no/a/an.*

a. If there is .... wind, wind farms cannot be efficient.

b. We haven't got .... news about the situation.

c. If you need .... advice, do not hesitate to ask your teacher.

d. This document contains .... very important piece of information.

e. They had to call the police because .... luggage was abandoned in the airport.

f. If you want to buy .... new furniture, you have the choice between many stores.

g. Society isn't making .... progress to curb global warming.

h. The airline company doesn't have .... information on the next flight.

2 Complétez les phrases suivantes avec *much* ou *many*.

a. The clerk couldn't give us .... information on the product.

b. We shouldn't buy too .... furniture because our office is small.

c. How .... people went to the mall today?

d. They haven't got .... money to spend on extras.

e. Too .... news can generate stress.

3 Traduisez les phrases suivantes en anglais.

a. Mon collègue m'a donné beaucoup d'informations importantes.

....

....

b. Il y a trop de meubles dans cette pièce.

....

....

c. Mon patron m'a donné de bons conseils.

....

....

d. Quelles sont les nouvelles ?

....

....

e. Il faut rester à côté de ses bagages dans les gares et les aéroports.

....

....

19 • *Pluperfect*

- **Construction : sujet + *had* + participe passé**
- **Emploi :**

a) Le *pluperfect* s'emploie dans un contexte passé. Il sert à marquer une antériorité par rapport à une action exprimée au prétérit.

b) Le *pluperfect* + *-ing* est l'équivalent du *present perfect* + *-ing*, mais dans un contexte passé. Il sert à mettre l'accent sur l'activité décrite.

c) Au style indirect, le prétérit comme le *present perfect*, sont transformés en *pluperfect* au style indirect passé.

20 • Préfixes et suffixes

On peut ajouter un suffixe à un nom, un verbe ou un adjectif, de façon à créer un mot dérivé. Les principaux suffixes sur les objectifs sont les suivants :
-ful (plein de, caractérisé par) : ***powerful*** → puissant.
Ce suffixe s'écrit avec un seul « *l* » à la fin !
-less (sans, dénué de) : ***childless*** → sans enfant.
-y ou ***-ly*** (pour marquer une qualité) : ***wealthy*** → riche, ***friendly*** → amical.
-ish (pour marquer quelque chose de négatif) : ***selfish*** → égoïste.
– La plupart des préfixes que l'on trouve devant les verbes sont ***under***, ***over***, ***mis***.

19 Pluperfect

1 Utilisez le plus que parfait dans les phrases suivantes.

Ex: If I had had more time, I would have chosen the blue design.

a. If they (arrive) one hour earlier, they would have seen their best friends.

....

b. If there (not be) a car industry, we would all have travelled by train.

....

c. Before moving to London, they (live) in New York.

....

d. She (buy) a new apartment before she came to visit us.

....

e. He would always have been single if he (not meet) his partner.

....

2 Traduisez en français.

a. It would have been better if he had said nothing.

....

....

b. Before considering her application letter, she had met the first applicant.

....

....

c. If he had told the truth, he would not have felt so bad.

....

....

d. They had had a first appointment before making the final decision.

....

....

e. She had decided to move away from California because of yearly wildfires.

....

....

3 Traduisez en anglais.

a. Elle a dit qu'il avait eu un accident.

....

....

b. L'entreprise avait accordé une augmentation de salaire à la suite des grèves.

....

....

c. Si jamais tu avais oublié de commander un taxi, j'aurais pu t'emmener.

....

....

d. Tu avais pensé que la guerre n'aurait pas eu lieu.

....

....

20 Préfixe et suffixe

1 Choisissez l'adjectif et/ou l'adverbe pour compléter les phrases.

Fearless / powerful / powerless / heartless /reluctantly

a. He is a .... child. He does not even know he is taking risks.

b. The online company is so .... that it has the biggest share of the market.

c. This man is .... He can never show any feelings for those who suffer.

d. She would .... ask the company for a salary raise.

2 Trouvez le mot composé d'un préfixe ou d'un suffixe.

a. She performs better than someone. She .... (do) everybody.

b. Companies produce too much. They .... (produce)

c. When a company lacks a normal work force, it is .... (staff)!

d. When somebody is crushed or destroyed by problems, s/he is .... (whelmed).

e. When judges rule against a decision, they .... (rule) the objection.

3 Trouvez le mot qui a la même racine et qui traduit le mot français.

a. Impuissant (power) : ....

b. Une erreur ou se méprendre (take) : ....

c. Amical (friend) : ....

d. Surmonter (come) : ....

e. Dépasser (take) : ....

f. Quiproquo (understand) : ....

g. Inattendu (expect) : ....

h. Le réveil (wake) : ....

Grammar

21 • Présent simple

Le présent simple (***the simple present***)
Il s'utilise pour exprimer une vérité générale, une caractéristique, une action habituelle, itérative (répétée).

→ *China still **dominates** the business* → La Chine domine toujours le commerce (comme par le passé et comme vraisemblablement dans le futur).

→ *It **supplies** nearly half of the European Union's garment imports*
→ La Chine fournit presque la moitié des imports de vêtements de l'Union européenne (comme par le passé et comme dans le futur).

Rappels :

– Seule la 3e personne du singulier modifie le verbe avec l'ajout du ***-s*** ou du ***-es*** suivant la terminaison du verbe :

→ *China supplies half of the European garment imports.*

– La forme négative et la forme interrogative se caractérisent par la présence de l'auxiliaire ***do*** pour toutes les personnes, sauf à la 3e personne du singulier pour laquelle on emploie ***does***.

– Attention à l'ordre des mots dans les questions :

→ *How much of the European garment imports **does** China supply?*

– Attention aux formes contractées à la forme négative :

→ *China **doesn't** supply 100% of the European garment imports.*

22 • Présent continu

Le présent continu : *be* + *-ing*
Le présent en ***be*** + ***-ing*** peut être utilisé pour décrire un événement qui continue au moment présent.

→ *But more orders **are shifting** to lower-wage economies such as in Cambodia and Vietnam, where garment factories **are mushrooming**.*
→ Les commandes se tournent en ce moment même (***are shifting***) vers des pays aux salaires plus bas, d'où les usines de textiles qui poussent comme des champignons en ce moment même (***are mushrooming***).

Rappel :
Le présent en ***be*** + ***-ing*** se forme avec les trois formes du présent du verbe ***be*** : ***am / is / are*** + **BV *-ing***.

21 Présent simple

1 Transformez les phrases suivantes :

1) à la forme interrogative en posant la question sur la partie soulignée.

2) à la forme négative.

a. Many customers appreciate online shopping.

1) ....

....

2) ....

....

b. They are looking for bargains.

1) ....

....

2) ....

....

c. Many companies care about their staff.

1) ....

....

2) ....

....

d. Many brands choose to relocate.

1) ....

....

2) ....

....

e. More and more people live next to their workplace.

1) ....

....

2) ....

....

2 Complétez les phrases suivantes an conjuguant le verbe entre parenthèses au présent simple.

a. Mot products (travel) by sea and by air.

....

....

b. The supermarket (open) every day at 9 am and (close) at 6 pm.

....

....

c. China and the USA (not agree) on trade tariffs.

....

....

d. A computer (cost) less today than 10 years ago.

....

....

e. Some people (not trust) new technologies.

....

....

22 Présent continu

1 Traduisez les phrases suivantes en utilisant un présent continu.

a. Les magasins sont en train de se tourner vers les produits bio.

....

....

b. Les prix sont en train d'augmenter.

....

....

c. Les ventes en ligne sont en train de dominer le marché.

....

....

d. Que font–ils ? Ils sont en train de réparer la vitrine.

....

....

e. Les clients se précipitent vers les caisses.

....

....

2 Complétez le texte suivant avec le présent qui convient.

Today, Mrs Parker .... (think) of the letter she must not forget to write to her client, Mr Jones. He .... (want) to know everything about the different products available, that is why Mrs Parker (list) all the details about the products' features. It isn't difficult for her because she .... (know) all the brands products by heart as she .... (work) at her desk 8 hours a day, five days a week. She .... (take) a lunch break every day at 12 am and she always.............. (go) for a cup of tea with her co-workers at 6 pm. But today, she (consider) leaving earlier because she .... (have) friends coming for dinner. She .... (need) time to cook.

TRAINING EXAMS EXERCISES INTERNSHIP

23 • Present perfect

- **Le *present perfect* simple (*have / has* + participe passé) s'emploie pour :**

a) Se référer à un événement, fait ou action qui n'est pas daté et qui n'a pas d'occurrence précise dans le passé.
→ *They **have chosen** a new manager.*
Attention : s'il y avait eu un repère temporel : *two years ago, during the war, etc.* le prétérit aurait été obligatoire.

b) Se référer à une action / un fait commencé dans le passé et qui perdure jusqu'à maintenant.
→ *He **has worked** with them since 1998.*
→ Il travaille avec eux depuis 1998.
Attention : ce cas précis d'emploi du *present perfect* se traduit par du présent de l'indicatif en français.

24 • Present perfect en ing et since/for

- **La différence entre *for* et *since* dans les phrases au *present perfect* :**

→ *He has worked with them **since** 1998.*
→ *He has worked with them **for** many years.*
On utilise ***since*** devant une date, un point de départ précis dans le passé.
On utilise ***for*** devant l'expression d'une durée.

- **Le *present perfect* progressif (*have* + *been* + BV-*ing*)** est utilisé pour donner plus de relief à la phrase.

Avec le *present perfect* progressif, l'intention / l'implication du locuteur (celui qui parle / écrit) change.
→ *He **has worked** with them for many years.*
→ Il travaille avec eux depuis de nombreuses années.
→ *He **has been working** with them for many years.*
→ Cela fait de nombreuses années qu'il travaille avec eux.

23 Present perfect

1 Choisissez le present perfect simple et/ou en ing.

a. We (follow) .... the latest news concerning the hurricane in Florida.

b. Ikea (launch) .... a new service to help customers assemble their furniture.

c. This summer's wild fires (bring) .... distruction in many californian towns.

2 Utilisez *for* ou *since* avec le present perfect simple ou progressif.

Ex: I have lived in Paris FOR 2 years.

a. .... I was born, I have been speaking English.

b. I have waited for you .... ages.

c. .... 2001 they have lived in a Spanish-speaking country.

d. Our corporate headquarters have been in Seattle .... 1994.

e. Our showroom has displayed our new technological devices .... April 2022.

3 Choisissez entre le present perfect simple ou en ing.

a. This week we (publish) a complex but important story.

....

b. Decades of scandals (make) clear that Swiss banks (attract) illicit funds from tax-evaders.

....

c. Deciding to publish these stories (be) a balancing act.

....

d. Previous reporting (spur) global action in favour of a fairer, more open banking.

....

e. It (already be) in operation for 21 years.

....

f. NASA (give) the go-ahead for one more decade.

....

g. The International Space Station (enable) one giant leap for science and mankind.

....

h. NASA (notice) signs of infrastructure and components slowing down.

....

i. The pandemic (make) us less, not more materialistic.

....

j. She (investigate) small scale acts of communal living.

....

k. This week we (publish) a complex but important story.

....

l. Previous reporting (spur) global action in favour of a fairer, more open banking.

....

4 Traduisez en anglais.

a. J'apprends l'anglais depuis 6 ans.

....

b. Elles se connaissent depuis la maternelle.

....

c. Cela fait 5 ans qu'il habite à Madrid.

....

d. Il fait des lasagnes pour le déjeuner le dimanche depuis au moins dix ans.

....

e. Elle travaille chez Coca Cola depuis moins de deux ans.

....

f. Cela fait un mois qu'elle envoie des lettres de candidature pour trouver un emploi.

....

5 Traduisez en français.

a. I have been speaking English since I was born.

....

b. They have been charged with wrongdoing.

....

c. She has been on her way for almost 2 hours now.

....

d. They have gone to Columbia.

....

e. They have bought themselves a new car. Look it is parked over there.

....

f. I have never been into binge viewing.

....

6 Que diriez-vous ? Soulignez la réponse la plus probable.

a. I have known them for 5 years. OR I have been knowing them for 5 years.

b. I have loved our hiking journey. OR I have been loving our hiking journey.

c. She has enjoyed your party. OR I have been enjoying your party.

d. They have been continuing their trip. OR they have continued their trip.

e. I have started my new job. OR I have been starting my new job.

25 • Prétérit simple

- **Construction du prétérit simple**

a) Le prétérit des verbes réguliers se forme en ajoutant ***-ed*** à la base verbale.
→ *The store **opened** 7 years ago.*

b) Beaucoup de verbes ont un prétérit irrégulier. Il faut les apprendre.

c) **Une phrase négative se construit sur le type :** ***did*** *+* ***not*** *+ base verbale.*
→ *The store **didn't open** in January.*

d) Pour poser une question, utilisez soit : auxiliaire + sujet + BV (pour les *yes/no* questions), soit : *wh-* + *word* + ***did*** + sujet + BV? (pour les *wh-* questions).

- **Emploi du prétérit simple**

Le prétérit (ou *simple past*) est utilisé pour quelque chose qui est complètement terminé et sans lien avec le présent. De ce fait, le prétérit est toujours associé (soit dans la phrase même, soit dans le contexte sans que cela ne soit exprimé) a une expression qui ramène à un moment précis du passé :
→ *5 years ago, yesterday, last year, on 22nd January 1957, when I was at school…*

26 • Prétérit continu

- **Construction du prétérit continu**

a) **Le prétérit en *-ing*** se construit avec ***be*** au prétérit + V-***ing***
→ *I **was going** to the market when I met you.*

b) **Une phrase négative**
→ *You **were not working** at your office when your sales assistant arrived.*

c) **Pour poser des questions**, soit : aux + sujet + V-***ing*** soit : ***wh-*** + aux + sujet +V-***ing***
→ ***Were you working*** *at your office when your sales assistant arrived?*

- **Emploi**

Le prétérit en ***-ing*** s'emploie souvent en lien avec le prétérit simple. Il souligne que l'action est présentée dans son déroulement et souvent interrompue par une autre action passée montrée dans sa brièveté.
→ *She **was preparing** a report when she received an email in which she was told to start preparing a business trip.*
→ Elle travaillait sur un rapport quand elle reçut un courriel lui demandant de préparer un voyage d'affaires.

25 Prétérit simple

1 Choisissez entre le prétérit simple ou le prétérit progressif.

Ex: While I was working from home, my colleagues were meeting via video calls.

a. We (debate) whether to make a decision or not when we (hear) that it was no longer necessary.

…………………………………………………………

…………………………………………………………

b. The CEO (listen) to the shareholders concerns while the meeting with the finance department (go on).

…………………………………………………………

…………………………………………………………

c. When they (agree) to our terms, we (feel) so happy.

…………………………………………………………

…………………………………………………………

d. The new applicant (meet) the human resources manager when we (find out) that the position had been filled.

…………………………………………………………

…………………………………………………………

e. When the merger negotiations (start) we (still prepare) the financial details of the report.

....

....

2 Choisissez entre le prétérit simple ou en ing.

a. While solar panels (create) enough shade to help the soil retain vital moisture, they (produce) electricity.

....

b. Last year California (suffer) its worst megadrought in 1,200 years.

....

c. Wolves (be eradicated) from many areas of Europe in the 19th century.

....

d. Nixon and Mao Zedong (meet) on Feb 21, 1972.

....

3 Choisissez le prétérit simple ou en ing.

a. They (load) containers when there (be) an accident.

....

b. While they (write) their application letter, their co-workers (make) phone calls.

....

c. When they (make) the decision, it (be) already too late.

....

d. President Joe Biden (introduce) the Build Back Better plan but it (be supported) by the Senate.

....

e. The 2022 winter Olympic Games (be) a real success.

....

f. As he (sit) on the soccer field, he (think) back to what his teacher had said about renewable-energy sources.

....

g. Sama (place) job ads in countries across Africa looking for people who could speak African languages.

....

h. Sama employees (stand) a better chance of having their demand met by acting as a group.

....

4 Traduisez en français.

a. While the company was negotiating the last detail, the labour force was on strike.

....

b. They were completing major tasks while the marketing manager was meeting her counterpart.

....

c. When I joined the company, employees were not working on the same premises.

....

d. They got to know their colleagues while they were working on the same project.

....

e. If they all stopped working at once, they could pressure on the head office.

....

5 Traduisez en anglais.

a. Elle rédigeait son rapport quand je l'ai rencontrée.

....

b. Elle n'était pas au bureau hier. Elle travaillait de chez elle.

....

c. Tandis qu'une réunion se tenait en visio-conférence, elle appelait l'agence de voyage.

....

d. Pendant que le voyage s'organisait, nous prenions les derniers rendez-vous.

....

e. Hier le personnel a visité les nouveaux locaux de l'entreprise.

....

27 • Pronoms personnels et possessifs

Pronoms sujets	Pronoms objets	Pronoms possessifs	FYI: Adjectifs possessifs	Pronoms réfléchis
I	Me	Mine	My	Myself
You	You	Yours	Your	Yourself
He	Him	His	His	Himself
She	Her	Hers	Her	Herself
It	It	Its	Its	Itself
We	Us	Ours	Our	Ourselves
They	Them	Theirs	Their	Themselves

28 • Propositions infinitives

a) Construction du verbe *want* (vouloir)

– ***Want***, lorsqu'il précède un verbe, est toujours suivi de ***to***.

→ *He wants to be the best.* → Il veut être le meilleur.

– ***Want* + CO + *to* + verbe :**

→ *He **wants** his company **to** improve to be the best.*

– Contrairement au français, qui utilise une subordonnée complétive (Il veut que son entreprise s'améliore pour être la meilleure), l'anglais utilise une proposition infinitive.

Remarque :
La 2e partie de la phrase, ***to be the best***, est aussi une proposition infinitive exprimant un but. Le français le traduit par : « pour être la meilleure ». Ne pas traduire « pour » par ***for*** en anglais. Le ***to*** suffit à exprimer le but.

b) Construction avec *would like* (voudrait / aimerait)

Would like est une formule atténuée de ***want*** qui se construit de façon identique :

→ *He **would like** his company **to be** the best.*

c) Construction du verbe *allow* (autoriser)

– ***Allow*** se construit toujours avec ***to***, comme ***want*** : ***allow*** + ***CO*** + ***to*** + verbe.

→ *We do not **allow** certain products to be sold in some shops.*

– ***Allow*** se construit fréquemment au passif.

→ *Some shops **are not allowed** to sell this product.*

d) Construction particulière du verbe *make* (faire)

Make **+ CO + verbe** signifie faire faire quelque chose à quelqu'un.

→ *The aim of the law is to **make shops stop selling** those products.*

e) Construction du verbe *let* (laisser, permettre)

Let se construit sans ***to*** : ***let*** **+ CO + verbe**.

→ *We shouldn't **let shops sell** those products.*

27 Pronoms personnels et possessifs

1 Utilisez un pronom personnel, un adjectif possessif et/ou un pronom réfléchi/réciproque.

Ex: Joan's commute takes her 45 minutes each way. But she Likes her office.

a. Self-driving cars will become more and more common in the future. .... will no longer be considered sci-fi devices.

b. Everybody has got .... favourite means of transport.

c. Some companies think of .... as the best.

d. To be productive when working with someone, you need to know .... well.

e. Retailers have to meet the needs of .... customers.

2 Traduisez en utilisant les pronoms possessifs.

Ex : C'est celui de Stella. C'est le sien. It is Stella's. It is hers.

a. C'est le manteau de ma mère. C'est le sien.

....

b. Ce sont les bénéfices de l'entreprise.

....

c. C'est de leur responsabilité.

....

d. C'est le discours du Premier ministre.

....

e. C'est leur décision.

....

3 Traduisez en français.

a. They have known each other for 10 years.

....

b. She knows herself well enough to figure out that it won't be a piece of cake.

....

c. She did it herself.

....

d. They love each other so they have planned to get married next July.

....

28 Propositions infinitives

1 Construisez des propositions infinitives à partir des éléments suivants.

a. The manager/want/the employees/improve/their results

....

b. Companies (not allow)/use/green washing/attract/customers

....

c. Everybody/would like/their children/succeed

....

d. Employees/would like/their salaries/be/higher/live better

....

e. It's difficult/make/people/stop/buying/unhealthy products

....

f. They need/better qualifications/join the team

....

g. Motorists/must/slow down/avoid/traffic accidents

....

h. We/shouldn't/let/robots/replace/human beings

....

i. Many British people/wished/remain/in the EU

....

j. Retailers/try/reconnect/with their customers

....

2 Traduisez les phrases suivantes en français.

a. Companies want their profits to increase every year.

....

b. People under 18 years old aren't allowed to buy alcohol in most countries.

....

c. To be sure to be on time you should take the 7 o'clock.

....

d. My boss would like me to work overtime, but I don't wish to right now.

....

e. Let me talk to her to try to clarify the situation.

....

29 • Propositions subordonnées concessives

Elle est introduite soit par ***although***, ***in spite of***, ***despite***, ***though*** (bien que, en dépit de, quoique).

→ ***Although*** *he missed his train, he arrived on time.*

→ ***Despite*** *heavy rains, the region was not flooded.*

→ ***In spite of*** *her hard work, she was not able to pass her exam.*

→ *She passed her exam with flying colours* ***though*** *she did not work hard.*

30 • Quantifieurs *few/fewer, less, much/many*

a) **Différencier *much* et *many* = beaucoup**
Les noms indénombrables (au singulier) sont précédés de ***much*** → ***much*** *money.*
En anglais, les noms dénombrables (au pluriel) sont précédés de ***many*** → ***many*** *employees.*

b) **Différencier *a little* et *a few* = peu**
Les noms indénombrables (au singulier) sont précédés de ***a little*** → ***a little*** *money.*
Les noms dénombrables (au pluriel) sont précédés de ***a few*** → ***a few*** *employees.*

c) D'autres adverbes et expressions adverbiales sont utilisés pour **exprimer une grande quantité** et sont utilisés indifféremment avec les noms dénombrables et indénombrables : *a lot of / lots of / plenty of.*

d) **Comparer des quantités**
Plus de : ***more*** + nom… → ***More*** *companies are involved in sustainable development today.*
De plus en plus : ***more and more***
Moins de : ***less*** + nom indénombrable (singulier) → ***less know how***
Fewer + nom dénombrable (pluriel) → ***fewer*** *applications*
De moins en moins : ***less and less/fewer and fewer***
Autant de : ***as much as ou as many as***
→ *You can have* ***as many*** *friends* ***as*** *you want on Facebook, but will you get* ***as much*** *real friendship?*

Remarque : *too much / too many* = trop
→ ***too much*** *money → trop d'argent*
→ ***too many*** *people → trop de gens*

29 Propositions subordonnées concessives

1 Complétez les phrases suivantes avec *although/despite/in spite of/though*.

a. .... many companies stopped their activities during the pandemic, they didn't go bankrupt.

b. Some car manufacturers continue to produce polluting cars .... the new standards.

c. People continue to buy industrial food .... they know it's unhealthy.

d. Many products are still available .... their impact on the environment.

e. The firm's CEO has decided to downsize .... the shareholders received a lot of money.

2 Traduisez les phrases de l'exercice 1 en français.

a. ....

b. ....

c. ....

d. ....

e. ....

30 Quantifieurs few/fewer, less, much/many

❶ Complétez les phrases suivantes avec *much* ou *many*, *a little /little*, *a few/few*.

a. There are .... people in the shops today; it seems they have .... money to spend. (*2 possibilities*)

b. Hurry up! We don't have .... time.

c. Parents give their children too .... toys to compensate for the .... time they spend with them.

d. Only .... staff members attended the meeting.

e. I don't have .... news about her project.

f. Only......... women have access to very high positions.

❷ Entourez la réponse correcte.

a. (Fewer/less) people buy processed food because they care for their health.

b. People have access to (much/many) information thanks to the internet.

c. In this new supermarket, cashiers earn (fewer/less)than in the previous one .

d. They have very (few/little) unsold products in this firm.

e. (Much/many) efforts are necessary to improve the company's bottom line.

f. Department stores and malls attract (less/fewer) customers than before.

❸ Traduisez en anglais.

a. De moins en moins d'enfants lisent des livres ; beaucoup préfèrent jouer avec leurs portables.

....

....

b. Les entreprises vendent moins de produits industriels.

....

c. Pour réussir il faut beaucoup d'argent et un peu de chance.

....

....

d. Cette startup recrute autant d'hommes que de femmes.

....

e. Seules quelques entreprises encouragent la diversité.

....

....

f. Beaucoup de salariés vont être licenciés car l'entreprise fait très peu de bénéfices.

....

....

....

g. Je n'ai pas beaucoup d'argent sur moi.

....

h. Il ne me reste que peu de temps avant mon départ.

....

....

i. Il y a beaucoup de gens qui sont un peu fous !

....

j. Combien en as-tu acheté ?

....

❹ *Much/Many* et *Few/fewer/little* ou *Less*. Faites le bon choix.

a. There are too much/many people in the room.

b. Too little/few water is in the bottle for the hike we contemplate.

c. How many/much advice would you give a job applicant?

d. How many/ much does a Tesla cost?

e. Media outlets have not given many/much information about the French Presidential election.

f. Too little/few is done for climate refugees.

g. I received fewer/little responses this year.

31 • Questions fermées et ouvertes

a) **Questions fermées**
On appelle questions fermées les questions auxquelles on ne peut répondre que par oui/non/peut-être/je ne sais pas.
En anglais ces questions débutent toujours par un auxiliaire et se construisent comme suit :
Aux + sujet+ verbe + reste de la phrase + ?
*Ex: **Do you like** your job?* → Aimez-vous/Est ce que vous aimez votre travail ?
***Did you see** the match last night?* → Avez-vous vu/Est ce que vous avez vu le match hier soir ?
***Will you come** to the meeting?* → Viendrez-vous/Est ce que vous viendrez à la réunion ?
Attention : l'anglais ne possède pas l'équivalent de la particule invariable « est ce que »

b) **Questions ouvertes**
On appelle questions ouvertes toutes les autres questions, c'est-à-dire celles auxquelles on ne peut répondre ni par oui/non/je ne sais pas / peut être.
Elles se caractérisent par la présence obligatoire d'un pronom interrogatif comme : ***what/where/how*** etc… et se construisent comme suit :
(Wh) + aux + sujet + verbe + reste de la phrase + ?
*Ex: **Where do you buy your groceries?*** → Où faites-vous vos courses ?
How long have you been working in this company? → Depuis combien de temps travaillez-vous dans cette entreprise ?
What can I do for you? → Que puis-je faire pour vous ?

32 • Subordonnées relatives

- **Emploi**
Les propositions relatives peuvent être ou non encadrées par des virgules. Il existe deux types de propositions relatives : certaines sont déterminatives, c'est-à-dire essentielles à la phrase, les autres sont dites non-déterminatives (ou appositives), car elles ne sont pas essentielles, mais donnent une information complémentaire.

→ *Mr Smith, **who** joined our chain in May 2010, said…*

- **Construction**
La proposition relative est introduite par un pronom relatif. Pour choisir le bon, il faut prendre en compte deux paramètres concernant l'antécédent : la nature (humain ou objet / idée) et la fonction (sujet /complément).

Remarques :
– Quand on annonce quelque chose, la proposition relative en début de phrase commence par ***what***.
– Quand on veut reprendre tout ce qui a été dit dans la proposition précédant la virgule, on utilise ***which***.

→ ***What** I mean is that more sales are expected.*
→ *More sales are expected, **which** means that…*

– Pour les relatives exprimant la possession (dont), on utilise le pronom relatif ***whose***.
– Il y a aussi les adverbes relatifs (utilisés comme pronoms) : ***where, when, why***.

→ *The place **where** I was born.*

Antécédent	Fonction du pronom relatif		
	Sujet	CO	Complément du nom
humain	*who, that*	*who(m), that*	*whose*
non humain	*which, that*	*which, that*	*whose, of which*

31 Questions fermées ouvertes

❶ Posez des questions qui donnent comme réponse soit oui soit non.

Ex: ***Will*** *you go to the swimming pool this summer? Yes, I* ***will.***

a. Q: ....

A: No, I am not. I am doing something else at the moment.

b. Q: ....

A: Yes, they would.

c. Q: ....

A: Yes, we can.

d. Q: ....

A: No, they won't. They will go on Sunday.

e. Q: ....

A: No, I didn't. I sent it yesterday.

❷ Posez des questions en WH – dites questions ouvertes avec *what, where, when, how, which, what time, how much,etc.*

Ex: When is Sarah's job interview? Sarah's job interview is on Monday at 10.

a. Q:.. ?

A: At ten o'clock.

b. Q:.. ?

A: 57,000 euros per year.

c. Q:.. ?

A: 15 candidates are on the shortlist.

d. Q:.. ?

A: I could start on the 15th of March.

e. Q:.. ?

A: because I really like New York.

32 Subordonnées relatives

❶ Complétez les phrases suivantes avec le pronom relatif approprié (voir encadré leçon)

a. Joseph King is the CEO .... organised yesterday's meeting with foreign investors

b. I'm sending you all the details about this client .... insurance policy has expired.

c. We have to listen to our customers to know .... they have to tell us about the product.

d. Sometimes between several products consumers do not know .... one to choose.

e. The problems .... many companies are faced to is the lack of skilled employees.

❷ Transformez les phrases suivantes comme dans l'exemple ci-dessous, en supprimant les pronoms relatifs en déplaçant les prépositions.

Ex: The sales representative ***with whom*** *I negotiated the sale was very professional.*

→ *The sales representative* ***I negotiated the sales with*** *was very professional.*

a. The position for which I applied was already taken.

→ ....

b. The operator with whom he spoke on the phone told him to call later this afternoon.

→ ....

c. The car with which he drives to work is the company car.

→ ....

d. The company with which we merged is very powerful.

→ ....

e. The staff members on whom the sales manager was counting proved to be unreliable.

→ ....

TRAINING EXAMS EXERCISES INTERNSHIP

Grammar

33 • Superlatif

a) **Le superlatif de supériorité = le plus**

- ***The*** **+ adjectif court +** ***-est*** **ou** ***The*** **+ adjectif terminaison en** ***y*** **+** ***iest***

→ *It is the **largest** company in the world.*
→ *New York is **the busiest** city in the USA.*

- ***The*** **+** ***most*** **+ adjectif long**

→ *One of **the most successful** entrepreneurs of our age.*

- **Les adjectifs irréguliers (à connaître)**

good / well → the best; bad → the worst; far → the farthest / the furthest

→ *They had* **the best** *results of the year.* ***The worst*** *is yet to* come. This is ***the furthest / farthest*** we can go.

b) **Le superlatif d'infériorité = le moins**

The least **+ adj**

→ *The product was abandoned by the brand because it was **the least successful**.*
→ Le produit a été abandonné par la marque car c'était le moins réussi.

c) **Le superlatif avec** ***ever*** **+** ***present perfect***

→ *He is the best manager the company **has ever had**.*

33 Superlatif

1 Complétez les phrases suivantes en transformant l'adjectif au superlatif de supériorité.

a. This company is (large) in the world in terms of revenue.

....

....

b. Customers always look for (good) bargains or (cheap) prices.

....

....

c. Fossil fuels are among (dangerous) energies for the environment.

....

....

d. Tesco, (famous) British retailer, has had (bad) sales results since it was created.

....

....

e. £50K per year is (far) the company can pay you.

....

....

2 Complétez les phrases en choisissant le superlatif de supériorité ou d'infériorité suivant le contexte.

a. He was (successful) sales representative, he had (bad) results in the department.

....

....

b. This fashion shop has (beautiful) design I have ever seen.

....

....

c. Shareholders have lost a lot of money; it is (profitable) investment of all times.

....

....

d. Tesla manufactures (clean) car in the world but also (expensive).

....

....

e. Coconut based products are very good, they are (healthy) on the market.

....

....

3 Traduisez les phrases suivantes en anglais.

a. Le plus grand centre commercial du monde a ouvert à Dubaï.

....

b. Vous trouverez le meilleur café de la ville dans ce bar.

....

c. C'est la nouvelle la plus étonnante que j'aie jamais entendue.

....

d. L'énergie solaire est l'industrie la moins polluante.

....

e. Les gens les plus riches du monde sont les moins inquiets pour l'avenir.

....

4 Complétez les phrases par l'un des adjectifs au superlatif.

The worst / The nicest / the most expensive / the least successful/ the farthest

a. She is .... sales manager I have ever met.

b. This is .... endeavour ever.

c. Summer is .... period to travel to Greece because it is much too hot.

d. Coca Cola with a cherry taste was .... beverage introduced to consumers.

e. Relocating our manufacturing to Romania is .... we would want.

5 Traduisez les phrases suivantes en français.

a. The worst solution for the employees would be massive job cuts.

....

....

b. China and India are the world's most populated countries.

....

....

c. The cheapest way to travel remains the train.

....

....

d. The best products are not necessarily the most expensive ones.

....

....

e. Because of a roadblock, the next village was the furthest destination we were able to reach.

....

....

f. You should wear your best clothes for the job interview.

....

....

g. This mission is the most exciting I have ever carried out.

....

....

h. She is the smartest woman on the team and the friendliest too.

....

....

i. The happiest day in his life was when he joined the company.

....

....

j. They always recruit the most qualified employees.

....

....

Vocabulary

1 Consumers

after sale service (n): *service après-vente*
aisle (n): *allée/rayon d'un supermarché*
age group (n): *tranche d'âge*
appeal (vb) appeal (n): *attirer/attrait*
average (adj): *moyen(nne)*
bargain (n): *affaire (faire une affaire)*
behaviour (n): *comportement*
brand (n): *marque*
brand awareness (n): *reconnaissance de la marque*
brick and mortar store (n): *magasin phsysique "en dur"*
buying/purchasing/spending power (n): *pouvoir d'achat*
cashier-free (adj): *sans caissier*
charity (n): *organisation caritative*
check-out (n): *caisse*
compulsive spender (n): *acheteur compulsif*
consumer behaviour (n): *comportement du consommateur*
consumer spending(n): *dépense des consommateurs*
consumption (n): *consommation*
consumption patterns/habits (n): *habitudes de consommation*
convenience foods (n): *plats préparés*
coupons (n): *bons d'achat/de réduction*
crowdfunding (n): *financement participatif*
customer service (n): *service client*
delivery (n): *livraison*
deliver (vb): *livrer*
discount (n): *rabais*
disposable(adj): jetable
endcap (n): *tête de gondole*
groceries/grocery shopping (n): *courses alimentaires*
home delivery (n): *livraison à domicile*
household (n): *ménage/foyer*
impulse buying (n): *achat impulsif*
income (n): *revenu*
item (n): *article/produit*
loyalty card (n): *carte de fidélité*
luxury brand (n): *marque de luxe*
mid-priced brand (n): *marque de moyenne gamme*
processed foods (n): *nourriture industrielle*
online review (n): *critique en ligne*
organic (adj): *bio*
popup ad (n): *fenêtre publicitaire sur Internet*
purchase decision-making process(n) : *processus de décision d'achat*
purchasing behaviour (n): *comportement d'achat*
retail/store brand (n): *marque de magasin*
retailer (n): *commerçant, détaillant*
sales (n): *ventes/soldes*
scheme(n): *dispositif/programme*
spend (vb): *dépenser (argent) passer (du temps)*
spending patterns (n): *habitudes de dépenses*
take away (adv): *à emporter*
fulfill basic needs (vb): *répondre à des besoins élémentaires*
go mainstream (vb): *devenir majoritaire*
go to waste (vb): *aller au rebus (à la poubelle)*
meet consumers' needs/expectations (vb): *répondre aux besoins/attentes des consommateur*
rate (vb) rate (n): *évaluer/taux*
target (n): *cible (vb): cibler*
tap a market (n): *pénétrer un marché*
trend (n): *tendance*
upscale brand (n): *marque haut de gamme*
voucher (n): *bon d'échange*
waste (n): *déchêt*

1 Complete the sentences with the following words.

Consume/discounts/bargains/habits/organic/spend/purchase/buy/attract/brands/target/customers/influencers/lay out/spending patterns processed.

a. .... do not necessarily .... the products they ....: for example, parents do not .... toys for themselves but for their children.

b. Today children are very strong ...., that is why .... do everything they can to .... them, even for products which do not .... children directly.

c. Price is a very important feature in customers' .... That is why most of them look for .... and ....

d. They .... more time and money when a store's .... is pleasant and attractive.

e. An increasing number of people are changing their .... by replacing .... food by .... food.

2 Match the definition with the corresponding word.

a. A customer who buys a product he/she had not planned to purchase •	• check out **1.**
b. The place where customers line up before they leave the store •	• delivery **2.**
c. The moment when the products arrive at a customer's home •	• household **3.**
d. The people who live in the same house/flat •	• impulse buyer **4.**
e. Their products are very expensive •	• loyalty card **5.**
f. A company selling products for individual customers •	• luxury brands **6.**
g. Something stores give to clients to make them come back •	• retailer **7.**

3 Translate into English.

a. Le processus de décision d'achat des clients est différent aujourd'hui.

....

b. Ils passent plus de temps en ligne sauf pour les courses alimentaires.

....

c. Un bon service client répond aux attentes des consommateurs.

....

d. Les ventes des produits jetables diminuent.

....

e. Les clients sont influencés par les avis en ligne.

....

f. La plupart des vieux vêtements vont au rebus.

....

g. Les têtes de gondole doivent attirer les clients.

....

TRAINING
EXAMS
EXERCISES
INTERNSHIP

Vocabulary

2 Marketing & distribution

advertisement /ad/advert (n): *un spot publicitaire, une annonce*
advertising (n): *publicité*
advertise (vb): *faire de la publicité, promouvoir*
apparel (n): *vêtement*
average (adj): *moyen(ne)* on average (adv): *en moyenne*
bargain (n): *une bonne affaire*
batch(n): *lot*
brand (n): *marque*
brick and mortar store (n): *magasin physique*
campaign (n): *campagne* (advertising campaign: *campagne publicitaire)*
click and mortar store (n): *magasin à la fois physique et en ligne*
commercial (n): (us) *spot publicitaire*
competitor (n): *concurrent*
competition (n): *concurrence*
consumer behaviour/pattern (n): *comportement du consommateur*
corner shop/convenience store (n): *magasin de proximité*
department store(n): *grand magasin (galeries lafayette/ macy's etc...)*
digital marketing (n): *marketing numérique*
digital media (n): *les média numériques*
fast fashion (n): *mode éphémère*
flagship store (n): *magasin pilote, navire amiral*
grocery shopping (n): *courses alimentaires*
high street store (n): *magasin de centre-ville*
label (n): *étiquette*
labelling (n): *étiquettage*
launch (vb): *lancer (sur le marché)*
layout (n): *agencement, disposition*
lifestyle (n): *mode de vie*
loyalty card (n): *carte de fidélité*
low end (adj): *bas de gamme*
lure (vb): *attirer dans le but de tromper*
outlet (n): *point de vente*
mall (n us): *centre commercial*
market research (n): *étude de marché*
midrange (adj): *milieu de gamme*
multi format store (n): *magasin décliné en plusieurs formats (i.e carrefour)*
niche (n): *créneau*
packaging (n): *conditionnement/ emballage*
pop up store (n): *magasin éphémère*
premium (n): *avantage, privilège*
price tag (n): *étiquette de prix*
product packaging (n): *conditionnement et emballage du produit*
product/ brand /company endorsement (n): *utilisation d'une personnalité ou d'une célébrité pour véhiculer l'image d'un produit, d'un événement, d'un service ou d'une marque.*
pure player (n): *magasin exclusivement sur Internet*
range (n): *gamme (prix/produits)*
retailer (n): *détaillant, commerçant*
retailing (n): *commerce de détail*
sample (n): *échantillon*
shoe-box store (n): *magasin rectangulaire en tôle dans les zones commerciales à l'entrée des agglomérations*
shop window (n): *vitrine d'un magasin*
showcase (n): *vitrine (sens figuré)*
showrooming (n): *consulter les produits en magasin pour les acheter ensuite en ligne*
target (n) (vb): *cible, cibler*
the spending/consuming power/purchasing power (n): *pouvoir d'achat*
address needs (vb): *répondre à des besoins*
buy in bulk (vb): *acheter en gros*
display (vb) (n): *étaler , étalage*
handle (vb): *manipuler (manier)*
hit the shelves (vb): *arriver sur les rayons (mis en vente)*
market products (vb): *commercialiser des produits*

multi channel (n): *multi canal*
omni channel (n): *omni canal*
provide (vb): *fournir*
supply (vb): *fournir*
target audience (n): *audience/public/consommateur/cible*
trade secret (n): *secret commercial*
trend (n): *tendance*
upscale / high end (adj): *haut de gamme*
welfare (n): *bien être* (animal welfare: *bien être animal)*
warehouse store (n): *magasin entrepôt*
wholesaler(n): *grossiste*
word of mouth (adj) (n): *bouche à oreille*
wrapping material (n): *papier/materiel d'emballage*
youth-targeted promotions (n): *des promotions destinées aux jeunes*

1 Choose the right answer:

a. A retailer without online presence is:

- ☐ a click and mortar store.
- ☐ a brick and mortar store.
- ☐ a digital store.

b. Fashion today changes all the time that's why it's referred to as:

- ☐ fashion victim
- ☐ fast fashion
- ☐ cheap fashion

c. Because it's less expensive and often more effective, many brands today rely on:

- ☐ TV commercials
- ☐ Pop up ads
- ☐ Word of mouth

d. People need them because they are local and their opening hours are longer:

- ☐ Malls
- ☐ Department stores
- ☐ Convenience stores

2 Complete the definitions with a word from the list on the opposite page.

a. A store proposing many different prices proposes a large .... of prices.

b. A company selling only to professional retailers is a ....

c. Customers seldom go online for their ....

d. Luxury products are also referred to as ....

e. Shopping centres are called .... in the USA.

f. Physical stores are worried about the new trend called ....

g. Shops located in town centres are called ....

h. What people buy depend on their ....

i. Big suburban stores are also referred to as ....

j. The Galeries Lafayette is a ....

3 Memory game : Translate

Hide the list opposite and test yourself. You have 20 seconds.

Concurrence/point de vente/grand magasin/magasin de proximité/audience cible/vitrine/agencement/emballage/commerçant/milieu de gamme/carte de fidélité/promotion ciblant les jeunes.

Vocabulary

3 Companies

accounting/accountancy (n): *comptabilité*
beverage (n): *boisson*
boom (n/vb): *explosion / exploser (sens fig)*
bottom line (n): *benefice net, résultat financier*
branch (n): *branche, filiale*
business (n): *activité, entreprise*
chairman (n): *président*
challenge (vb): *défier*
challenger (n): *concurrent pricncipal*
charity (n): *organisation caritative*
check out (n): *caisse (dans un magasin)*
chief executive officer (CEO) (n): *directeur général, dirigeant*
company (n): *entreprise*
compete with (vb): *faire concurrence à*
competition (n): *concurrence*
competitor (n): *concurrent*
conglomerate (n): *conglomérat*
corporation (n): *entreprise*
cut (n/vb): *coupe sombre/couper → faire baisser*
decrease (n/vb): *diminution, diminuer*
downsize (vb): *réduire (taille d'une entreprise)*
downturn (n): *crise (économique)*
drop (n/vb): *chute, chuter*
employee (n): *employé(e) salarié(e)*
employer (n): *employer*
environmentally-friendly (adj): *écologique, bon pour l'environnement*
executive (n): *cadre dirigeant*
factory (n): *usine*
fail (vb): *échouer*
failure (n): *échec*
fair trade (n): *commerce équitable*
file for bankruptcy (vb): *déposer le bilan*
firm (n): *entreprise, firme*
food industry (n): *industrie agroalimentaire*
go bankrupt (vb): *faire faillite*
greenwashing (n): *éco- blanchiment*
grow (vb): *augmenter, croître*
growth (n): *croissance*
head (n): *dirigeant*
headquarter (n): *siège social*
human resources (n): *ressources humaines*
increase (n/vb): *augmentation, augmenter*
innovate (vb) : *innover*
jumpstart (vb): *rebondir*
launch (vb) (n): *lancement, lancer (un produit sur le marché)*
lead (vb): *mener, diriger, être en tête*
leader (n): *meneur, numéro un*
leadership (n): *direction*
management (n): *direction/gestion*
manager (n): *dirigeant/gestionnaire*
manufacture (vb): *fabriquer*
merge (vb): *fusionner*
merger (n): *fusion*
operating costs (n): *coûts de fonctionnement*
outsource (vb): *externaliser*
outsourcing (n): *externalisation*
overheads (n): *frais généraux*
partnership (n): *partenariat*
payroll (n): *registre du personnel*
policy (n): *stratégie*
position (n): *poste (dans une entreprise)*
profit (n/vb): *profit, bénéfice, bénéficier*
profit margin (n): *marge bénéficiaire*
profitability (n): *rentabilité*
raw materials (n): *matières premières*
relocate (vb): *délocaliser*
relocation (n): *délocalisation*
research and Development (n): *Recherche et Développement*
restructure (vb): *restructurer*
revenue (n): *chiffre d'affaires*
sales department (n): *service commercial*
shareholder (n): *actionnaire*
shortage (n): *manque, pénurie*
slow down (vb): *ralentir*

small and medium size company (SME) (n): *petite et moyenne entreprise → PME*
staff (n): *personnel (d'une enterprise)*
start up (n): *petite entreprise innovante*
state-owned company (n): *entreprise publique*
subcontractor (n): *sous-traitant*
subsidiary (n): *filiale*
subsidize (vb): *subventionner, financer*
supplier (n): *fournisseur*
supply chain (n): *chaîne d'approvisionnement*
sustainable (adj): *durable* (sustainable development = *développement durable)*
utilities (n): *fournisseurs d'eau de gaz et d'électricité*
venture (n): *entreprise risquée*

1 Choose the right word from the opposite page corresponding to the following clues.

a. A period when companies can lose profits: ....

b. A company belonging to a bigger one: ....

c. What companies often do when they are confronted to financial problems: ....

d. A company owning several businesses: ....

e. A word meaning that some companies decide to operate some of their services abroad: ....

f. The main rival of the market leader: ....

g. When a company puts a new product or service on the market: ....

h. Companies working together for a limited period of time: ....

i. Two companies combining into one: ....

j. The person leading a company: ....

2 Translate into English.

a. Certaines entreprises délocalisent, d'autres externalisent certains services.

....

b. Un nombre croissant d'entreprises suivent une politique bonne pour l'environnement.

....

c. Le Directeur Général veut réduire la taille de l'entreprise.

....

d. Il y a plus de personnel dans le service commercial que dans le service Recherche et Développement.

....

e. Les frais généraux sont en augmentation.

....

f. La marque va lancer un nouveau produit sur le marché.

....

g. La chaine d'approvisionnement rencontre un problème à cause du manque de matériaux bruts.

....

h. Beaucoup d'entreprises utilisent l'éco blanchiment pour attirer les consommateurs.

....

i. Les actionnaires s'intéressent seulement aux profits.

....

j. Les fournisseurs d'eau de gaz et d'électricité devraient être des entreprises publiques.

....

Vocabulary

4 Work

applicant (n): *candidat*
application letter (n): *lettre de candidature*
apply for a job (v): *poser sa candidature*
at work (n): *au travail*
automated tasks (n): *tâches automatisées*
baby boomers (n): *baby-boomers (nés entre 1946 et 1964)*
bargaining power (n): *pouvoir de négociation*
be jobless/unemployed (v): *être au chômage ; sans emploi*
be on a maternity/parental leave (v): *avoir un congé maternité/parental*
be on a sick leave (v): *avoir un congé maladie*
be out of work/job (v): *être sans emploi*
benefits (n): *avantages sociaux*
blue-collar workers (n): *les ouvriers*
burnout (n): *burn-out/épuisement*
career (n): *carrière*
child labour (n): *travail des enfants*
compete with (v): *concurrence*
competition (n): *concurrence*
competitive (adj): *concurrentiel*
competitor (n): *concurrent*
cover letter (n): *letter de motivation*
CV/resumé (n): *un CV*
face-to-face meeting (n): *réunion en présentiel*
to be made redundant (v): *être licencié*
fixed term job/contract (n): *CDD*
full time/part-time job (n): *emploi à temps plein/à temps partiel*
go on strike (v): *faire grève*
hand in one's notice (v): *remettre sa démission*
hire (v): *embaucher*
industrial dispute (n): *conflit social*
in-person work (n): *travail en présentiel*
internship/work placement/training session (n): *stage*
job interview (n): *entretien d'embauche*
joblessness (n): *chômage*
job-seeker (n): *demandeur d'emploi*
labour market (n):*marché du travail*
labour movemen t(n): *mouvement des travailleurs*
labour shortage (n): *pénurie de manoeuvre*
labour union (n): *syndicat des ouvriers*
lay off (v):*renvoyer*
low paid jobs (n): *emplois mal payés*
mandatory overtime (n): *heures supplémentaires obligatoires*
open position (n): *poste à pouvoir*
overworked (adj):*surchargé, surmené*
pay rise (n): *augmentation de salaire*
pension (n):*allocation retraite*
pensioner (n): *retraité/e*
picket line (n): *piquet de grève*
quit/to resign(v): *donner sa démission/ démissionner*
raise salaries (v): *augmenter les salaires*
redundancy (n): *licenciement*
remote work (n): *travail à distance*
retire (v):*prendre sa retraite*
retiree (n): *retraité/e*
salary/pay/wage (n):*salaire*
set up union (v): *organiser/monter/établir un syndicat*
sexual harassmen t(n): *harcèlement sexuel*
sexual misconduct (n): *conduite répréhensible*
shift (n): *work in shifts: faire les trois huits/ travailler par rotation*
skilled/qualified (adj): *qualifié*
stage a strike (v): *organiser une grève*
strike (n): *grève*
strike-breaker (n): *briseur de grève*
teleworking (n): *télétravail*
tight labour market (n): *marché du travail tendu*
trainee/an intern (n): *un/e stagiaire*
underpaid (adj): *sous-payé*
unfair labour practice (n): *pratiques professionnelles illégales*
unionisation rate (n): *le taux de syndicalisation*
vacancy (n): *poste à pourvoir*

warehouse (n): *entrepôt*
watershed (n): *tournant/un moment décisif*
white-collar workers (n): *cadres*
work life balance (n): *équilibre vie privée/vie de travail*
work (n): *travail*
workforce :*labour force (n): population active*
working conditions (n): *conditions de travail*
working cost (n): *coût salarial*
working hours (n): *horaires de travail*
workload (n): *charge de travail*
workplace (n): *lieu de travail*

1 Complete each sentence with the correct word from the list below:

Watershed/workplaces/strike-breakers/workloads/burned out/surging/quit/picket line

a. According to the Bureau of Labor Statistics, more than 4,2 million Americans .... their jobs in August 2021.

b. There's no single factor driving workforce behavior. Wages aren't keeping up with .... prices.

c. As workers across industries face lower wages greater .... and higher risk.

d. Americans, economists say, are simply .... – and emboldened by the current labor market.

e. Labor unions have initiated strikes at nearly .... across the US.

f. Starbucks union vote sets up a .... moment for U.S. labor.

g. It was the same day Kaajal took her to the .... for the first time.

h. A factory lorry transporting .... was blocked by a blockade.

2 Complete the following sentences with the words in parenthesis.

a. The average paid maternity leave is 29 weeks and (paid paternity leave/16 weeks)...................................

b. Some employees have long-term work contacts and (self-employed)...

c. Harassment (classify/as sexual misconduct).............

d. To combat workplace sexual harassment, bills (sign/Congress)..

e. Working remotely two days a week (to be unusual).......

f. Mandatory overtime, low pays and long hours (to be the fate of the American worker)..................................

3 Underline the right word.

a. She has a lot of (work/job) at the Christmas season.

b. (Child labour/Children's labour) is forbidden in most countries but is not unusual in Bangladesh.

c. Getting an education means among other things having access to (children's books/child books).

d. Chinese traditional industries are confronting (rising/raising) labour costs thanks to a declining working population.

e. (Productivity/production) is when an employee is able to do more within the same amount of time.

4 The words are jumbled up: find the right order.

a. Appeal/will/ hybrid approach/ pool of applicants/a more diverse/a ....

b. Austin, Texas/a crucial component/in/has remained/remote work. ....

c. Employees/ highly/ can work/effectively/from home. .....
....

d. Underestimated/in-person interactions/the impact of/should not be. ....

Vocabulary

5 Transports

accommodation (n): *hébergement*
airliner (n): *avion de ligne*
all inclusive tour (n): *voyage tout compris*
amount to (v): *s'élever à*
an increase in fuel price (n): *une augmentation du prix de l'énergie*
be battery-powered (vb): *fonctionner avec une batterie*
be hauled (v): *être transporté*
boarding pass (n): *carte d'enregistrement*
breed corruption (v): *générer de la corruption*
bulk commodities (n): *marchandises en vrac*
bulk freighter (n): *navire de charge en vrac ; cargo*
by road (n): *par route*
charge (v): *charger (batterie)*
charging network (n): *réseau de bornes de rechargement*
charging time (n): *temps de recharge*
charter its ships (v): *affréter ses porte-containeurs*
check in (v): *enregistrer*
clear goods (v): *dédouaner les marchandises*
commodities (n): *marchandises*
commodity flows (n): *mouvements des marchandises*
commute (v): *faire le trajet domicile/travail*
commuter (n): *personne qui prend les transports pour aller au travail*
congested roads (n): *routes encombrées/embouteillées*
cruise ship (n): *paquebot*
cruiser (n): *yatch de croisière*
cushion the effect (v): *amortir l'effet*
eco-friendly tourism (n): *tourisme vert*
flight (n): *vol*
freight forwarder (n): *transitaire*
full board (n): *pension complète*
haul (n): *voyage/trajet*
holiday maker (n): *vacancier*
impediment (n): *obstacle*
journey (n): *excursion*
landscape (n): *paysage*
mark the route (v): *faire l'itinéraire*
mass tourism (n): *tourisme de masse*
ocean liner (n): *paquebot*
oil infrastructure (n): *l'infrastructure pétrolière*
package tour (n): *voyage organisé*
plug into a socket (vb): *brancher dans une prise*
refill (v): *faire le plein*
removal(n): *un retrait*
remove (v): *retirer*
runways (n): *pistes d'atterrissage*
sea resort (n): *station balnéaire*
sea side (n): *le bord de mer*
seascape (n): *paysage maritime*
shipment (n): *expédition*
shipping container (n): *conteneur*
shipping routes (n): *itinéraires maritimes/de transport*
shipping terminals (n): *baies/quais de chargement*
Shipping (n): *transport*
side-step/ bypass (v): *contourner*
stopover (n): *une correspondance*
subsidised public transport (n): *transports publics subventionnés*
supply chains (n): *chaîne d'approvisionnement*
the era of the ocean liner was over (exp): *l'ère des paquebots est finie*
tour operator (n): *voyagiste*
transport fare (n): *prix du transport*
transport grant (n): *aide au transport*
travel (v): *voyager*
trip(n): *voyage*
truck drivers (n): *chauffeurs de poids lourds*
vacationer (n): *vacancier*
winter resort (n): *station balnéaire*

1 The words are jumbled up: put them in the right order.

a. the end user/to/is shipped/the finished good.

....

b. 40 feet long/in a container/is/most of the shipping.

....

c. by truck/or by train/the container/will be moved.

....

d. powerful cranes/require/typically/shipping containers.

....

e. the ship/a specific route/sails.

....

f. has become/concentrated/highly/ due to/mergers/over the years/the international ocean shipping industry.

....

g. Houston/has docked/also/Amazon/at the port of.

....

h. on time/to customers/it's dispatching/to get packages/half-full trucks.

....

i. has/Amazon/its own transportation network.

....

j. phenomenal/were/Amazon's prices/ compared with/$4,000 to ship a container/ from China/the $12,000/ by other freight forwarders/demanded.

....

2 Find the words corresponding to the following clues on the opposite page.

a. To provide the world with the necessary energy you need this equipment.

....

b. When you want to avoid an obstacle, you tend to act that way.

....

c. We are lucky troopers as we commute with it for a decent price.

....

d. There was a shortage of people in this activity in the UK as it is badly paid and the working conditions are difficult.

....

e. If ever you have an electrical appliance or a computer, for it to work smoothly, you need first to make sure you have access to electricity. So what do you do?

....

f. when your car is almost running out of gas, you must do this otherwise you will end up walking back home.

....

g. When commuting to work in England by car, you will certainly be stuck on the road because of this major problem.

....

h. When arriving at the airport, this is the first thing you need to do with your luggage.

....

i. This is how you are called when you travel every morning from home to work.

....

j. It can be used as a synonym for trip.

....

3 Complete the following sentences with the following words

Grounding/traffic jam/prestigious luxury brand/cargo records/exports/container ships

a. In March 2021, the Suez Canal was blocked for six days after the .... of Ever Given.

b. Southern California is dealing with .... unlike any other

c. A record number of .... have been stuck waiting in the waters outside the ports of Los Angeles and Long Beach to unload cargo.

d. The ports have broken monthly .... regularly since last summer

e. .... to China in France decreased to 1911 EUR Million in November from 1961 EUR Million in October of 2021.

f. This .... opened thousands of stores in the world.

Vocabulary

6 World challenges

ai (artificial intelligence) (n): *intelligence artificielle*
alternative energies (n): *énergies alternatives*
a solar powered battery (n): *une batterie qui fonctionne à l'énergie solaire*
automation (n): *automatisation*
aware (adj): *conscient(e) averti(e)*
bad weather conditions (n): *intempéries*
big data (n): *méga données, données massives*
carbon emission (n): *émissions de dioxyde de carbone*
organic (adj): *bio*
carbon footprint (n): *empreinte carbone*
cattle breeding/raising (n): *élevage (bovins, ovins etc)*
insect breeding (n): *élevage d'insectes*
chemical (n): *produit chimique*
climate change (n): *changement climatique*
collect (vb): *rassembler, collecter*
cost-efficient (adj): *économique (qui économise)*
crop (n): *récolte*
crude (adj): *brut (pétrole)*
cryptocurrency(n): *monnaie virtuelle*
curb (vb): *diminuer, freiner*
data (n pl): *données*
deforestation (n): *deforestation*
digital (adj): *numérique*
disease (n): *maladie*
drought (n): *sécheresse*
energy efficient (adj): *qui ne consomme pas beaucoup d'énergie*
environmentally-friendly (adj): *écologique, respectueux de l'environnement*
exhaust (n): *gaz d'échappement*
fair trade (n): *commerce équitable*
farming (n): *agriculture/élevage*
flood (n): *inondation*
flooding (n): *submersion*
forecast (n): *prévision*
fossile energy (n): *énergie fossile*
fuel (n): *carburant*
global warming (n): *réchauffement climatique*
gmo (genetically modified organism) (n): *ogm (organisme génétiquement modifié)*
green energies (n pl): *énergies vertes*
greenhouse gas (n): *gaz à effets de serre*
health (n): *santé*
health oriented (adj): *tourné vers la santé*
human enhancement (n): *être humain augmenté*
hurricane (n): *ouragan*
ict (information communication technology): *tic (technologies de l'information et de la communication)*
natural disasters (n): *catastrophes naturelles*
nuclear energy (n): *énergie nucléaire*
nutrient (n): *nutriments*
oil (n): *pétrole*
organic (adj): *bio*
overfishing (n): *surpêche*
pollutant (n): *polluant*
predict (vb): *prédire*
recycle (vb): *recycler*
rise of the sea level (n): *montée des oceans*
set (vb): *fixer, établir*
shortage (n): *pénurie → set rules : fixer des règles*
smog (n): *brouillard généré par la pollution (smoke + fog)*
standard (n): *norme*
storm (n): *tempête*
landslide (n): *glissement de terrain*
state of the art (adj): *dernier cri, à la pointe de la technologie*
sustainable (adj): *durable*
sustainability (n): *durabilité*
solar panel (n): *panneau solaire*
storm (n): *tempête*

tide (n): *marée*
tidal wave (n): *raz de marée*
transhumanism (n): *transhumanisme*
waste (n): *déchets*
waste (vb): *gaspiller*
water table (n): *nappe phréatique*
wetland (n): *zone humide*
weather conditions (n): *conditions météorologiques*
wild fire (n): *incendie/feu de forêt*
wildlife (n): *la faune sauvage*
wind farm (n): *parc éolien*

---

1 Complete the sentences with the following words:

Energy- efficient / carbon footprint / global warming / AI / environmentally friendly / sustainability / natural disasters / fair trade / aware / GMOS

a. Consumers do not want to buy food containing ....

b. Everybody must do their best to reduce their ....

c. Hurricanes are part of .... due to ....

d. Some scientists believe .... is the solution to achieve ....

e. Thanks to .... small producers can send their children to school.

f. Today, new technologies have to be ....

g. Most people are .... of the necessity to save the planet.

h. New buildings today must be ....

2 Find the word corresponding to the following clues on the page opposite.

a. Cutting down forests: ....

b. Covid 19 is one: ....

c. It shouldn't be intensive any more: ....

d. The bitcoin is the most famous: ....

e. Improving human beings artificially: ....

f. They produce energy thanks to the wind: ....

g. It is threatening life in the sea: ....

h. When there is not enough materials: ....

i. The effect causing global warming: ....

j. A new type of breeding reducing the environmental impact: ....

3 Translate into English.

a. Le réchauffement climatique provoque des catastrophes naturelles.

....

b. Les intempéries augmentent chaque année.

....

c. L'intelligence artificielle ne peut remplacer l'intelligence humaine.

....

d. Des milliards de données sont collectées chaque jour. On les nomme méga données.

....

e. Les batteries fonctionnant à l'énergie solaire sont très économiques.

....

4 Put the words in the right order to make a correct sentence.

a. can/AI/greenhouse/decrease/help/effect/the

....

b. by/wild/global/generated/fires/are/droughts

....

c.Future/breeding/cattle/insect/replaced/be/by/near/the/farming/in/will

....

d. Aware/everyone/footprint/measures/carbon/should/its/impact/their/be/decrease/take/and/to/of

....

e. Gas/environmental/curb/to/respect/oil/should/standards/greenhouse/new/companies/the

....

TRAINING
EXAMS
EXERCISES
INTERNSHIP

Vocabulary

7 Global issues

Assess (v): *évaluer*
balanced trade (n): *échange équilibré*
be compatible with (vb): *en adéquation avec/ compatible*
be instrumental in (v): *contribuer à*
benefit from (v): *tirer profit de*
bilateral and/or multilateral agreements (n): *accords bilatéraux/multilatéraux*
border (n): *une frontière*
boundaries (n): *limite/frontières*
brexit campaign (n): *campagne pour le Brexit*
brexiteer (n): *Britannique pro Brexit*
cap exports (vb): *mettre un plafond/limiter les exportations*
comprehensive (adj): *exhaustif*
design new regulatory systems (vb): *élaborer un système réglementaire/des législations réglementaires*
digital trade (n): *échanges commerciaux facilités par le numérique*
dispute settlement (n): *résolution des conflits*
domestic issues (n): *problèmes/questions nationales*
dutyfree (n): *sans taxes douanières*
economic damage (n): *dégâts économiques*
economic recovery (n): *reprise économique*
emerging sectors (n): *nouveaux secteurs d'activité*
enter into force (v): *entrer en vigueur*
exert influence (v): *exercer son influence*
expel (v): *expulser*
exploratory talks (n): *négociations*
free trade commitment (n): *engagement en faveur du libre échange*
FTAs (Free Trade Agreement(s)): *accord de libre échange*
gain achievements (v): *obtenir des réalisations*
government procurement (n): *marché public*
growth (n): *croissance*
implement a deal (v): *mettre en place un accord*
impose duties on imports (vb): *imposer des taxes à l'importation*
impose/lift sanctions (v): *imposer/lever des sanctions*
Incentive (n): *incitation*
key issue (n): *question clé*
lawsuits (n): *actions en justice*
like-minded (adj): *qui est sur la même longueur d'ondes/qui partage les mêmes valeurs*
migrant (n): *immigré*
mischaracterize (v): *donner une image fausse/ erronée*
open up the market (v): *ouvrir son marché*
partnership (n): *partenariat*
protectionist measures (n): *mesures protectionnistes*
pull out of a deal (vb): *se désengager*
put in jeopardy (vb): *mettre en danger*
recover from (v): *se rétablir de*
regenerate (v): *régénérer/redynamiser*
regulatory practices (n): *pratiques réglementaires*
relevant assets (n): *atouts appropriés*
reliant (adj): *dépendant*
relocating/relocation (n): *délocalisation*
relocating/re-shoring (n): *s'implanter sur son territoire national*
reluctantly (adv): *avec réticence/à contre cœur*
remainer (n): *Britannique anti Brexit*
run counter (v): *aller à l'encontre*
self-sufficient (adj): *autosuffisant/indépendant*
Shape new Brexit regulations (vb): *réécrire la législation européenne*
small and medium-sized companies (n): *petites et moyennes entreprises*
sovereignty (n): *souveraineté*
take steps (v): *prendre des mesures*
tariff barriers (n): *barrières douanières*
the dairy market (n): *marché laitier*
the EU member-states (n): *les Etats membres de l'EU*
the European legal order (n): *la législation européenne*
the New Normal (n): *la nouvelle normalité 60*

the Northern Ireland Protocol (n): *Le protocole de l'Irlande du Nord*
the withdrawal agreement (v): *l'accord de retrait*
think out of the box (vb): *penser en dehors des sentiers battus*
trade war (n): *guerre commerciale*
US customs (n): *douanes américaines*
USCMA (US- Canada-Mexico Agreement): *Accords nord-américains*
windfall (n): *aubaine, une manne*
withdraw (v): *se retirer*

1 Complete the sentences with one of the words below.

Goods/shortages/pandemic/around/oversupply/picked up/containers

a. Some suppliers still have too few .... to sell, there will be others with too many.

b. Everything was about .... in 2021.

c. Once the demand had been satisfied, there was suddenly an ....

d. Demand for cars .... again a few months later, there were not enough chips to go around.

e. Shipping .... move some 1.9 billion tonnes per year by sea alone

f. A typical container now spends 20% longer in transit than before the ....

g. Even a 10% increase in container freight rates can reduce industrial production by .... 1%.

2 The sentences are jumbled up. Rewrite them in the right order.

a. He says/twice the amount of/than the US does/with the region's 10 economies/China now conducts/trade/-£650 billion worth.

....

b. Laos/there's/train/a new high speed/in.

....

c. Southeast Asia/to strengthen/with/the US/is working/ties.

....

d. The leaders/in five years/of the US, Mexico and Canada/for the first North American summit/are meeting.

....

e. Are now returning to Iraq/had been trying/to get into the European Union/hundreds of migrants who/from Belarus.

....

f. And what/ foreign countries/should/in ending the crisis in Sudan/play/?

....

3 Match the words with the definition: the words are on the opposite page.

a. An unexpected reward or gain: ....

b. When two countries agree on decisions concerning trade: ....

c. What separate countries: ....

d. Somebody from Britain who wanted to leave the EU: ....

e. Whatever you exchange online is part of it: ....

f. Problems related to your country: ....

g. When somebody is kicked out of the country: ....

h. When you are involved in easing exchanges between countries: ....

i. People who think the same: ....

j. People who make the decision to cross the border to improve their life: ....

4 Find out words that have the same roots.

Ex: **job: jobless, joblessness, jobber, and jobseeker**

a. Applicant: ....

b. Work: ....

c. Settle: ....

d. Damage: ....

e. Domestic: ....

TRAINING EXAMS EXERCISES INTERNSHIP

INTERNSHIP

1 Faire un CV (CV *and/or resume*)

Un CV (curriculum vitae) est un document qui se modifie au fil des années et qui se modifie aussi en fonction de l'entreprise à qui vous le soumettez. Il doit permettre d'être lu rapidement et de montrer votre expérience professionnelle ainsi que vos qualifications. N'oubliez pas les activités périscolaires qui priment chez les employeurs anglo-saxons.

Your name
Address
Country
Phone
Email

Career Objective
To obtain an entry-level position in international trade utilising my language skills in Spanish and Russian

Education
2018-2020: Victorine H Business School, France
BTS CI (2-year technical diploma in International Commerce)
2015-2018: Lycée XXXXX, France
Economics and Social Studies Baccalaureate (A-level/High School Diploma)

Work Experience
2019: A 2-month work placement at Louis Vuitton, NYC. Prospecting clients in the USA by mail and phone; designing a leaflet for the summer season and writing a questionnaire for retailers in American department stores to improve our visibility.
2018: A 2-month summer job at the local bakery. Handling the cash register, taking orders and organising delivery at weddings, summer festivals.
2017: A 2-month summer job at a summer camp that enrolled children and managed recreational facilities. Managing a team and programming activities.

Languages
French: Mother tongue
Spanish: Mother tongue
Russian: European Level B1 (intermediate)

IT skills
Excel, Word, PowerPoint and Sage

Interests
Sports: Aikido instructor
Volunteer work as a firefighter, reading, cinema and drama (in a drama club for 10 years)
References available upon request

Info Dans votre CV :
- ⊘ pas de photo ;
- ⊘ pas de nationalité ;
- ⊘ pas de date de naissance.

Tips → Le CV donne les grandes lignes de vos activités professionnelles. Notez que vous utiliserez des verbes en -ING pour introduire les tâches accomplies, ex : *handling customer queries, scheduling activities according to age groups*.

Method

When applying for a training course, a work placement or a job, a well-organised and well-presented CV is important.

In some countries like the US there are two different types of document: – a resume is a one-page summary of your work experience in relation to the job you're applying for – whereas a CV is longer as it includes all your experience and lists much more information.

In both cases, there are rules to follow.

1 Comply with the layout codes

- The CV should fit on one page (only one side) and if possible on white paper.
- Use a classical and readable font. Pick the right font size (14pt for section titles, 11pt for normal text). Use consistent formatting for dates.
- Prioritize the information but limit the number of levels.
- Do not write "Curriculum Vitae" at the top of your CV.
- Do not use too many colours, it would be difficult to decipher and wouldn't be attractive.
- Comply with usual layout rules: headings levels, space between sections and so on...
- Save your CV as PDF (so that the format will not change when printed).

2 There is no perfect CV

- There's no perfect type for a CV but there are many templates that can correspond to you.
- CV templates vary according to countries.
- A good CV must sum up your career path in one page so you have to say a lot in a few words.
- A CV is a complement to your motivation letter.

3 Express yourself correctly

Check your spelling and expression: it is essential.

Be careful about your language level.

2 Faire un CV – Practise Part 1

For your BTS, you have to write your CV to apply for a training course or a work placement. Prepare your educational and professional background assessment by filling the following grid.

	Period of time	The tasks you performed	Positive points	Difficulties
School studies				
High School studies (BTS)				
Work experience (training periods, part-time jobs...)				
Personal / leisure activities				

Practise Part 2

1. Prepare a sketch or a draft of your CV.
2. Write your CV on your computer.
3. Format your CV according to the guidelines below (the layout is only an example: it helps to organise sections).

	Photo (not compulsory)	**FULL NAME** Address Phone number | Email address
	Personal profile statement	
	Education	
(timeline)	....	• .... • ....
	Work experience	
(timeline)	....	• .... • ....
	Skills	
	Languages	• ....
	Computer	• ....
	Hobbies and interests	
		• ....

3 Rédiger une lettre de demande de stage ou de candidature spontanée

Pour mettre toutes les chances de votre côté, il faut, au préalable, faire un travail de recherche sur l'entreprise à qui vous allez envoyer votre lettre. Dans votre courrier, vous joindrez votre CV et vous indiquerez pourquoi cette entreprise vous permettrait de mettre en pratique vos connaissances. Vous montrerez que vous connaissez l'entreprise, que ce courrier n'est pas un hasard.

My NAME
My ADDRESS
Phone number
Email address

DATE

COMPANY'S ADDRESS

Name of the person you are writing to
Her/his title
Name of the company

Dear Mrs O'Leary/Dear Sir/Madam,

LOOKING FOR A WORK PLACEMENT

I am a first/second year student preparing a post-baccalaureate degree specialised in small and medium-sized companies at the Lycée .... in Gennevilliers. Part of the curriculum is based on a work placement that I have to carry out from the beginning of May to the end of June.
I would like very much to gain work experience with a local company that would give me the opportunity to use my skills.
Your company appeals to me as you are a small, progressive firm where there may be opportunities to work as part of a team on various projects. A student from our school recommended your company where she was fortunate to obtain a placement in the past. She spoke highly of her work placement and mentioned that your company gave her the possibility to use and develop her skills.
As you will see from my enclosed CV, I believe I have the necessary skills to contribute to your company.
Previously I had a summer job at the company................................ where I learned to supervise a team.
I believe it has enabled me to learn communication and organisation skills.
I am available for an interview to discuss my qualifications in relation to a potential placement with you.
I thank you in advance for considering my application.
I look forward to hearing from you.

Yours sincerely/Yours faithfully,

Name

Signature

Method

When applying for a training course, a work placement or a job, a cover letter or a motivation letter are necessary. There are rules to follow.

1 Difference between a cover letter and a motivation letter

A cover letter is an introductory letter that you address to a manager in response to an advertised job in his company. A motivation letter (or "letter of interest") is an introductory letter too but you address it to a HRM (Human Resources Manager) in an organization that may not have a job available at the moment. In many countries, the content is not different.

2 Comply with the layout codes

The letter should fit on one A4 white page (only one side).

Write in black ink, in straight lines (you can use guide lines under your sheet of paper).

Use a simple to read, regular font (size 10pt or 12pt).

Type the letter if you send it by mail (as PDF). Otherwise write it by hand.

Follow the rules of presentation used for writing letters (date, heading signature...).

3 Organise the structure

Write three paragraphs: the introduction, the body and the conclusion.

4 Express yourself correctly

Check your spelling and expression: it is essential.

Be careful about your language level.

Use short sentences.

4 Rédiger une lettre de demande de stage ou de candidature spontanée – Practise Part 1

For your BTS, you have to write a motivation letter to apply for a training course or a work placement.

1 Prepare your training assessment by filling the following grid.

	What I know	Qualities required	My assets and my know-how
Enterprise/ service	……………… ………………	……………… ………………	……………… ………………
The type of job I seek	……………… ………………	……………… ………………	……………… ………………
The type of missions	……………… ………………	……………… ………………	……………… ………………

2 Take the Personality traits test. Then write your letter, complying by the rules given.

Your basic contact information as in your CV.	**FULL NAME** ……………… ………………
Date	
Contact details	To:
Introduction	………………
Body	……………… ……………… ……………… ………………
Conclusion	………………
(Request a meeting)	
Closing formula	
Signature	

In order to prepare your motivation letter, take this personality test filling the following grid.

Personality traits

Ambition

- ❑ Most of the time, I am satisfied with what I have.
- ❑ I am ready to give the best of myself in order to succeed.
- ❑ I am motivated but I don't have any precise long-term goal.

Self-confidence

- ❑ I often doubt about myself and my skills.
- ❑ I only move to the foreground if I feel allowed to do so.
- ❑ I am generally self-assured.

Care, reliability, rigour

- ❑ I am not really careful, I like doing things fast.
- ❑ I take my time to get things right.
- ❑ I like getting to the bottom of things. I am a perfectionist.

Sense of initiative

- ❑ I am rather careful. I need to know where I am going.
- ❑ I like to innovate but I need to anticipate.
- ❑ I rather like new situations and taking risks.

Spirit of dialogue

- ❑ I usually stick to my ideas.
- ❑ I can easily change my point of view.
- ❑ I rarely have a clear-cut opinion.

Listening skill

- ❑ I do not like being influenced. I like to decide by myself.
- ❑ I like to listen to other people's point of view. I like dialogue.
- ❑ I sometimes lose track of what I wanted to say or do.

Independence

- ❑ I like being supervised.
- ❑ Most of the time, I can do with what I know.
- ❑ I like to prove I can do things alone.

Self-control, stress tolerance

- ❑ I am rather anxious as to what others expect.
- ❑ I am usually able to step back when necessary.
- ❑ I am very calm most of the time.

Sense of organization

- ❑ I am not very organised, I rely on intuitions.
- ❑ I always follow the work methods I am given.
- ❑ I am able to develop a complex organization.

Decision-making abilities

- ❑ I often hesitate. I don't really like choosing.
- ❑ I need to take my time to think before choosing.
- ❑ Generally speaking I make good decisions quickly.

Availability, punctuality

- ❑ « Always be on time »: this is worth for me and everybody else.
- ❑ A few extra minutes won't matter.
- ❑ The most important thing is to get the job done.

Methods

- ❑ I get mentally prepared before I start working.
- ❑ I usually get immediately confronted with what I have to do.
- ❑ I navigate between theory and practise.

Self-control, touchiness

- ❑ I get angry easily.
- ❑ I am a peaceful easy-going person.
- ❑ I can make efforts to remain calm, but it sometimes shows.

Team spirit

- ❑ I need to work alone and to get organised by myself.
- ❑ I enjoy dialogue and cooperation.
- ❑ I adapt easily to any situation.

5 Rédiger un rapport de stage

Part 1

A. How I found the company where I carried out my work placement

– It took me quite a lot of time to find a company that was interested in having a trainee.
– I was helped in my internship search by my teacher.
– I secured a work placement interview and met with my tutor.
– The job interviewer wanted to find out if I would be a keen trainee.

Part 2

B. Presenting the company

– The company is located in (place).
– It is a small company run by the (name) family.
– The company was founded in (year) by (name).
– The company activity is to provide hospitals, clinics and pharmacies with medical equipment.
– Their main supplier is located in Switzerland.
– The company has specialised in (name of items).
– The CEO is (name), Mr/s (name) is the Human Resources Manager ; etc.

Part 3

C. The tasks I was responsible for

– I was in charge of setting up appointments with suppliers and clients.
– My task was to double check that orders placed by our customers had been forwarded to our transport company to be delivered on the date stated on the order form.
– One of my assignments was to go through the emails, answer the most urgent ones, and forward the others to my mentor.
– Sorting out the mail when it arrived and bringing it to the relevant department was a daily activity.
– Once I had to organise a meeting with the heads of every department to draw up a work schedule for a special project that needed to be completed within three weeks.
– I had to deal with angry clients or unhappy suppliers.
– I had to call companies that had not settled their invoices.

Part 4

D. Point of view

– I like the company where I was a trainee. First, my colleagues were very helpful; second, they let me take initiatives and third, I could interrupt them, they would always listen to my inquiries.
– However, it was sometimes a little dull as I started the day with the emails, then I sorted the letters, and I really started working on my project late in the morning.
– I wish I had had an extra week to finish my project.

Tips
→ Faites un plan en quatre grandes parties que vous suivrez.
→ Ajoutez des documents de l'entreprise.
→ Votre présentation doit durer 2 minutes.

Method

At the end of a working placement you have to write a report. It will be assessed by a jury. Once again there are rules to follow.

1 Comply with the layout codes

The title page must include your name, your form, the name of the company you have worked for and the dates of the training period.

Number the pages of the report. Use a readable font.

Do not forget a detailed numbered table of contents.

Append long documents such as catalogues, press articles, estimates...)

Number appendices and give them a title.

2 Organise the structure and content

The structure must be clear, with titles and subtitles. Try to balance the different parts.

Write distinct paragraphs and connect them using transitions.

Write your report with professional and technical terms.

Make complete sentences. Be careful about your language level, the syntax and your spelling.

3 Organise your report

The structure	The content
Introduction	Tell about the context and the goals of the training course. Present the structure of your report.
Company	I. Present the company and its market 1. Tell briefly about its history and its line of business. 2. Present the financial aspects: type of company, sales figures, market share... 3. Analyse the company's offerings and market. 4. Draw the organization chart of the company.
Body	I. Describe your mission(s) 1. Your tasks and goals 2. How you carried out your missions 3. The problems you encountered II. Personal and professional assessment Present the positive and negative aspects of your training course Tell about what you learnt.
Conclusion	Give your impressions after this training course. Explain your future prospects.

6 Rédiger un rapport de stage – Practise Part 1

For your BTS, you have to write a report after a working placement.

The introduction in your report is particularly important since it is what the jury will read first.

Write this introduction according to the indications in the margin.

1 Start by presenting...

- what led you to this placement (BTS)
- the professional context (company, line of business...)

2 Tell about the goals of the placement.

3 Present the structure of your report.

In order to prepare your report, here is a grid you can complete with the notes you took down during your training course. This grid is a synthesis: you don't need to write full sentences, you can simply jot down the key details and ideas using dashes or bullets to make a list.

1 The company and its market

	Key ideas
1. Short history / line of business	
2. Financial aspects: type of company, sales figures, evolution, market share...	
3. Analysis of the company's offerings and market: their know-how, market positioning, their image, their marketing strategies, their customer base	
4. Organization chart of the company	

2 Describe your mission(s)

	Key ideas
1. Your tasks and goals	
2. How you carried out your missions	
3. The problems you encountered and the results you achieved	

3 Personal and professional assessment

	Key ideas
1. Positive points: technical, methodological and human benefits	
2. Negative points: professional and relational difficulties	

7 Mener un exposé oral

Method

Whether at school or at work, you may have to report orally. It is important to know how to do so well.

1 Get prepared

Organise what you are going to say, develop a clear structure. Think of a precise timing.
Choose the right visual material for your notes:
Do not write on the two sides of your sheets of paper.
Only write key ideas: do not write complete sentences.
Colour-code your notes: for example, key ideas in green, examples in blue...
Practise presenting orally your report before the D-Day and check the time.

2 Use visual supports for your presentation

You can use the white board or the digital board to write key-words, definitions, references...
Do not forget to prepare a document you will pass out with your detailed plan on it.
Prepare your PowerPoint presentation carefully: one slide = one idea
Avoid too much written text. Prefer visual elements. Use dashes or bullets to list your points.
Choose a clear layout. Leave blank space. Avoid too dark a background.
Check your spelling.

3 Work on speaking in front of others

Do not sit down.
Face the audience.
Speak clearly and loud enough. Vary your voice.
If you give your presentation with other students or colleagues, do not forget to allocate the roles beforehand.

7 Mener un exposé oral – Practise Part 1

1. Either alone or in a group choose a subject and look for information you'll report orally.
2. Build and write down the structure.
3. Prepare your presentation using the grid below.
4. Practise orally and time your speech.

Structure	Duration and roles allocation	Visual documents	Key ideas and references
Introduction – – – **Part I**: .... 1) – – – 2) – – – 3) – – – **Part II**: .... 1) – – – 2) – – – 3) – – – **Conclusion** – – –			

TRAINING EXAMS EXERCICES INTERNSHIP

Cartes

English as a world language

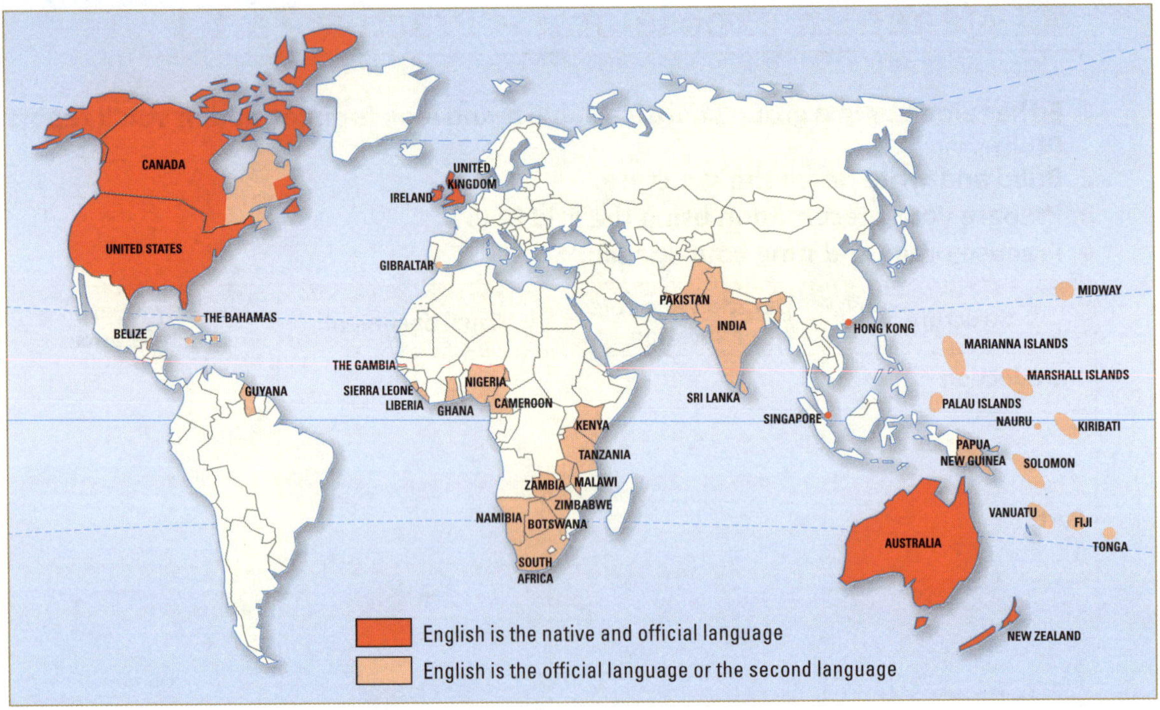

The United Kingdom: geography

The Republic of Ireland

The United Kingdom: economy

- ▲ (orange) Most dynamic urban centres.
- ▲ (grey) Urban centres undergoing regeneration.
- Main North Sea oil and gas fields. Since 1980, Britain has kept increasing the amount of energy it produces thanks to its offshore gas and oil fields. But these supplies are now diminishing and Britain is looking for alternative sources of energy.
- Coastal areas whose economy was boosted by North Sea oil and gas production.
- The South-East, with its fast-growing and booming economy, and low unemployment (mainly finance and service industries).
- Areas in the process of adapting to new technologies. These are areas which were affected by the decline of traditional manufacturing industry (textile, steel, iron, ship-building and coal-mining), mainly in the Midlands, Scotland and South Wales. They are now beginning to be revitalized thanks to new businesses (e.g. high technology, banking, insurance, catering...).
- Intensive agriculture.
- Main fish-farming area (trout and salmon).
- More marginal regions.

Members of the Commowealth

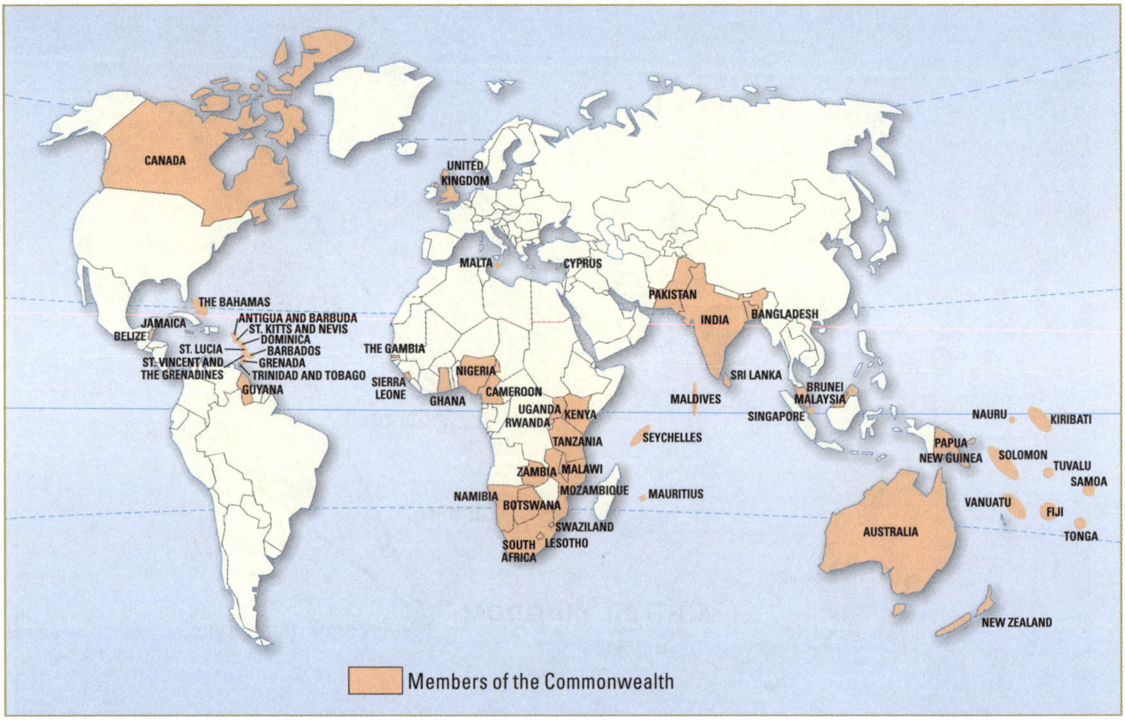

Australia

New Zealand

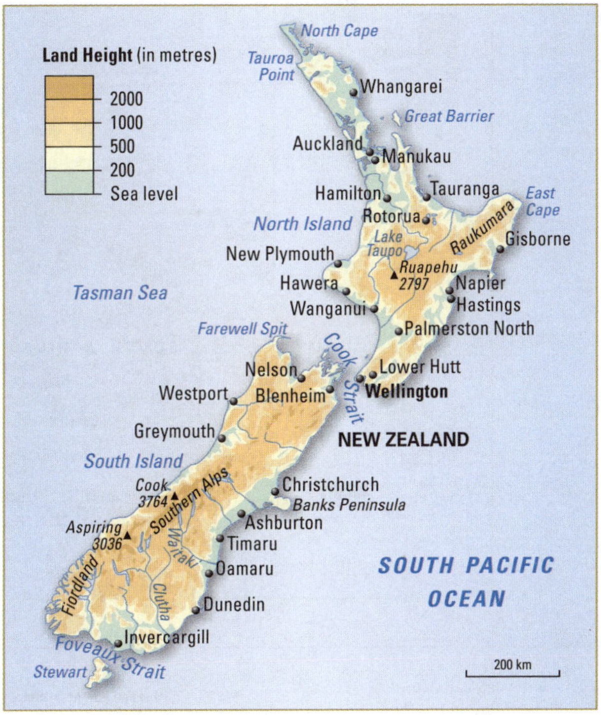

Canada

Cartes

South Africa

India

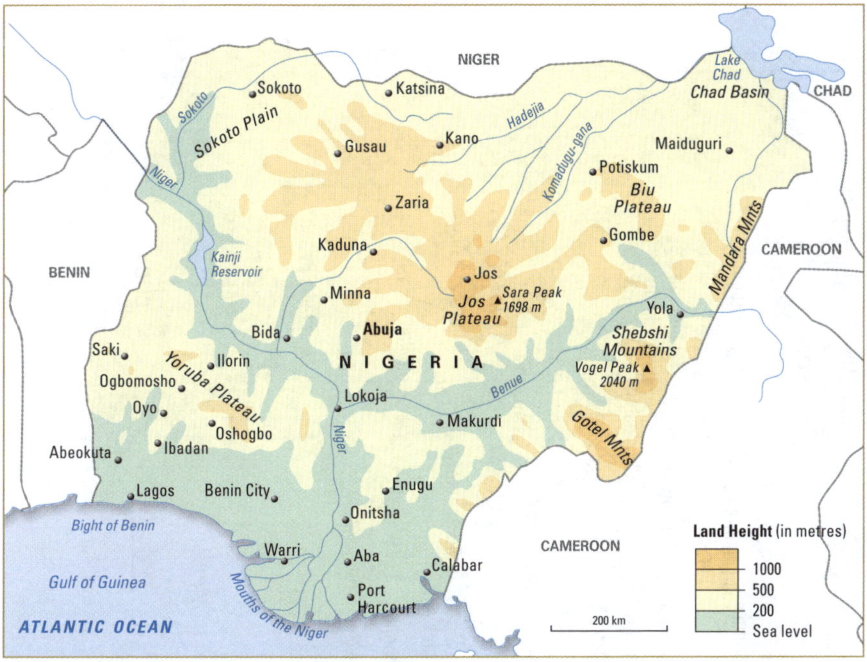

Nigeria

Jamaica

Cartes

The United States: geography

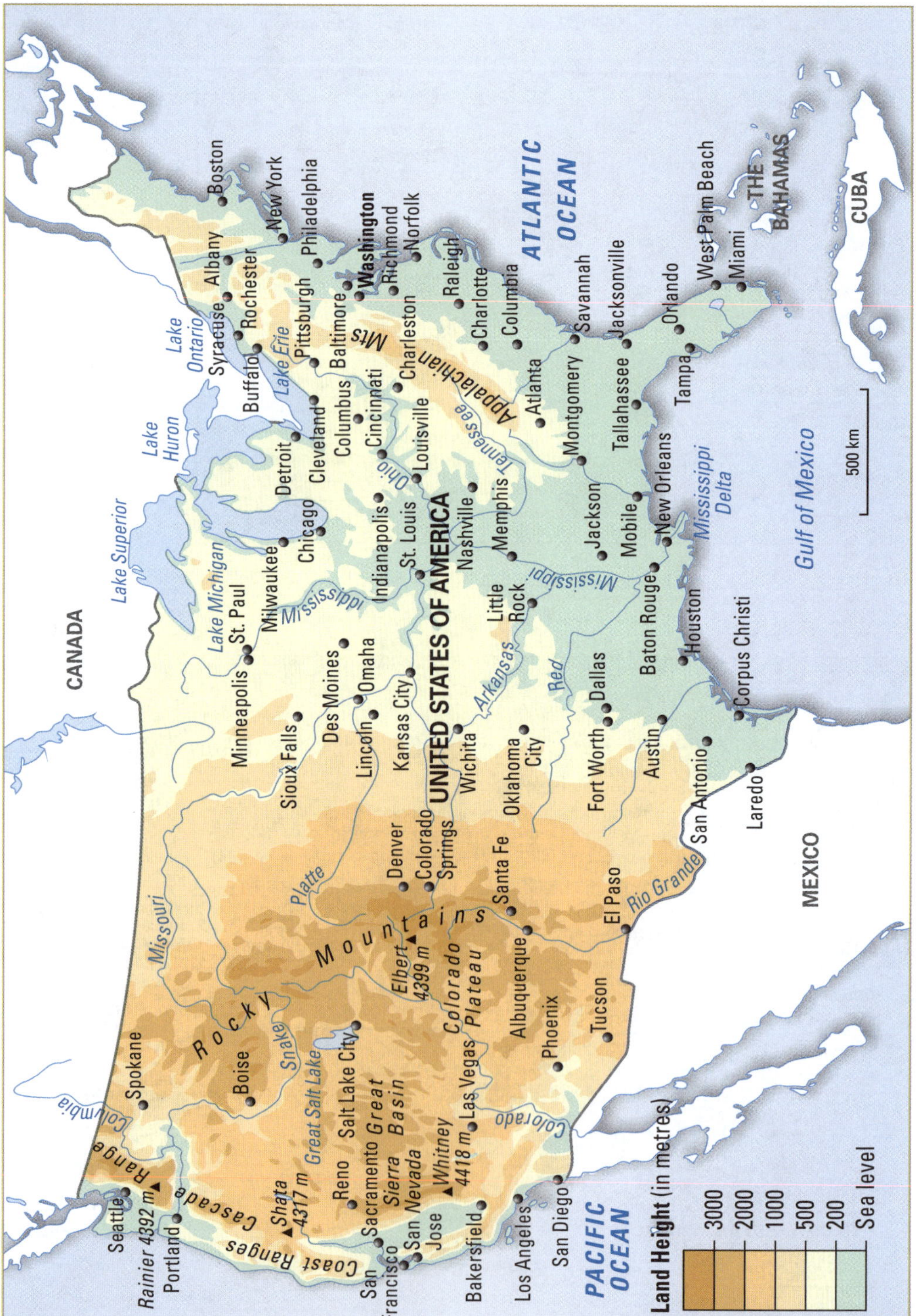

The 50 states

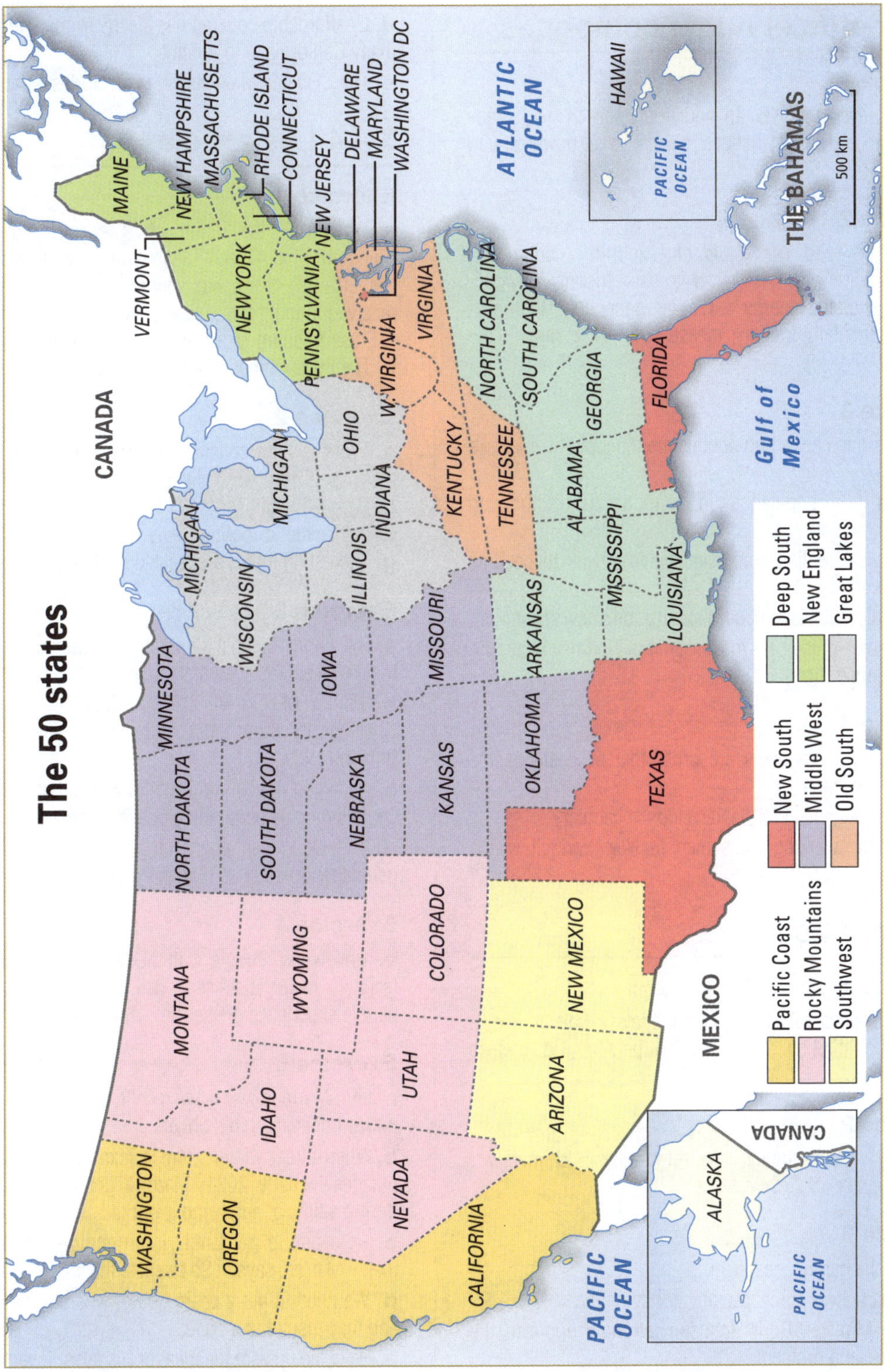

Grammar Corrigés

1 Adjectifs et noms composés

Exercice 1

a. A blue-eyed boy; **b.** an hour-long speech; **c.** a red-haired man; **d.** a left-handed baker; **e.** a power-driven president.

Exercice 2

a. Hybrid-powered cars ; **b.** oil exporting countries ; **c.** a Covid-induced crisis ; **d.** a user friendly device ; **e.** solar-generated energy ; **f.** solar generated factories ; **g.** environmentally-friendly measures ; **h.** a large-scale strategy.

Exercice 3

a. Dark-skinned elves and hobbits are the topic of amazon's new series.

b. Foreign-born populations in the uk are decreasing with brexit.

c. Work visa holding europeans go to the uk to become seasonal workers.

d. Non-white actors are chosen for amazon's new adaptation.

e. Enjoy some of the UK's most scenic rail journey including a steam-hauled trip.

Exercice 4

a. These food producers are proof that neccesity is the mother of invention.

b. The online game, Wordle, develops vocabulary.

c. For many working class men in New York, it was a revolution

2 Adverbes

Exercice 1

a. A smokeless tobacco ; **b.** an ageless beauty ; **c.** a powerless institution ; **d.** a skillful person ; **e.** tireless person.

Exercice 2

a. Warily ; **b.** faithfully ; **c.** reluctantly ; **d.** merely ; **e.** heartily.

Exercice 3

a. Today she hardly goes there.

b. They had never purchased any goods online.

c. Prime Minister, Boris Johnson, strongly opposed the Northern Ireland protocol.

d. Unaffordable housing has clearly triggered the coming of many Californians to Austin.

e. The CEO had often visited the factories of her company.

3 – 4 Les articles

Exercice 1

a. President Joe Biden; **b.** The queen of the United Kingdom; **c.** Queen Elizabeth II; **d.** France; **e.** The Netherlands; **f.** she was sent evidence of his guilt; **g.** she received good news; **h.** Do not forget to take luggage; **i.** Press freedom is a right; **j.** The Obama Administration; **k.** The 2022 Chines Olympic games.

Exercice 2

a. Work is time-consuming ; **b.** A good job is for some a well-paid job ; **c.** Politics is being able to compromise ; **d.** Domestic politics is different from international politics ; **e.** Pat made a politic reply ; **f.** Tim is good at art ; **g.** Interesting topics are tackled by the news.

Exercice 3

a. The world's biggest corporations have found an agreement to take measures against the rise of the sea level.

b. Pankaj Mishra will talk to Guardian columnist Aditya Chakrabortty about India, globalisation and his new novel, Run and Hide.

c. An expert in economic affairs writes that a major conflict could seriously derail the global economy.

d. The world can count on the highly motivated young generation to address human rights issues.

Exercice 4

a. Brexit ; **b.** People with ADHD ; **c.** Hoarding disorder leads to major distress ; **d.** Evidence does indicate that people experience greater problems ; **e.** There is a link.

Exercice 5

a. Lino Marreno was leaving cello practice one day when he noticed blisters on his fingers.

b. When a freak winter storm in Texas caused massive power outages in early 2021, Marrero got to test his invention during a time of need, and it worked.

c. « No one in my family is an engineer or anything like that, » Marrero says. « So I went to the library, I went online. »

d. We need to get a chain going, where I inspire someone and they inspire someone.

e. He came up with the idea for his latest invention.

Exercice 6

a. True ; **b.** False : Vice President Kamala Harris fights for justice alongsie journalist Helen Zia ; **c.** True : Youth can make a difference ; **d.** False : Her maternal great-grandmothe, a political activist in Korea, is her personal hero ; **e.** True ; **f.** False You should treat everyone with respect and Kindness ; **g.** False : He believes that real change is in legislative action ; **h.** True ; **i.** False : He launched a collective of middle-school activists.

Exercice 7

a. Comme la plupart des adolescents, elle a le chic/la technique/le coup avec les réseaux sociaux.

b. J'ai pris la parole/j'ai parlé de l'avenir de l'éducation.

c. Elle veut réglementer le harcèlement sur Internet.

d. Quel est le prochain projet pour l'année à venir ?

e. Cela a été un grand tourbillon/une grande tornade d'émotions.

5 Auxiliaire modal *can/could*

Exercice 1

a. I am sorry but I couldn't attend yesterday's meeting.

b. The delivery may have been delayed because of the transport strike.

c. May I ask you a question ?

d. I'm sorry, I can't drive, I haven't got a driving license.

e. The CEO might decide to raise the salaries, but it's quite unlikely.

Exercice 2

a. Unsatisfied employees can ask their trade unions for advice.

b. Because of the metro strike, many people won't be able to go to work tomorrow.

c. The customs were able to seize one thousand counterfeit watches last week.

d. I'm afraid I won't be able to travel to the USA.

e. If you have reached your targets, you will be able to get a pay raise.

Exercice 3

a. Les employés mécontents peuvent demander conseil à leur syndicat.

b. À cause de la grève du métro, beaucoup de gens ne pourront pas aller travailler demain.

c. Les douanes ont pu saisir un millier de montres de contrefaçon la semaine derrière.

d. J'ai bien peur de ne pas pouvoir me rendre aux États Unis.

e. Si vous avez atteint vos objectifs, vous pourrez demander une augmentation de salaire.

6 Auxiliaire modal *may/might*

Exercice 1

a. The employees may go on strike to protest against their working conditions.

b. The CEO wasn't able to answer the journalist's questions.

c. We won't be able to reduce global warming before the next century.

d. May I ask you to wait here for a few minutes ?

e. The ice cap might have melted more than what the experts had predicted.

Exercice 2

a. Customers may change their habits after the pandemic.

b. Children can't own a credit card.

c. This deal couldn't be fairer.

d. We will ask the cashier if we may pay with a check.

e. He is sitting too far away, he won't be able to hear the speaker.

7 Auxiliaire modal *must*

Exercice 1

a. I must go to the dentist's.

b. The meeting has not started yet. There must be a problem.

c. When I worked at Tesco, I had to arrive 30 minutes before the opening of the supermarket.

d. I must not wear a face mask at the cinema now.

e. I will have to arrive at the airport 2 hours before boarding the plane.

Exercice 2

a. They must not smoke in that building.

b. British people should have known that Brexit would make their life harder.

c. With a Republican Senate, President Biden must know his bill won't pass.

d. Schools ought to be peaceful places.

8 Auxiliaire modal *should* et expression du conseil

Exercice 1

a. Online buyers should/had better beware of credit card phishing.

b. Packaging should/had better respect the environment.

c. Companies should/had better pay their employees a living wage.

d. If they want to restore their brand image they should/had better change their advertising campaign.

e. If you xant to make profits, you should/had better invest in AI companies.

Exercice 2

a. You should work less/you had better work less/I advise you to work less/you oght to work less.

b. You should arrive on time for your appointments/you ought to be on time.../you had better be on time.../I advise you to be on time...

c. You should answer/meet your customers needs/ You ought to answer.../ You had better answer.../ I advise you to answer

Exercice 3

a. He should stop smoking.

b. She had better be on time.

c. The Head of the school advises parents to spend time talking to their kids/children.

d. You ought not to be late.

e. She should have noticed it.

Exercice 4

a. He should help her much more.

b. They should really work hard at school/they should do their homework to improve their marks.

c. We should take the time to visit her.

d. He had better start working.

e. You ought to be on time/You ought to dress up.

9 Comparatifs

Exercice 1

a. The Covid-19 pandemic has had more impact on the world's economy than the 2008 great recession.

b. Wind farms produce much more energy when the wind blows.

c. Trading with the UK is slower than when the UK was a EU member state.

d. Higher demand for natural gas will impact energy prices.

e. Nuclear power plants will be built more rapidly now that oil prices have gone up.

Exercice 2

a. Electric vehicles are less polluting but less autonomous than regular cars.

b. Employees have been on strike to earn better salaries.

c. Sweatshops in Dacca are known for being more exploitative than factories in the western world.

d. California is experiencing more and more wild fires and higher and higher housing prices, so californians are leaving.

e. Austin in Texas has attracted more people as renting is cheaper than in california.

10 Complément du nom et cas possessif

Exercice 1

a. St Valentine's Day ; **b.** Yesterday's newspaper ; **c.** In two weeks›time **d.** A bachelor›s degree in law **e.** My little sister's red Pullover ; **f.** Jane Austen's novel ; **g.** St Patrick's Day ; **h.** Every school's decision.

Exercice 2

a. Right; **b.** right; **c.** right; **d.** wrong: the Clinton administration is most common; **e.** wrong: the London Olympic games.

11 Conditionnel *if* clauses

Exercice 1

a. Si elle avait le temps, elle visiterait la Californie.

b. S'ils avaient eu le savoir-faire, ils auraient produit ce nouveau produit.

c. S'il pleut, je prendrai mon parapluie.

d. Elle aurait été incapable d'aller à Genève, si elle n'avait pas emprunté la voiture de sa meilleure amie.

e. Elle n'aurait pu se rendre à Genève si elle n'empruntait pas la voiture de sa meilleure amie.

Exercice 2

a. If demand was lower, energy prices would not have increased.

b. Consumers would have consumed more during Covid-19 if they had not been in lockdown.

c. If Nord-Stream 2 operated, Germany would meet its demand.

d. Re-locating manufacturing will be implemented if it means that it is less costly.

e. Remote working will be considered a good solution especially if employees have a long commute.

Exercice 3

a. If Lucie was broke, she would take any job available.

b. If Tony had not broken his leg, he would have been part of the football tournament.

c. They would have visited Japan if the pandemic had not broken out.

d. Nord Stream 2 would deliver natural gas if the regulators signed the contract.

12 Discours rapporté

Exercice 1

a. She asked her at what time her job interview was.

b. They assured them that everything would go well.

c. They answered that they would be ready on time.

d. She asked her how she would go to her appointment.

e. The media outlets reported that some industries did not abide by the labour regulations.

Exercice 2

a. She told her not to be late.

b. She asked her to be on time.

c. They ask him to bring his resume at his job interview.

d. She suggested they went.

e. She ordered him to do it right away.

Exercice 3

a. Yesterday she said that she did not want to have a salary below £50,000.

b. She said that he was the boss of the company.

c. He said that he was worried for his job.

d. Two days ago Laura said that she had already maxed out her hours.

Exercice 4

a. She asked her why she had decided to change job. OR she asked her why she decided to change job.

b. His colleague asked him where he was going for the interview.

c. Her boss asked her how long her commute was.

13 *Ever* et ses composés

Exercice 1

a. CCTVs are supposed to see customers wherever they are in the store. ; **b.** With online shopping, you can place your order whenever you want and wherever you are. ; **c.** Whoever the company recruits, she or he will have to possess. ; **d.** We can meet at 10 AM or at 2 PM, whichever time best suits you. ; **e.** Wherever you go, your smartphone will track you. ; **f.** However hard you hit, this material won't break.

Exercice 2

a. Call me whenever you want.

b. Wherever you are, your computer must be connected.

c. Whatever you think, you must/have to do the job.

d. Whoever is here must answer the phone.

e. Don't think you can do whatever you like/want!

14 Expression de la fréquence

Exercice 1

a. How often must the head of department write a report?

b. How often does the company organise a trip for its staff?

c. How often do employees telework?

d. How often are trains delayed?

e. How often do staff members clock in and out?

f. How often does she start at 9?

g. How often do co-workers organize a get together?

Exercice 2

a. Generally, employees get a pay raise every two years.

b. Most people must pay their taxes once a year.

c. The price depends on how often you travel.

d. In the USA TV shows are interrupted by commercials every 20 minutes.

e. Nowadays, hurricanes happen more than twice a year.

f. 965 tons of avocados are sent every year from Mexico to the US.

g. Sea levels will rise by about a foot on average along the US coast by 2050.

Grammar Corrigés

15 Forme passive

Exercice 1

a. L'article s'intitule « La pandémie ».

b. On nous a dit que 20 personnes ont péri dans un accident de la route.

c. Trois voleurs furent arrêtés à la gare à 3 heures du matin hier.

d. La naissance du bébé de la famille royale a été couvert par tous les organes de presse.

e. On m'avait envoyé une lettre d'excuse.

Exercice 2

a. Two books were given to me.

b. Two ordinators were stolen.

c. It is reported/said that Freench people will suffer from inflation.

d. A waiter is wanted.

e. It is reported/thought that purchasing power will decrease.

Exercice 3

a. Containers are offloaded with container cranes as soon as container ships reach their final destination.

b. Container ships are met by tugs.

c. Proper preparations should be made so that the cargo loading procedure can be carried out in a quick and safe manner.

d. In case any defective lashing equipment is found it should immediately be replaced.

e. Containers are lifted off the ship two at a time by quay cranes.

Exercice 4

a. Your CV should be sent by email.

b. A promotion was obtained by Ben.

c. I was told there was a training in the first month.

d. Days off are requested by one of your employees all the time.

e. The offer will be turned down (by you).

16 Futur en *will*

Exercice 1

a. When I am 18, I will take my driving license.

b. It will cost much/ it is going to cost much.

c. As long as you are safe, they will not ask questions.

d. They will host the next olympic games/ they are going to host the next olympic games.

e. You will be on time there is a strike.

Exercice 2

a. As soon as he is hired, he will move to a new apartment.

b. If demand keeps going up, prices will rise.

c. Emma is going to double check the report.

d. In Britain the purchasing power will decline as prices increase.

e. As long as there are people of good will, wars and conflicts will be avoided.

Exercice 3

a. Unless we come to an agreement there won't be a solution.

b. They are going to write a cv and a cover letter as students are applying to business schools.

c. The American working class will /is going to suffer from not having access to affordable housing.

d. The Great Resign movement in the US will impact the labour market.

e. The pandemic in the US is going to reveal that child care centers are very expensive.

17 Gérondif

Exercice 1

a. Reading is much more pleasant than watching TV.

b. She is committed to hiring a diverse labour force.

c. Before taking the train, I double check that there is no strike.

d. Instead of going on holiday abroad, I have made the decision of going hiking.

e. By changing its one-child policy to a three-child policy, China wanted the Chinese to have bigger families.

Exercice 2

a. Right ; **b.** right ; **c.** wrong ; **d.** right ; **e.** right.

18 Indénombrables

Exercice 1

a. If there is no wind, wind farms cannot be efficient.

b. We haven't got any news about the situation.

c. If you need some advice, do not hesitate to ask your teacher.

d. This document contains a very important piece of information.

e. They had to call the police because some luggage was abandoned in the airport.

f. If you want o buy some new furniture, you have the choice between many stores.

g. Society isn't making any progress to curb global warming.

h. The airline company doesn't have any information on the next flight.

Exercice 2

a. The clerk couldn't give us much information on the product.

b. We shouldn't buy too much furniture because our office is small.

c. How many people went to the mall today?

d. They haven't got much money to spend on extras.

e. Too much news can generate stress.

Exercice 3

a. My colleague gave me /has given me much important information.

b. There is too much furniture in this room.

c. My boss gave /has given me some good advice.

d. What is the news?

e. You have to stay next to your luggage in stations and airports.

19 Pluperfect

Exercice 1

a. If they had arrived one hour earlier, they would have seen their best friend.

b. If there had not been a car industry, we would all have travelled by train.

c. Before moving to London, they had lived in New York.

d. She had bought a new apartment before she came to visit us.

e. He would always have been single if he had not met his partner.

Exercice 2

a. Cela aurait été mieux s'il n'avait rien dit.

b. Avant de prendre en compte sa lettre de candidature, elle avait rencontré un premier candidat.

c. S'il avait dit la vérité, il ne se serait pas senti si mal.

d. Elles ont eu un premier rendez-vous avant de prendre la décision finale.

e. Elle avait décidé de quitter la Californie à cause des feux d'incendie annuels.

Exercice 3

a. She said that he had had an accident.

b. The company had granted a salary rise after the strike.

c. If ever you had forgotten to call a cab, I could give you a lift.

d. You had thought that the war would not happen.

20 Préfixe et suffixe

Exercice 1

a. He is a fearless child. He does not even know he is taking risks.

b. The online company is so powerful that it has the biggest share of the market.

c. This man is heartless. He can never show any feelings for those who suffer.

d. She would reluctantly ask the company for a salary raise.

Exercice 2

a. She outdid everybody.

b. They overproduce.

c. It is understaffed or undermanned.

d. She is overwhelmed.

e. They overrule the objection.

Exercice 3

a. Powerless ; **b.** mistake ; **c.** friendly ; **d.** overcome ; **e.** overtake ; **f.** misunderstanding ; **g.** unexpected ; **h.** awake.

21 Présent simple

Exercice 1

a. What do many consumers appreciate? / Many customers don't appreciate oline shopping.

b. What are they looking for? / They aren't looking for bargains.

c. What do many companies care about? / Many companies don't care about their staff.

d. What do many brands choose to do? / Many brands don't choose to relocate.

e. Where do more and more people live? / More and more people don't live close to their workplace.

Exercice 2

a. Most products travel by sea and by air.

b. The supermarket opens every day at 9 am and closes at 6 pm.

c. China and the USA do not/don't agree and trade tariffs.

d. A computer costs less today than 10 years ago.

e. Some people don't trust new technologies.

22 Présent continu

Exercice 1

a. Stores are turning /shifting to organic products.

b. Prices are increasing /rising.

c. Online sales are dominating the market.

d. What are they doing? They are repairing the shop window.

e. Customers are rushing towards the check outs.

Exercice 2

Today, Mrs Parker is thinking of the letter she must not forget to write to her client, Mr Jones. He wants to know everything about the different products available, that is why Mrs Parker is listing all the details about the products' features. It isn't difficult for her because she knows all the brands products by heart, as she works at her desk 8 hours a day, five days a week. She takes a lunch break every day at 12 am and she always goes for a cup of tea with her co workers at 6 pm. But today, she is considering leaving earlier because she is having friends coming for dinner. She needs time to prepare a proper dinner.

23 Present perfect

Exercice 1

a. We have been following the latest news concerning the hurricane in Florida.

b. Ikea had launched a new service to help customers assemble their furniture.

c. This summer's wild fires had brought distruction in many californian towns.

Exercice 2

a. Since I was born, I have been speaking English.

b. I have waited for you for ages.

c. Since 2001 they have lived in a Spanish-Speaking country.

d. Our corporate headquarters have been in Seattle since 1994.

e. Our showroom has displayed our new technological devices since April 2022.

Exercice 3

a. This week we have published a complex but important story.

b. Decades of scandals have made clear that Swiss banks have been attracting illicit funds from tax-evaders.

c. Deciding to publish these stories has been a balancing act.

d. Previous reporting has spurred global action in favour of a fairer, more open banking.

e. It has already been in operation for 21 years.

f. NASA has given the go-ahead for one more decade.

g. The International Space Station has enabled one giant leap for science and mankind.

h. NASA has been noticing signs of infrastructure and components slowing down.

i. The pandemic has made us less, not more materialistic.

j. She has been investigating small acts of communal living.

k. This week we have been publishing a complex but important story.

l. Previous reporting has spureed global action in favour of a fairer, more open banking.

Exercice 4

a. I have been learning English for 6 years.

b. They have known each other since kindergarten.

c. It has been 5 years since he lived in Madrid/ He has lived in Madrid for 5 years.

d. He has been preparing lasagne for Sunday lunch for at least 10 years.

e. She has been working for Coca Cola for less than 2 years.

f. She has been sending application letters to find a job for a month now.

Exercice 5

a. Je parle anglais depuis que je suis née.

b. Ils ont été inculpés de malversations.

c. Cela fait presque deux heures qu'elle est partie.

d. Ils sont partis en Colombie.

e. Ils se sont acheté une nouvelle voiture. Regarde, elle est garée là-bas.

f. Je n'ai jamais été fan de marathon télé / de regarder l'intégrale d'une série.

Exercice 6

a. I have known them for 5 years – la phrase au present perfect avec *know* est fausse.

b. I have loved our hiking journey – les verbes de sentiment supportent mal la forme en ing.

c. She has enjoyed your party.

d. They have continued their journey.

e. I have started my new job.

25 Prétérit simple

Exercice 1

a. We were debating whether to make a decision or not when we heard that it was no longer necessary.

b. The CEO was listening to the shareholders concerns while the meeting with the finance department went on.

c. When they agreed to our terms, we felt so happy.

d. The new applicant was meeting with the human resources manager when we found out that the position had been filled.

e. When the merger negotiations started we were still preparing the financial details of the report.

Exercice 2

a. While solar panels were creating enough shade to help the soil retain vital moisture, they produced electricity.

b. Last year California suffered its worst megadrought in 1,200 years.

c. Wolves were eradicated from many areas of Europe in the 19th century.

d. R. Nixon and Mao Zedong met on Feb 21, 1972.

Exercice 3

a. They were lading containers when there was an accident.

b. While they were writing their application letter, their co-workers were making phone calls.

c. When they made the decision, it was already too late.

d. President Joe Biden introduced the Build Back Better plan but it was supported by the Senate.

e. The 2022 winter Olympic Games were a real success.

f. As he sat on the soccer field, he was thinking back to what his teacher had said about renewable-energy sources.

g. Sama placed job ads in countries across Africa looking for people who could speal African languages.

h. Sama employees stood a better chance of having their demand me by acting as a group.

Exercice 4

a. Alors que la société négociait les derniers détails, le personnel était en grève.

b. Ils finissaient/mettaient la dernière main à des taches d'importance tandis que le/la directeur/rice du marketing rencontrait son homologue.

c. Quand je suis entré dans l'entreprise, les employés ne travaillaient pas dans les mêmes locaux.

d. Ils apprirent à la connaître alors qu'ils travaillaient sur le même projet.

e. S'ils s'arrêtaient tous de travailler, ils feraient pression sur la direction.

Exercice 5

a. She was writing her report when I met her.

b. She was not at the office yesterday. She was working remotely.

c. While a meeting via Skype was held, she was calling the travel agency.

d. While the business trip was organised, we were making our last appointments.

e. Yesterday the staff visited the nex premises of the company.

27 Pronoms personnels et possessifs

Exercice 1

a. Self-driving cars will become more and more common in the future. They will no longer be considered sci-fi devices.

b. Everybody has got their favourite means of transport.

c. Some companies think of themselves as the best.

d. To be productive when working with someone, you need to know each other well.

e. Retailers have to meet the needs of their customers.

Exercice 2

a. It is my mother's coat. It is hers. **b.** These are the company's profits. **c.** The responsibility is theirs. **d.** It is the Prime Minister's speech. **e.** The decision is theirs.

Exercice 3

a. Ils se connaissent depuis dix ans.

b. Elle se connaît bien pour savoir que ce ne sera pas facile.

c. Elle l'a fait elle-même.

d. Ils s'aiment donc ils ont décidé de se marier en juillet prochain.

28 Propositions infinitives

Exercice 1

a. The manager wants the employees to improve their results. ; **b.** Companies aren't allowed to use green washing to attract customers. ; **c.** Everybody would like their children to succeed. ; **d.** Employees would like their salaries to be higher to live better. ; **e.** It's difficult to make people stop buying unhealthy products. ; **f.** They need better qualifications to join the team. ; **g.** Motorists must slow down to avoid traffic accidents. ; **h.** We shouldn't let robots replace human beings. ; **i.** Many British people wished to remain in the EU. ; **j.** Retailers try to reconnect with their customers.

Exercice 2

a. Les entreprises veulent que leurs bénéfices augmentent tous les ans.

b. Les moins de 18 ans ne sont pas autorisés à acheter de l'alcool dans la plupart des pays.

c. Pour être sûr d'être à l'heure, vous devriez prendre le train de 7 heure.

d. Mon patron aimerait que je fasse des heures supplémentaires, mais je ne souhaite pas en faire pour le moment.

e. Laissez moi lui parler pour tenter d'éclaircir la situation.

29 Propositions subordonnées concessives

Exercice 1

a. Although many companies stopped their activities during the pandemic, they didn't go bankrupt.

b. Some car manufacturers continue to produce polluting cars despite/in spite of the new standards.

c. People continue to buy industrial food though/although they know it's unhealthy.

d. Many products are still available despite/in spite of their impact on the environment.

e. The firm's CEO has decided to downsize although the shareholders received a lot of money.

Exercice 2

a. Bien que de nombreuses entreprises aient cessé leur activité pendant la pandémie, elles n'ont pas fait faillite.

b. Certains constructeurs automobiles continuent de produire des voitures polluantes malgré les nouvelles normes.

c. Les gens continuent d'acheter de la nourriture industrielle bien qu'ils sachent que c'est mauvais pour la santé.

d. Beaucoup de produits sont encore disponibles malgré leur impact sur l'environnement.

e. Le Directeur Général de l'entreprise a décidé de réduire les effectifs bien que les actionnaires aient reçu beaucoup d'argent.

30 Quantifieurs *few/fewer, less, much/many*

Exercice 1

a. Fewer, little / autre possibilité : many, much ; **b.** much ; **c.** many, little ; **d.** a few ; **e.** much ; **f.** a few.

Exercice 2

a. Fewer ; **b.** much ; **c.** less ; **d.** few ; **e.** many ; **f.** fewer.

Exercice 3

a. Fewer and fewer childred read books ; many prefer playing with their smartphones.

b. Companies sell fewer industrial products.

c. In order to succeed, you need much money and a little luck.

d. This startup recruits as many women as men.

e. Only a few companies encourage diversity.

f. Many employees are going to be laid off because the company makes very few profits.

g. I haven't got much money on me.

h. I've got a little time left before I leave.

i. Many people are a little bit crazy !

j. How many have you bought ?

Exercice 4

a. Too many people ; **b.** Too little water is in the bottle ; **c.** How much advice would you give a job applicant ? ; **d.** How much does a Tesla cost ? ; **e.** Media outlets have not given much information about the French Presidential election. ; **f.** Too little is done for climate refugees ; **g.** I received fewer responses this year.

31 Questions fermées et ouvertes

Exercice 1

a. Q: Are you working on the invoice of our new customer ?

b. Q: Would they enjoy having lunch with us on Monday ?

c. Q: Can we make a decision about the price of this new device?

d. Q: Will they visit the new factory next Saturday?

e. Q: Did you take care of that business last Monday?

Exercice 2

a. Q: What time is your job interview?

b. Q: How much do you earn per year?

c. Q: How many candidates are on the shortlist?

d. Q: When could you start?

e. Q: Why do you want to work there?

32 Subordonnées relatives

Exercice 1

a. Joseph King is the CEO who organised yesterday's meeting with foreign investors.

b. I'm sending you all the details about this client whose insurance policy has expired.

c. We have to listen to our customers to know what they have to tell us about the product.

d. Sometimes between several products consumers do not know which one to choose.

e. The problems that many companies are faced to is the lack of skilled employees.

Exercice 2

a. The position I applied for was already taken.

b. The operator he spoke on the phone with told him to call later this afternoon.

c. The car he drives to work with is a company car.

d. The company we merged with is the leader in its field.

e. The staff members the sales manager was counting on proved to be unreliable.

33 Superlatif

Exercice 1

a. This company is the largest in the world in terms of revenue.

b. Customers always look for the best bargains or the cheapest prices.

c. Fossil fuels are among the most dangerous energies for the environment.

d. Tesco, the most famous British retailer, has had the worst sales results since it was created.

e. £50K per year is the furthest the company can pay you.

Exercice 2

a. He was the least successful sales representative, he had the worst results in the department.

b. This amazing fashion shop has the most beautiful design I have ever seen.

c. Shareholders have lost a lot of money; it is the least profitable investment of all times.

d. Tesla manufactures the cleanest cars in the world but also the most expensive.

e. Coconut based products are very good, they are the healthiest on the market.

Exercice 3

a. The largest Mall in the world opened /has opened in Dubai.

b. You will find the best coffee in town in this bar.

c. It's the most surprising news I've ever heard.

d. Solar energy is the least polluting industry.

e. The richest people in the world are the least worried for the future.

Exercice 4

a. She is the nicest sales manager I have ever met.

b. This is the most expensive endeavour ever.

c. Summer is the worst period to travel to Greece because it is much too hot.

d. Coca Cola with a cherry taste was the least successful beverage introduced to consumers.

e. Relocating manufacturing to Romania is the farthest we would want.

Exercice 5

a. La pire/plus mauvaise solution pour les salariés sera une suppression massive de postes.

b. La Chine et l'Inde sont les pays les plus peuplés du monde.

c. La manière la moins chère de voyager reste le train.

d. Les meilleurs produits ne sont pas nécessairement les plus chers.

e. À cause d'un barrage routier, le prochain village a été la destination la plus lointaine que nous ayons pu atteindre.

f. Vous devriez porter vos plus beaux vêtements pour l'entretien d'embauche.

g. Cette mission est la plus palpitante que j'aie jamais effectué.

h. Elle est la femme la plus intelligente de l'équipe et également la plus chaleureuse/sympathique/aimable.

i. Le plus beau jour de sa vie a été quand il a rejoint l'entreprise.

j. Ils embauchent toujours les salariés les plus qualifiés.

Vocabulary Corrigés

1 Customers

Exercice 1

a. Customers ; buy ; consume ; purchase.

b. Influencers ; brands ; attract ; target.

c. Spending patterns ; bargains ; discounts.

d. Spend ; layout.

e. Habits ; processed ; organic.

Exercice 2

a-4. Impulsebuyer ; **b-1.** checkout ; **c-2.** delivery ; **d-3.** household ; **e-6.** luxurybrands ; **f-7.** retailer ; **g-5.** loyalty card.

Exercice 3

a. Customers' purchase decision making process is different today.

b. They spend more time online except for groceries.

c. A good customer service answers customers' expectations.

d. Sales of disposable products are declining.

e. Customers are influenced by online reviews.

f. Most worn out clothes end up in landfills.

g. Endcaps have to attract customers.

2 Marketing, digital & distribution

Exercice 1

a. A brick and mortar ; **b.** Fast fashion ; **c.** Word of mouth ; **d.** Convenience stores.

Exercice 2

a. range ; **b.** wholesaler ; **c.** upscale ; **d.** malls ; **e.** showrooming ; **f.** high street stores ; **g.** purchasing power/spending power ; **h.** shoe box stores ; **i.** department store ; **j.** mall.

Exercice 3

Competition ; outlet ; department store ; convenience store ; target audience ; shopwindow ; layout ; packaging ; retailer ; middle range ; loyalty card ; youth oriented promotion.

3 Companies

Exercice 1

a. Downturn ; **b.** subsidiary/branch ; **c.** downsize ; **d.** conglomerate ; **e.** outsource ; **f.** challenger ; **g.** launch ; **h.** partnership ; **i.** merger ; **j.** CEO.

Exercice 2

a. Some companies relocate, others outsource some of their departments.

b. An increasing number of firms follow an environmentally friendly policy.

c. The CEO wants to downsize the company.

d. There is more staff at the sales department than at the Research and Development department.

e. Overheads are increasing/rising.

f. The brand is going to launch a new product on the market.

g. The supply chain is having a problem because of a raw material shortage.

h. Many companies use greenwashing to attract consumers.

i. Shareholders are only interested in profits.

j. Gas and electricity providers should be state-owned.

4 Work

Exercice 1

a. According to the Bureau of Labor Statistics, more than 4,2 million Americans quit their jobs in August 2021.

b. There's no single factor driving workforce behavior. Wages aren't keeping up with surging prices.

c. As workers across industries face lower wages greater workloads and higher risk.

d. Americans, economists say, are simply burned out – and emboldened by the current labor market.

e. Labor unions have initiated strikes at nearly workplaces accros the US.

f. Starbucks union vote sets up a watershed moment for U.S. labor

g. It was the same day Kaajal took her to the picket line for the first time.

h. A factory lorry transporting strike-breakers was blocked by a blockade.

Exercice 2

a. The average paid maternity leave is 29 weeks whereas the paid paternity leave is 16 weeks.

b. Some employees have long-term work contacts and self-employed do not have any contract.

c. Harassment classifies as sexual misconduct.

d. To combat workplace sexual harassment, bills were signed by Congress.

e. Working remotely two days a week will no longer be unusual.

f. Mandatory overtime, low pays and long hours were the fare of the American worker.

Exercice 3

a. She has a lot of workat the Christmas season.

b. Child labour is forbidden in most countries but is not unusual in Bangladesh.

c. Getting an education means among other things having access to children's books.

d. Chinese traditional industries are confronting rising labour costs thanks to a declining working population.

e. Productivity is when an employee is able to do more within the same amount of time.

Exercice 4

a. A hybrid approach will appeal to a more diverse pool of applicants.

b. Remote work has remained a crucial component in Austin, Texas.

c. Employees can work from home highly effectively.

d. The impact of in-person interactions should not be underestimated.

5 Transports

Exercice 1

a. The finished good is shipped to the end user.

b. Most of the shipping is in a container that's 40 feet long.

c. The container will be moved to a port by truck or by train.

d. Shipping containers typically require powerful cranes.

e. The ship sails a specific route.

f. The international ocean shipping industry has become highly concentrated over the years due to mergers.

g. Amazon has also docked at the port of Houston.

h. It's dispatching half-full trucks to get packages to customers on time.

i. Amazon has its own transportation network.

j. Amazon's prices were "phenomenal," $4,000 to ship a container from China compared with the $12,000 demanded by other freight forwarders.

Exercice 2

a. oil infrastructures.

b. bypass/side step.

c. transport grant.

d. truck drivers.

e. plug into a socket.

f. refill.

g. congested road.

h. check in.

i. commuter.

j. travel.

Exercice 3

a. In March 2021, the Suez Canal was blocked for six days after the grounding of Ever Given.

b. Southern California is dealing with a traffic jam unlike any other.

c. A record number of container ships have been stuck waiting in the waters outside the ports of Los Angeles and Long Beach to unload cargo.

d. The ports have broken monthly cargo records regularly since last summer.

e. Exports to China in France decreased to 1911 EUR Million in November from 1961 EUR Million in October of 2021.

f. This prestigious luxury brand opened thousands of stores in the world.

6 World challenges

Exercice 1

a. GMOS ; **b.** carbon footprint ; **c.** natural disasters global warming ; **d.** AI sustainability ; **e.** fair trade ; **f.** environmentally friendly ; **g.** aware ; **h.** energy efficient.

Exercice 2

a. Deforestation ; **b.** disease ; **c.** farming ; **d.** crypto currency ; **e.** human enhancement ; **f.** wind farms ; **g.** overfishing ; **h.** shortage ; **i.** greenhouse gas ; **j.** insect breeding.

Exercice 3

a. Global warming generates natural disasters.

b. Bad weather conditions increase every year.

c. AI can't replace human intelligence.

d. Billions of data are collected every day. They are called Big Data.

e. Solar powered batteries are very cost efficient.

Exercice 4

a. AI can help decrease the greenhouse effect.

b. Droughts are generated by global wild fires.

c. In the near future, cattle farming will be replaced by insect breeding.

d. Everyone should be aware of their carbon footprint and take measures to decrease its impact.

e. Oil companies should respect the new standards to curb greenhouse gas.

7 Global issues

Exercice 1

a. Some suppliers still have too few -goods- to sell, there will be others with too many.

b. Everything was about shortages in 2021.

c. Once the demand had been satisfied, there was suddenly an oversupply.

d. Demand for cars picked up again a few months later, there were not enough chips to go around.

e. Shipping containersmove some 1.9 billion tonnes per year by sea alone.

f. A typical container now spends 20% longer in transit than before the pandemic.

g. Even a 10% increase in container freight rates can reduce industrial production by around 1%.

Exercice 2

a. He says China now conducts twice the amount of trade with the region's 10 economies than the U.S. does - $650 billion worth.

b. There's now a new high-speed train in Laos.

c. The U.S. is working to strengthen ties with Southeast Asia.

d. The leaders of the US, Mexico and Canada are meeting for the first North American summit in five years.

e. Hundreds of migrants who had been trying to get into the European Union from Belarus are now returning to Iraq.

f. And what role should foreign countries play in ending the crisis in Sudan?

Exercice 3

a. windfall.

b. FTA (Free Trade Agreement).

c. border.

d. brexiteer.

e. digital trade.

f. domestic issues.

g. expel.

h. dispute settlements.

i. like-minded.

j. migrant.

Exercice 4

a. Application ; apply for ;

b. Workplace ; worker ; workingman ; working-class ;

c. Stettlement ; unsettling ; unsettled ; settler ;

d. Damaged ; damageable ; damaging ;

e. Domesticated ; domesticity ; domestication.

Crédits photo

12 ht © Pe3k / Shutterstock ; 13 ht © Patrick Lefevre / Belpress / Andia ; 14 bas © Hootsuite ; 15 bas © Sentavio / Shutterstock ; 15 ht © Eurostat ; 20 m © Prizma / Shutterstock ; 22 bas g Droits réservés ; 22 bas d © Singh_lens / Shutterstock ; 25 ht Reuters / Alamy Banque D'Images / Photo12 ; 26 bas d Baloo Rex May / CartoonStock ; 30 ht © Quarta / Adobe Stock ; 31 ht © TY Lim / Shutterstock ; 32 bas © Nils Versemann / Shutterstock ; 33 ht © Carpenter, Dave / CartoonStock ; 33 bas Droits Réservés ; 38 bas Droits Réservés ; 40 bas © Hakinmhan / Adobe Stock ; 42 bas g © Nezabudkina / Shutterstock ; 45 bas Droits Réservés ; 45 © Tero Vesalainen / Shutterstock ; 52 © Frederic Legrand - Comeo / Shutterstock ; 53 © Fortune Magazine ; 54 m © Zacarias da Mata / Adobe Stock ; 55 ht Droits Réservés ; 55 bas © wowomnom / Shutterstock ; 60 © Onephoto / Adobe Stock ; 62 Droits Réservés ; 64 ht Droits Réservés ; 70 m Droits Réservés ; 71 ht © Otto Dettmer / Ikon images / Akg-images ; 73 ht © Elms Art / Adobe Stock ; 73 bas © Terovesalainen / Adobe Stock ; 78 bas © Wachiwit / Shutterstock ; 80 bas © Bojan / Adobe Stock ; 82 ht Sundry Photography / Shutterstock ; 88 ht © Jag_cz / Adobe Stock ; 89 ht © Vessels Value ; 90 © Travel mania / Adobe Stock ; 91 ht Droits Réservés ; 96 bas © Quality Stock Arts / Adobe Stock ; 98 bas © Marina Ignatova / Adobe Stock ; 100 ht © encierro / Adobe Stock ; 101 bas d © Mike Mareen / Adobe Stock ; 106 m © Smash / Adobe Stock ; 108 ht g Droits Réservés ; 114 bas Droits Réservés ; 116 bas Droits Réservés ; 118 ht Droits Réservés ; 124 ht © Blue Jean Images / Adobe Stock ; 125 ht Harmony Video Production / Shutterstock ; 126 bas Droits Réservés ; 127 bas Droits Réservés ; 132 bas Droits Réservés ; 134 bas © Jonathan Ernst / Reuters / Adobe Stock ; 137 m © Yaroslav astakhov / Adobe Stock ; 152 © Maria / Adobe Stock ; 155 bas © Maria / Adobe Stock ; 155 ht © Maria / Adobe Stock ; 162 m © Andreaobzerova / Adobe Stock ; 164 bas © Andrewesterland / Adobe Stock

Conception couverture :
Lucas Cholewa et Vincent Rioult

Conception maquette intérieure :
David Bart

Mise en pages :
Nord Compo

Fabrication :
Laura Milhomme

Code éditeur : 223739
Numéro de projet : 10295043
Dépôt légal : avril 2022
Achevé d'imprimer en juillet 2023 en Espagne par Macrolibros SL (17511)